D0597057

METAMORPHOSIS

ROBERT A. FERGUSON

Metamorphosis

HOW TO TRANSFORM PUNISHMENT IN AMERICA

Yale
UNIVERSITY PRESS

NEW HAVEN AND LONDON

Published with assistance from the Louis Stern Memorial Fund.

Yale University Press books may be purchased in quantity for educational, business, or promotional use. For information, please e-mail sales.press@yale.edu (U.S. office) or sales@yaleup.co.uk (U.K. office).

Set in Scala type by IDS Infotech, Ltd.
Printed in the United States of America.

ISBN 978-0-300-23083-3 (hardcover : alk. paper)
Library of Congress Control Number: 2017957275
A catalogue record for this book is available from the British Library.

This paper meets the requirements of ANSI/NISO Z39.48-1992 (Permanence of Paper).

10 9 8 7 6 5 4 3 2 1

We like to run to the cliffs over the sea and watch people die when the wind pushes their boats against the rocks. You feel relieved the problems are not yours.

—Lucretius, *On the Nature of Things*

This seems the most important of all, it is impossible to overlook the extent to which civilization is built up upon a renunciation of instinct.

—Sigmund Freud, *Civilization and Its Discontents*

We need not remain trapped in inherited answers. An awareness of the causes and implications of past choices should encourage us to a greater experimentation with our own solutions.

—David J. Rothman, *The Discovery of the Asylum*

CONTENTS

ACKNOWLEDGMENTS

THE SPIRIT AND GENEROSITY OF DEAN Gillian Lester of Columbia Law School enabled me to finish this book. Seven research assistants across recent years also made it possible: Dina Hoffer, Caitlin Smith, Alexander Lemann, Ian MacDougall, David Pucino, Michael Chang-Frieden, and Zander Weiss. They were the best one could wish for. Two anonymous reviewers through Yale University Press corrected mistakes and saw ways to emphasize important themes with greater power. William Frucht, my editor, gave invaluable encouragement and direction along with Philip King, in production, and Glenn Perkins, my copy editor. Each of them improved the book. Daniel Robinson schooled me on military personnel and organization. Dr. Richard H. Fulmer, a psychoanalyst, taught me a great deal about the stages a person goes through in dealing with rejection.

Too many colleagues to mention gave of themselves in our weekly discussions of each other's work. Nonetheless, three deserve special mention. Jim Liebman's scholarship on punishment and his commentary have been vital assets. Bernard Harcourt, the leading scholar on interdisciplinary study on the faculty, made important suggestions on particulars and approaches. Most important of all, Brett Dignam, the best lawyer you will ever find in litigation work with prisoners, gave unstintingly of her own research, experience, and penetrating knowledge of prison culture. At another level, the 200 letters I have received from the incarcerated have allowed me glimpses of the inside. Their despair, mordant humor, information, courage, and insight have touched me deeply.

At our monthly meetings and other exchanges, Kenji Yoshino, the crucial professional friendship in my academic life, helped to bring out the best in my work and shared his own vast knowledge and profound grasp of constitutional nuance. No one is more important to the study of law at this moment. My greatest debt, as always, is to my closest intellectual companion, wife, and the light of my life, Priscilla Parkhurst Ferguson. Her advice, sympathy, and unstinting help, sacrificing her own scholarly work, kept the book and me alive.

METAMORPHOSIS

Introduction: The Need for New Answers

THE RETURN TO A POLITICS OF LAW and order has brought new urgency to the reform of our penal institutions. Otherwise our prisons and jails will continue to march down a blind alley of hostility, occasional revolt, and withering failure. This book makes an argument, and it tells a story. It argues that retributive theory can be modified to reduce the misery at the core of incarceration. It also shows how small changes at every stage of the process, an architectonics of reform, can change prison culture.

Any book written from outside should begin with a disclaimer. No one knows what prison really means except those who are incarcerated. Yet everyone who reads or views anything about the subject knows that the punitive impulses that put and keep people in prison today are brutal and ineffective. There are many ways to approach the unknown within the known of this problem. Statistical, descriptive, anecdotal, comparative, historical, sociological, and legal descriptions surround the subject in all of its immensity, and the diversity of institutional arrangements in federal, state, municipal, and county incarceration complicates every approach.[1]

Metamorphosis takes a different tack without challenging the importance of others. It looks to the elemental forms in punishment. It argues that legally sanctioned theories of retribution have allowed vindictiveness to flourish everywhere in sentencing and our penal systems. The established forms of punishment are elemental in two senses of the word. First, they are near reflexes in thought. Second, in their intractability, they explain why a new approach must correct mistreatment in a broken system. Only transformation in the forms themselves, change from the inside out, can answer these problems.

Legal punishment changes for good or ill. It either heals or it hurts. Either way, it changes the individuality of the recipient. Debate naturally centers on these alternatives. It is the central issue in punishment. A transgressor must be made to adjust one way or the other. To punish means to alter another's behavior, often with further alterations in status, wherewithal, and identity. So extraordinary is such enforced change that it requires a further concept, and the earliest monody on punishment gave it one: metamorphosis.

The Roman poet Ovid, first to study punishment in depth, came up with the name. He devoted 12,000 lines of haunting verse to the subject and called it *Metamorphoses*. His title, new to the Latin language, reached beyond change to the more profound idea of transformation. The power in the term—change beyond recognition—gave him an additional insight.[2] Ovid recognized that the cruelty in hurting overwhelmed any thought of healing and that it therefore had better be understood and controlled. In chapter 3, his obsessive rendition will mark one turn in what can be done about the imbalance in punishment.

This book accepts Ovid's terms for two reasons. It agrees that punishment must seek a more balanced transformation, and it argues that a better understanding of human nature in its active parts can adjust that balance toward healing instead of hurting. The words "metamorphosis" and "transformation" are organic in significance: the tadpole turns into a frog under accommodating environmental circumstances. Penal reform is similarly possible if the right conditions can be made to prevail.

One of the first great American theorists of human behavior rendered organic transformation in more philosophical terms. "New truth is always a go-between," wrote William James, "a smoother over of transitions. It marries old opinion to new fact so as ever to show . . . a maximum of continuity." "A new opinion," he added, "counts as 'true' just in proportion as it gratifies the individual's desire to assimilate the novel in his experience to his beliefs in stock."[3]

One cannot change many of "the beliefs in stock" on imprisonment. Locking some people up will always be necessary in some form, but with "new facts" come "new opinions," and with them one can begin to change the spirit of incarceration, the organic thought behind its processes, its profoundly negative current purposes, its understanding of its practices, and its current inability to turn lives around.

Change as the touchstone in punishment, hurting or healing, provides an ignored opportunity. It tells us that the intransigence of the status quo need not dominate reform. George Orwell may have said it best. In "Politics and the English Language," he declared, "if thought corrupts language, language can also corrupt thought."[4] New thought comes from new language, and it can help us toward a better balance in punishment for what it should be.[5]

Hurting far outweighs healing in the criminal justice system today. Severe punishments with casual as well as more deliberate forms of cruelty and even malice have become a dangerous national habit, and more Americans have come to recognize the problem in these terms. Harsh sentencing, overcrowding in prisons, frequent abuse, the much higher percentages of minorities held, inexcusable deaths among those behind bars, too many ruined lives, and the dramatic increase of women incarcerated—each of these documented facts has brought new apprehension and hence more attention to institutions of incarceration.

The first penitentiaries in America tried to heal instead of hurting. The purpose in confinement was "to join practicality to humanitarianism" by inscribing "the fundamentals of proper social organization" that "the social deviant" lacked in outside life. Another goal, less practical, aimed "to separate the offender from *all* contact with corruption both within and without its walls." Punishment is a difficult business. The absence of a sufficient infrastructure and naïveté about corruption would soon give way in these early institutions to "a mechanical application of discipline" on the way toward neglect and abuse, but whatever its faults, the original policy had a working benevolence that should not be forgotten; it wanted to help.[6]

Can the current infrastructure of our penal system yield a similarly positive agenda? Rhythms in communal understanding are important here. It is a truism in policy formation but worth repeating: negative conditions turn into problems only when we come to believe that we should do something about them, and we have come to that point on prison reform.[7] Something is up when judge after judge demands that the country "jettison the madness of mass incarceration" and insists that most criminals are "not evil incarnate." Gauging success by the number of years given in prison, they add, makes no sense for offenders acting out of "weakness, need, sometimes desperation . . . without schooling, skills, hope or direction."[8]

Change is in the air; how much remains unclear. In 2015 the president of the United States, notably the first president ever to visit a federal prison, looked at a typically small prison cell and exclaimed, "Nine by 10—three grown men in a 9-by-10 cell." Anyone could join in the inevitable conclusion: "Overcrowding like that is something that has to be addressed." This kind of realization spreads when a president says it and then adds, "we want to make sure that we're seeing what works and build off that."[9]

What works! Build off that! Barack Obama's words are doubly apt. Aspiration to one side and pragmatism to the fore, the rationale and power of existing arrangements have their purposes. What should be kept and what must change? How long do we allow culpability to trump the development of capability in those we punish? My title, *Metamorphosis,* acknowledges that change must come directly out of what is already there. The correction of existing understandings of punishment must be organic. It must take what is given to transform it into something better.

Prison culture is currently driven by retributive instincts, impulses as natural as they are repressive. This is where all theories of punishment begin, but they don't have to end there. At some point, further development turns into a likely response when both citizens and experts see that the stress on retribution is overwhelming penal institutions. Seeing also comes from within those institutions. Some of the greatest experts on punishment are inside of correctional facilities.

A previous study I published in 2014, *Inferno: An Anatomy of American Punishment,* produced an unsolicited outpouring of several hundred letters from people in prison eager to offer their own grounded knowledge of the subject. At no point did I seek or initiate a correspondence, but I have responded to every letter that I have received on the terms it presented, and I now have a file cabinet drawer full of them. These private communications make a general plight striking and specific. In every instance they have urged me on against the forms of injustice and dismissal that flourish in American prison life.

Prison letters are invariably long. Most are hand printed and average six to eight pages, double-sided. The incarcerated have time. Their letters reminded me of an often overlooked passage in Martin Luther King Jr.'s famous "Letter from Birmingham Jail, April 16, 1963": "Never before have I written so long a letter," wrote King from jail. "I'm afraid it is much too long to take your precious time. I can assure you that it would have been much shorter if I had been writing from a comfortable desk, but what else can one do when he is alone in a narrow jail cell, other than write long letters, think long thoughts and pray long prayers?" As one ten-page letter to me began, "I'm not sure how long this letter will be, so be ready."[10]

Think about it. In the electronic continuum of the twenty-first century, the main source of formal letters written in script may well end up being those sent by prisoners, full of yearning, in search of someone who might listen. Here are the six things they gave me—always in a more visceral sense than what I knew from published sources or from the close surveillance that always accompanies a visit to prison.

First, people in prison have their own language distinct from that used against them, and the language is subtle and nuanced even when very basic in meaning. The tones and import of these writers range across irony, comedy, veiled allusion, and despair in covert reduction of the authority exercised over them. Second, many long-timers in prison are an unused resource. They could improve prison life if given the chance. Third, education helps the incarcerated dramatically, and it is a poorly understood resource in most correctional facilities. Many of my letters have come from self-taught people more aware of their deficiencies than their underlying eloquence.

Fourth, prison letters show that meaningful growth starts inside, within the individual, away from the social norms of correction facilities. The incarcerated begin with feelings of embittered victimization, and those emotions often remain dominant. If and when attitudes change, the move is toward gradual acceptance of the role a person played in coming to prison. "I did this to myself," the writer realizes, and it logically follows that "I have to do something about it." This intellectual journey is a lonely one, and it is rarely helped by institutional compulsions. Fifth, writing out one's thoughts to another about the stages of one's understanding has enormous benefit to anyone in prison. It is all about being heard in a place where no one cares. Sixth, and finally, contact with the outside world through communication and visitation is a crucial ingredient in mental health.

The prison letters that come to me confirm something else. Published prison narratives only manage to reach print by emphasizing the melodramatic rather than the tedium and boredom that rule in confinement. To get published, the writer must stress the abuse in confinement. But how much abuse is there? The private letters I receive—handwritten on page after page of ruled yellow paper—answer that question. They prove that prison abuse is endemic rather than episodic. I find it everywhere embedded in pages of jumbled paragraphs and casual asides where the emphasis is on other subjects.

Unnecessary cruelty and ritual humiliation in American jails and prisons are not peripheral phenomena based on crowded conditions. They are intrinsic to current understandings of punishment. The unrestrained abuse recorded by these prison writers also explains why I keep their identities and even their locations confidential when I refer to them in these pages. Retaliation against those who have written to me, if they are identifiable, is not a possibility; it is a certainty. So I refer to these private accounts only as Prison Letters, 2014–2017.

What does it actually mean to be human and treated like one? This is an unavoidable if often implicit topic in theories of punishment, and philosophical concern surrounds the subject without direct address. Such terms as "the value of an individual soul," "redemption," "personal dignity," "individual integrity," "human rights," "responsibility," "sinfulness," "intent," "duty," and "rational norms" all vie for attention. They also belong to conflicting frames of religious and secular thought. Yet no use of these worthy concepts reduces the severity of punishment in American prisons. Perhaps that is so because most of these words welcome explanation by the punisher as much as the need of the punished.

My approach to the role of human nature in punishment turns on a simpler fact. We know ourselves through our ability and need to develop in some way. Most animals fulfill their nature. Human beings define themselves through growth in individual capacities, and if they are not allowed to develop their capabilities positively they will develop them negatively.

Here in a nutshell is the problem in every prison in the country: negative development. The incarcerated have no room to succeed in personally relevant terms.

Those nine-by-ten-foot prison cells for three people that President Obama gazed into tell their own story, but so do the president's words when he says "that is something that has to be addressed." Neither fatalism nor despair is a tolerable end point in a country claiming to live by justice as fairness. How can we change what no one wants but so many see as inevitable? Each chapter takes up that question from a different angle. Together they say, we can change this, but we have to do it from the ground up, from inside out!

New answers within elemental forms are needed in a way that can change the forms themselves. I ask only that you read these pages without preconceived ideas on the subject. The intractability of the problem comes not from an absence of available answers. It comes from competing and now compacted interests that are equally unhappy over existing policies, conditions, and risks in penology. In the conflict of interests, these positions grow narrow and intense. All sides are constricted by habits of thought and a combativeness that makes everything worse.

Fatalism over incarceration policies is certainly understandable. A culture of fear wants its criminals locked up for as long as possible. The public debate often comes down to this. How many people do we need to incapacitate and for how long? The country holds 2.2 million people in prisons and jails, and it is a profitable arrangement for those who hold them. We spend over $80 billion on incarceration and its aftermath.

Our punishment regimes are the third largest employer in the nation. One in nine government employees works in some form of corrections. A more enormous number, one out of every thirty-seven Americans, lives under some kind of legal surveillance. It is one out of seven for black men. The culture of fear puts a particular emphasis on corralling minorities. Roughly 60 percent of black men who do not finish high school will go to prison if current rates continue. That's a majority! The figure remains at 30 percent of black men with a high school education—still far too high.[11]

Punishment levels thrive in part because this is one of the few utterly secure domestic industries. If you are paid for watching the convicted or have invested in it as a profitable enterprise, you don't have to worry about layoffs, shifts in global markets, and other economic fluctuations. If you want to understand the covert limits on reform, follow the wealth in penology and what it worries about.

This country will always put large numbers of people away no matter the cost, and the public will pay for it through taxes and governmental subsidies. Whole communities, many in depressed areas, depend on correctional facilities for their livelihood, one reason we sentence six and seven times longer than France or Germany for the same offense. Count on it. Incarceration will be profitable into the foreseeable future, and reform must deal with that certainty by using it for better purposes.

How do we challenge such a cultural, economic, and institutional juggernaut? Well, first off, punishment regimes in America are decentralized. That is a disadvantage in general reform, but there is opportunity in its separate parts. We are not looking at an aircraft carrier in danger of capsizing or running aground if we try to turn it around too quickly. Penology in America consists of thousands of smaller ships in many places at the federal, state, and county levels, and if you make some of them better, others will take notice.

The Trump administration is calling for ever more severe punishment, but at least twenty states, facing increasing prison costs, have begun to reduce sentences and have experimented with alternative forms of correction. There is enough progress here to suggest a trend.

Take a singular example of possible reform. Officials at the Bedford Hills Correctional Facility, a maximum security prison in New York state with a capacity for 972 women and a family-centric approach, encourage the people they hold to advance their educations, and these programs have achieved roughly 80 percent involvement, an unheard level of participation in most facilities. For years one of the most innovative wardens in prison life, Elaine A. Lord, kept those levels high.

How did she do it? She walked the corridors. She knew her people, both keepers and kept, and she held to a larger principle. "This place," she said, "has to be a community to work." Observed one ex-prisoner, "Warden Lord was a bright light in a dark place."[12] Notably, that light came from the top and reached all the way to the bottom. The situation is ripe for experimentation in many different places. Everyone involved would prefer to sail better than we now do in the polluted waters of penology.

Legal punishment cannot avoid being a distasteful and dangerous enterprise. There will always be much to worry about in it. Superintendents dread prison revolt. Correction officers have higher injury rates than other occupations, and they retire as soon as they can. No one on the front lines likes this job. From the other side, the incarcerated cannot help but fear everyone around them. All levels in corrections hate where they are even if everything is going well, and it is not going well in America today.

Prolonged loss of freedom is the volatile condition of imprisonment in an industry where no one wants the product that comes out of it. Nor, in consequence, can anyone deny the need for new thought on the subject. We simply have to do this better than we now do it in a republic that prides itself on ideals of democracy and equality.

New thought currently fails because pragmatic levels of enforcement are caught in a vicious circle. The top echelons of authority in American prisons know they are in trouble and want to do better, but they cannot keep legislators from proposing heavy penalties to please special interests and electorates. They are also challenged by the leadership of powerful correction officer unions. The lowest echelon on the prison blocks cannot be taken for granted either. Correction officers working the cells are the managers of a dangerous environment. Their problems and wishes cannot be ignored. All sides, not just those held in prison, are kept in place. The convicted are not the only ones entrapped by present circumstances.

If size, intransigence, and intractability are handicaps in reform, they point to unfairness everywhere. How do we square the appalling numbers, the lengths of sentences, the targeting of minorities, and so many ruined lives with the communal pledge of "liberty and justice for all"? The easy answer no longer suffices. Yes, law turns on the clash between reality and aspiration, but that doesn't mean current practices should win out. The social organization of power makes sense in legal institutions only if power has prior legitimacy in meaning, and much of current penology has lost its meaning. We have to think past where we are.

I have said there is a chance if we take on the federated system of prisons and jails separately, facility by available facility, instead of accepting the staggering dimensions of incarceration and its collective understandings. Organizations work by how they are structured. Structure, in turn, is a matter of how authority is expressed and how it is understood down a line of command.

Prison problems begin here. Policy in penology is imposed from above, but confinement, by its very nature, is run from below. Language from above has difficulty imposing itself on prison practice in the way intended. Well-meant official understandings do not preclude "atrocity-producing situations" from emerging—situations in which ordinary people learn to inflict unnecessary cruelty on those under their power through habit and circumstance.[13]

Coping with the dilemma of levels in penal structures is one key to turning a problem into a solution. A great deal depends on what we think of the power of language in guiding thought and determining action. Again, in Orwell's understanding, is the language used "a natural growth" of the circumstance that requires it, or is it "an instrument, which we shape for our own purposes"?[14] Either way, we can only think with the language that we understand.

This linguistic puzzle dominates what follows. Cruelty, poorly defined in American punishment, grows out of the justifications and habits of a punisher, and those justifications and habits become easy ones when coupled to retributive instincts. The calculated absence of exchange across penal hierarchies allows cruelty—"the disposition to inflict suffering" or, more subtly, "delight or indifference to the pain or misery of others"—to develop into regular patterns.[15] "Vocal silence" across levels separates agency (what is done on the ground) from apparatus (what the institution officially says it stands for).[16]

Everyone in penology is thereby protected when bad behavior becomes the settled norm, especially when something goes seriously wrong, as in the permanent injury or death of a prisoner. The hush about behavior, vast in the institutional setting of a prison, has to be opened and articulated. Top-down authority must find a language to ensure bottom-up accountability, one that will recognize cruelty for what it is.

Easier said than done? Yes, but there are attributes in all of us to call upon. Human nature is not defined by cruelty, despite its presence. We are social animals, and we prefer cooperation to enforcement even in an imposed situation. No one wants uncontrolled conflict. The Golden Rule—do unto others as you would have them do unto you—has a secular equivalent: the best predictor of how we will act depends on how we are treated.[17] The negative equivalent is certainly obvious enough. "I want the same respect I give you," testified one ex-prisoner in a trial of abusive guards in the summer of 2016. "If you threaten me, I'm going to threaten you."[18]

There is more to reciprocity than a "tit-for-tat strategy," and it is one place to start. How might a more nuanced and positive strategy work in prisons? Most correction officers fear an attack and respond by acting aggressively when minimally crossed. These insecurities breed the hostility in behavior that everyone in prison fears. Would guards insult and attack prisoners or prisoners insult and attack each other or an abusive guard if all realized that cooperation could produce a life without fear? Some would, but how many? The number seeking cooperation, as the warden at Bedford Hills Correctional Facility knew, will depend on the possibilities in community.

Communal possibilities begin in common courtesy. "Manners are of more importance than laws," Edmund Burke famously wrote. "Upon them, in a great measure the law depends. The law touches us but here and there, and now and then. Manners are what vex or sooth, corrupt or purify, exalt or debase, barbarize or refine us. . . . [T]hey aid morals, they supply them, or they totally destroy them."[19] Behavior is more than a matter of communication or even exchange. It depends on felt reciprocities that we learn to respect and express. My letters from prison indicate that the best moments for writers come when they are treated like people.

Right now the absence of mannered exchange, the lack of visible good will, and an ingrained hostility prevent the recognition of capabilities and normative growth in prison life. When moral registers are "totally destroyed," to use Burke's terms, corruption follows. Manners are a matter of education, sadly lacking in this context. Still, there is an answer. Where all see the advantage in it, education is possible. But how to begin? Where do we start in such a conflicted and hostile environment?

Metamorphosis is going to be possible because the elemental forms of punishment vary according to circumstance and gender. Men in prison live in isolation from each other, with physical prowess ruling the roost. Violent offenders feed on the vulnerable. Trust and engagement are foreign commodities, and resistance to education can be profound. There are ways to deal with these problems.

By way of contrast, women in prison are less violent and more likely to form groups, and they generally welcome educational initiatives, but many more of them suffer from previous abuse, sexual harassment, devastating familial dislocation, and a paralyzing loss of esteem. More stigma attaches to a woman in prison. You can "make yourself a man" in prison in some communal understandings. You never turn into "a lady" there. There are other ways to deal with these problems.

The different consequences of punishment require different approaches. Even so, we can only change treatment of the convicted if we first recognize a universal corrosion that controls everything. Contempt for the punished and dismissal of their worth are bottomless in the punisher. You become a cipher in prison, and that reduction leads directly to one form or another of inhuman treatment.

It need not be. An architectonics of reform, built piece by piece across the following chapters, shows how change can come from within these structures. Ideas do not evolve by themselves. As in any metamorphosis, they evolve when time and circumstance call for them. Legal, linguistic, technological, educational, and structural norms are all at issue in a broken system today, and each is taken up in turn to diagnose what does not work well and how it might work better. For unmistakably, each of these norms in practice has also reached a stage of development and recognition where interactive reform has become either possible or necessary.

A coda at the book's end steps out of the frame to illustrate how simple practices can become solutions. The subject of punishment is unpleasant only if we rest within it. Pockets of positive development are instructive. Shame and despair from the waste, indifference, humiliation, and hostility in our punishment complexes have answers right in front of us.

Reform always requires the right questions. Each chapter asks "where does advantage lie for change in institutions that are never far from violence and numbing despair?" And behind that question is a larger theoretical one about punishment as such. "Are the convicted placed in prison *for* punishment or *as* punishment?" The answers to these questions may be tentative and will vary, but they are cumulative in implication.

People can and do change the way they behave. Asking another kind of more personal question—"What is my advantage in a situation I do not like?"—takes some practice, but it lends itself to answers that challenge conventional understandings. Ignorance, anger, and mistake are not easily conquered. They can, nonetheless, shift the prisms of self-interest and curiosity over what occurs and why it occurs.[20]

At stake is more than rectification. The transformations called for seek a new institutional being, a different organic approach to what we are now doing. There are many concrete propositions for reform that are desirable, and often suggested: shorter sentences, greater discretion in sentencing, fairer control of plea bargaining, better arrangements with outside relationships, and broader parole policies, to name just a few of the most important. The goal here is greater. Something beyond the particularities is necessary if we are to end the patterns of destructive behavior in imprisonment today.

Metamorphosis: How to Transform Punishment in America insists on new definitions, better communication from those definitions, and hence more comprehensive understandings than we now have. Theories of punishment are, after all, relatively new in history. Nuanced thought about punishment begins to emerge only on the edge of modernity, and we haven't moved far beyond those eighteenth-century origins. Current debate still hinges on the same old language. We still hold to the differences between retribution and utilitarianism set forth in the Enlightenment by Immanuel Kant and Jeremy Bentham.

After two hundred years and counting there is surely more to learn. Is it too much to ask for an intellectual advance worthy of the best instead of the worst in us? Only in that way can one hope to change the hearts and minds of the people involved in punishment. We need to find the language and therefore the thought that will allow that to happen. Sooner or later, a truly civilized society will want better results than we now have. This book is about how it can happen sooner rather than later.

1

The Linguistic Tangle in Treatment of the Incarcerated

Punishment Known

CONFINEMENT RESTRICTS THE BODY AND, through it, mental well-being. You see it in the moment anyone has been convicted of a crime in an American courtroom or cannot make bail. Right after the decision from a judge, the person destined for confinement is put in handcuffs; it makes no difference if the application is unnecessary to prevent escape or resistance. It makes no difference because the importance of the moment lies elsewhere. The symbolism in handcuffing initiates the continuum in confinement at the same time that the image of it satisfies retributive alignments. This is all most people see of incarceration.

Put yourself in the situation. When so restricted, you are already seriously hampered. Try taking care of yourself in a bathroom with your hands bound either in front or in back. Your balancing mechanisms, freely swinging arms, are also lost. You are vulnerable if you trip without the protection of hands to break your fall. Scratching some itches becomes difficult or impossible. The handcuffs hurt. Any change in position is awkwardly managed. You must depend on others. Most of all, you are being shown. You are being displayed for what you were previously not: you have become the held property of the state.

Handcuffing represents the basic element in all of punishment: it visualizes your helplessness in the hands of others. Concreteness is important here. You are treated reasonably well in court, but those courtesies are not always apparent even there, and they disappear in the next moment when you are alone with your handlers.[1] For that, imagine the following five incidents. Actually you don't have to imagine them. All five happened in prison or jail, and recently. Concentrate instead on the linguistic tangle in confinement that governs them. Its elements—words controlling thought and justifying behavior—are malice, cruelty, and habit, and they combine in escalating levels of severity.

Malice and cruelty have normative implications. No one wants to be identified as malicious or cruel, and there are more practical reasons for avoiding the accusations. The same words point to legal terms of art in which punishment, as in "malice aforethought" and "cruel and unusual punishments," might make a penal perpetrator accountable. But we do not punish habit. Nor do we think of it in moral or legal terms. Mostly, we excuse it, even though it represents the root of all evil in American penal systems.

The first three incidents come from personal letters written to me from prison, and their casual tones relegate them to the realm of habit.[2] The first takes place in a federal prison in a southern state. A long-term but completely cooperative convict has a serious cavity that he has discovered through a toothache. Under prison rules, he should see a hygienist, who identifies the problem, and then, often after a considerable wait, maybe as much as a year, he can get to see a dentist. There is, however, a hitch. This federal prison has no hygienist, so under prison rules nothing at all happens. The prisoner's predicament gives new meaning to a phrase often used to dismiss the incarcerated: "Let 'em rot." Many people in this prison are walking around with blackened teeth.

Second, in a medium-security state prison in a northern locale, we have a man incarcerated for twenty-five years to life on a charge of armed robbery when he was a teenager. He has more time coming, too, but he has turned his life around. He has taken responsibility for his crime and given himself a high school education and a college education, and he is now leading classes for other prisoners who seek their high school general education degree, their GED. This prisoner has never been in trouble in a world full of trouble, and on this day he has stopped by an office, with permission, to pick up his teaching materials. A guard there leans over his desk and knocks the materials out of the prisoner's hands and says, "Pick that up, you clumsy bastard, and get the hell out of here."[3]

A third event, in a midwestern state prison, involves another long-term model prisoner on his way to scheduled work. A guard stops him in the hallway and asks, "Where are you going?" It is a reasonable question and the prisoner responds reasonably: "I am a counselor on my way to lead a scheduled discussion section with new prisoners in the small conference room in B Block." The guard answers with a non sequitur: "You're just an inmate." Says the prisoner, "Yes, but I'm also a counselor on my way to lead a scheduled discussion section." The guard lets the prisoner proceed but follows close behind him down the corridor saying a single word, over and over and louder and louder. "Inmate!" "Inmate!" "Inmate!!" "INMATE!!!"[4]

The fourth incident, more serious and hence in the public record, occurs in a city jail on the West Coast, where guards punish a prisoner by announcing to a cellblock that the prisoner is gay. They then force the young man to walk naked through the block and lock him in a cell with two predatory gang members who sexually assault him for hours. The guards know what will happen. They might not know that the gang members stick their victim's head in the toilet while raping him. Nor do they care.[5]

The last item is a group activity with many single episodes, and it has added significance. Deputies, again in a city jail on the West Coast, have given themselves tattoos on the back of their necks in celebration of a particular activity. They amuse themselves by awarding each other points every time one of them breaks a prisoner's bones. Regular beatings of prisoners are a matter of habit here.[6] Solidarity binds everyone in while guaranteeing that no one will talk about this behavior outside of the group.

Punishment Explained

No considerate person wants any of these occurrences to take place. They are all reprehensible, although some are worse than others. The first incident, the dental quandary, seems simple enough, but nothing is ever simple in prison. How important is a toothache to you or anyone? Serious tooth decay can lead quickly to an abscess, which, if untreated, may perforate bone and spread internally, with infection entering the bloodstream and reaching vital organs, such as the heart. Irrespective of these dangers, the pain can be excruciating, and indifference, as we have seen, is also a form of cruelty.

The second instance cited is clearly malicious but comparatively trivial in physical implications. Correction officers need to appear tough, capable, psychologically confident, and ready to act in a crisis while managing difficult clientele. Here, though, the guard who knocks the folder of class notes out of the hand of the prisoner has no need for appearances. The person accosted is known to be a model prisoner who has never presented the slightest difficulty. He is, in fact, the wished-for solution in prison life. He's proof that someone can improve while incarcerated, and his education has done more than make him a better person. He is using that education to benefit other prisoners around him—prisoners who might, in turn, improve themselves. Isn't that the goal of corrections?

Turning a serious felon into a balanced lawful person through education in the harsh environment of a medium-security prison is no small feat. Shouldn't the guard applaud that? Why doesn't he? There is a reason. Long-time prisoners have had plenty of time on their hands and some turn it to use by giving themselves a real education—often with help from resources in the institution, sometimes on their own. Either way, the prisoner is now a more educated person than the guard, who has at best a high school diploma from long ago. The guard resents the education in front of him and strikes out against it. The superior legal status that the guard demands from prisoners has been threatened by the success that the institution has enabled one of its charges to achieve.

The great irony in the incident should be lost on no one. Accomplishment has become a problem for the convict who has made himself the law-abiding figure that the system tries to promote. The angry guard needs to reduce what he hates to a level that he is comfortable managing. The teacher in front of him must be turned back into a worthless number behind bars. The prisoner, like all prisoners, must be shown to be incapable of managing his life well. He must be made to see that he is still just an object that requires control. He cannot be someone contributing to larger communal needs. By knocking the folder out of the prisoner's hand then blaming him for it, the guard signals his charge's incompetence. That understanding also allows the guard to issue a peremptory order. The file and scattered papers must be picked up immediately.

There is a considerable test for the prisoner in this moment. If the prisoner as teacher, in the legitimate pride in what he is doing, reacts with even a minimal response to the arbitrary hostility directed at him, the need to put him in his place will grow more intense. The barest flicker of protest to such intimidation will mean discipline for insubordination. Loss of privileges, cancelation of the class, and loss of points toward reentry into society—none are out of the question. Neither is a blow. The guard would welcome any excuse for a physical confrontation that only he can win.

Apparent worth is the problem in front of the guard, and it cannot be allowed to stand. How must the prisoner respond, and what internal discipline does it take with what personal cost to personal dignity? In this case, the prisoner did what he had to do rather than what anyone in the situation would want to do. He said, "I have no problem with you, sir."

Our third event is similar but has a different trajectory. The prisoner, a counselor on his way to help new prisoners, has been taunted repeatedly by a guard chanting the word "inmate." Again, we have a model prisoner and again the guard in question has no interest in recognizing the helping hand that might make his job easier. The correction officer has the right to know where the prisoner is going, and the right answer is politely given, but the answer—"I am a counselor on my way to lead a scheduled discussion section with new prisoners"—contains special identity, and it unleashes a vituperative barrage. As before, a prisoner has dared to take on another role, this time in language spoken, so the guard's hostility against that articulated identity has another purpose.

How language is used determines the nature of social interaction everywhere, and here it is about who controls identity. The guard is irritated by the prisoner's explanation of who he is, a person on a mission to help others: "I am a counselor." The inkling of authority and purpose must be removed. The guard therefore reduces the prisoner to his sentenced category: "You're just an inmate." People in prison do not like the term. So when this prisoner holds to the hard-won role of counselor, a title gained through many years of good behavior, the guard makes the term "inmate" deeply pejorative. With childish glee, a tactic one might find in a kindergarten playground, the guard chants it over and over again. He is insisting on the last word.

The ability to hold absolute power over the articulation of language on every occasion is a special form of tyranny. "Inmate" is not inherently a term of abuse, but it is a misnomer. A "mate" is a friend or accepted acquaintance. The term refers to "one who is the mate or associate of another or others in the same dwelling." It suggests companionship, maybe even a collectivity. Only secondarily does the term refer to "a person confined or kept in an institution," and in that peculiar instance a prefix is preferred: the word becomes *in*mate. Between the two meanings of "mate" is a third: "one not originally or properly belonging to the place where he dwells; a foreigner, stranger."[7]

Notice that there is no antonym to inmate. We do not talk of "outmates." Use of the term implies that you are *in,* or held, and hence *less* than a mate. You are understood to be without recourse. "You're just an inmate." Guards want the incarcerated to be isolated. "Inmate" implies presence without belonging. Confinement denies active will and with it a degree of personhood that goes with will.

Prisoners belong through the will of others. Lack of choice defines them. The guard does not say "you are one of the inmates." Isolated status without support lies behind the guard's words. "Just an inmate" says that well. As long as he is "in," nothing the sentenced prisoner can do will change that status. The guard's offensive chant says several things over and over again. "You dwell as an unwelcome stranger with a partial identity that I can take away at any moment. You are less than you think you are or are ever capable of becoming as long as you are here."

It is worth adding that in this incident the guard's behavior requires continuous effort. There is, in other words, a clear element of malice beyond impulse. How much malice is there in what might be called casual cruelty? The guard's behavior falls under the prison category of "ritual harassment." It belongs to habit, and it goes on everywhere in the punishment of the incarcerated.

There are predictable consequences to ritual harassment. Abuse reaches more disgusting and obvious levels of malice and cruelty in the fourth and fifth incidents described. Sexual abuse planned and orchestrated by prison guards and serious physical harm deliberately inflicted are inexcusable under any circumstances. They are so full of malice and cruelty that they transcend habit. The guards who encouraged the rape and physical abuse of a prisoner, and the guards who celebrated the breaking of a prisoner's bones, have left physical evidence of their illegal behavior, and they should be fired and prosecuted. Those above them should be relieved of command for claiming ignorance of practices that could have been discovered and answered by the damage caused.

Does that happen? Not in the world of penology today. In these publicized instances of especially terrible misbehavior an agreement is reached to have an oversight panel recommend general reforms, but no individual is punished for the acts identified. Nor does the responsible sheriff's department have to admit any wrongdoing on its part.[8] Nothing has been done to correct behavior in any of the five events described.

Fixing Punishment

The dental problem would seem to be the easiest to fix. If there is a rule that a prisoner must see a hygienist to identify a problem before seeing a dentist, then you either require the prison to hire a hygienist or you change the rule and send the prisoner directly to the dentist. The first option meets the rule, the second option applies a standard above the rule; it gives priority to minimal health needs while pragmatically saving the cost of a hygienist. Federal prisons have governmental oversight. If neither option occurs, with hiring a hygienist definitely preferred, you fire superintendents until one of them does occur.

The really impossible behavioral problems to counter come in the second and third events described. These incidents certainly deserve to be labeled "ritual humiliation." Both confrontations with model prisoners have been unprovoked and represent pointless, regular forms of degradation, what you might call identity theft. There are far more serious instances of abusive treatment of the incarcerated, and these two incidents are certainly mild in comparison to the other three indicated.

Still, the examples of ritual harassment are especially germane. As deplorable as these episodes are on the level of courtesy in human exchange, nothing will ever be done about them under current practices and understandings in penal punishment. Both are daily fare in correctional treatment.

Why will nothing happen? For a prisoner to seek effective redress for bad treatment through the prison hierarchy or a legal proceeding, there must be serious physical damage and clear evidence that the poor treatment in question was not provoked in any way. Even then, nothing will happen. Guards claim provocation where there is none. They are believed by their superiors and, often enough, by juries, in courtrooms packed with observing correction officers on the rare occasions that a case goes to trial. In any grievance that might lead to punishment of a correction officer, the likelihood of a finding for the prisoner remains slim. The far more frequent consequence of abuse will be harassment of a prisoner for daring to complain. No seasoned person in prison would think of filing a complaint for incidents two and three.[9]

Why are unnecessary put-downs more than just unpleasantness, mild affronts when compared to the other three events noted? Why is it so important to change this level of behavior? And if we wanted to change it, how can we go about it? That is what this book is about, and here are the reasons why the difficulty in reform should not stop us.

The discourtesies displayed in these seemingly more innocuous incidents belong to a continuum with no end point. As Aldous Huxley once noted, "we constantly speak of human beings in ways that implicitly deny their humanity—in words which reduce them to being mere representatives of a class, mere symbolical representations of some principle."[10] Incarceration dehumanizes the convicted with the all too predictable consequences we have found in incidents four and five.

We have to remember what we are all capable of doing. In the further words of Huxley, "most people would hesitate to torture or kill a human being like themselves. But when that human being is spoken of as though he were not a human being, but as the representative of some wicked principle, we lose our scruples." In the same vein, a lawyer of abused prisoners indicates why "successful prosecutions of corrections officers for misconduct and abuse of prisoners are rare": "Regrettably, some people think of prisoners as less than human. It's very troubling and unfair, but it's also an undeniable perspective animating these cases."[11]

An important key to malice and cruelty in the treatment of people in prison, one reinforced and maintained by habit, is the self-righteous assignation of absolute difference between punisher and punished. When that happens, the belief in retribution has no end. One other contributing factor in the two incidents of ritual harassment? We are looking at black prisoners in exchange with white correction officers.

Well over 60 percent of the people in prison belong to ethnic minorities; an even higher percentage identify as racially white in correction officer unions. Race is a factor with disparaging epithets at the center of many prison confrontations. It is so much easier to be severe with someone who can be utterly separated from yourself, and the difference quickly slides from race to racial assumptions about who has the capacity to be law abiding and who must be handled as a congenital lawbreaker.[12]

Consider, as well, the price that these black prisoners, and by extension the basically white institutions controlling them, must pay in tolerating the humiliations bestowed. Whatever they say, the teacher with his class notes and the counselor on his way to a discussion group can only avoid feelings of degradation by discounting the worthiness of the correction officers who are trying to bring them down. Inwardly they must decide that the challengers to their humanity lack moral authority and deserve no respect beyond what the situation demands. A needed integrity in reciprocity is lost in these exchanges and in all others like them.

The parallel in corrosive relations becomes exact. Just as the communications of correction officers with prisoners turn pernicious, so prisoners feel contempt for those they must regard as mere captors—so much so that any active compliance by a prisoner with the system stigmatizes that person.[13] The reciprocity on which a functioning community can thrive does not exist here. The correction officers "belong" to community no more than the incarcerated that they guard.

Untangling the Tangle

To break these patterns, we have to think about them in a different way, and we must start with the controlling tangle of malice, cruelty, and habit that dominates prison behavior on all sides. Is current treatment of the incarcerated, and simmering resentment in response to it, unavoidable? Such thinking acquiesces to the rule of habit and allows routine acts of cruelty to be the price of incarceration.

Case law over the abuse of prisoners under the "cruel and unusual punishments" clause of the Eighth Amendment to the U.S. Constitution finds accountability only in the severest cases, the kind where guards can actively be shown to have encouraged the rape of a prisoner or to have deliberately broken bones of prisoners. Even then, under strict court interpretations, the circumstances must be blatant enough and observable enough to prove unwarranted initiative on the part of the punisher for a case to have the chance to succeed.

What do we become if only in such extreme situations a perpetrator must worry about punishment inflicted because it *is* unusual and because it *has* required a special act of will connected to physical harm, a level of intent and practice in which malice and cruelty can be found and proved? Think about how much malice and cruelty that leaves untouched. If we accept the status quo, we must acknowledge significant levels of malice in the *usual* cruelties allowed in prison today because they are not *unusual*. So much of cruelty, what a punisher can justify, comes from ordinary people who have long practice in holding the upper hand in a situation. It connects, in other words, with habit.

Concern in cases of malice lies in how easily it can be masked. Cruelty, the product of malice, can be obvious without being traced to the instigating mask. Here, in the vagaries of such terminology, is one of the serious problems in reform. Malice is an inner attitude or feeling. It is always reprehensible but hard to ascertain. Cruelty, by way of contrast, is a visibly discoverable act, but habit can take over from malice to keep perpetrators and those around them from assigning cruelty to regular practice. The euphemism used in courts to cover both terms is "deliberate indifference," one of the definitions already noted of cruelty.

Follow the dynamics in play. Habit, a reflexive mental function reinforced by repetition, is the passive antidote to the active intent in malice. Ever since John Locke published *Some Thoughts on Education* in 1693, we have understood that habit controls much of human behavior.[14] The acceptance of habit obscures the ability to recognize malice and impedes the perception of cruel behavior. It cuts directly across the outrage we associate with cruelty. Habit is what we expect. Only something unusual fuels outrage over cruelty.

The hollowing out of relevant legal language is crucial here. The use of current definitions enmeshes us in the tangles, and hence the tentacles, of punishment. "Malice in law" only works by turning a feeling into an act, "the intentional doing of a wrongful act without just cause or excuse," which carries with it the presumption that said act is "reasonably calculated to injure another or others." If proved, and therein lies the difficulty, its presence can be definitive in a legal determination of punishment, as in the discovery of "malice aforethought."[15]

"Cruel and unusual punishments" is an even harder concept to work with, even though the act of cruelty is more palpable than the attitude in malice. Under the Eighth Amendment, the clause "cruel and unusual punishments" reaches the use of unwarranted force in prison only for malicious acts that cause pain, and even here the standard is loose rather than a fixed rule. Subject to interpretation, really to court discretion, the clause does not invoke a flat requirement when applied.

Here is the most serious tangle in the language of legal punishment. "Cruel and unusual punishments" clearly covers torture, when torture has been so defined. It also covers "any degrading punishment not known to the Common Law," "any punishment so disproportionate to the offense as to shock the moral sense of a community," and "punishment which is excessive for the crime committed." Cruelty, in other words, changes with the understanding and, alas, the convenience of communities and the common practices of their legal regimes. "It cannot be defined with specificity" and must be gauged by whether or not "a society tends to pay more regard to human decency and dignity and becomes, or likes to think it becomes, more humane."[16]

No one really knows what "cruel and unusual punishments" stands for against these diverse and open-ended standards. The Supreme Court, in its wisdom, has decided that "severe, mandatory penalties may be cruel, but they are not unusual in the constitutional sense," and some of its members have tried to restrict the doctrine to death penalty cases. In *Harmelin v. Michigan,* "cruel and unusual" is used to prove that the death penalty can, in fact, be "usual."[17]

Justice William Brennan has come closest, back in 1972, to a full standard in the always muddled accounts of "cruel and unusual punishments."

He does it in the equally muddled opinions of *Furman v. Georgia*, the case that led to a temporary moratorium on the death penalty. In his separate contribution, one of five concurrences in a decision with no majority and four separate dissents, Brennan offers "four principles" in finding cruel and unusual punishment.

Here they are. Punishment might be cruel and unusual if "by its severity [it is] *degrading* to human dignity"; if it "is *obviously* inflicted in *wholly arbitrary* fashion"; if it "is *clearly* and *totally* rejected throughout society"; or if it is "*patently* unnecessary."[18] The devil is not in the details but in the adjectives and adverbs, all of which use wording to take away most of what they might have given.

If this and later judicial renditions of the phrase have been unhelpful in fashioning an effective legal tool, it may be because cruelty is a bottomless concept dependent as much on circumstance as on historical trajectory. Montaigne saw this most graphically in his essay on the subject. He called cruelty "the extreme of all vices" in all of us, observing that "Nature herself, I fear, attaches to man some instinct for inhumanity." Extremity, by definition, knows no limits. Cruelty exists in us as an unlimited capacity. Montaigne knew that some would torment at increasing levels just to enjoy the sight. He argued that "the best apprenticeship" in life was "to unlearn evil."[19] William Blake saw the same thing when he claimed, "Cruelty has a Human Heart," one that opens into a "hungry Gorge."[20]

When does indifference to the pain of others turn actionable in law? The question is fraught with too much difficulty to give a set answer, one reason why deeply divided justices all write an aggressive opinion, point counterpoint, in *Furman v. Georgia*. Chief Justice Warren Burger, in his own fervent dissent in the case, conveys the frustration involved: "of all our fundamental guarantees, the ban on 'cruel and unusual punishments' is one of the most difficult to translate into judicially manageable terms." The Court, he accuses his colleagues, has further complicated "the haze that surrounds this constitutional demand."[21]

Malice is, if anything, just as troubling a concept to work with in common understanding, and hence in law. As "active ill will or hatred" the term eliminates the problem of indifference, but it is very hard to identify and then assay, and that is why law turns it into an implied action. Malice is "the state of mind required for a person to be found guilty of certain criminal offences." But how much ill will is too much? And how must it be identified to justify prosecution for an action in which malice and intent are often confused? How far does a little bit of malice extend, or is it an absolute designation whenever tied to action?[22]

The leading practitioner in American theories of jurisprudence, Judge Richard A. Posner of the Court of Appeals for the Seventh Circuit, has taken up these terminological difficulties repeatedly. He dissects them in case after case. "Unfortunately," he begins, "the word 'malice' does not have a settled meaning in law. Sometimes it means ill will, hatred, 'evil design,' or, in short, 'malice' in its everyday sense. But it can also mean 'simply knowledge of the harmful consequences of an act.' "[23] As for "willful and malicious," he writes "courts are all over the lot in defining this phrase." The courts fall into "redundancies" and resort to "oxymoron" when they have not "confused a state of mind (malice) with the consequence of an act (harm)." These confusions have extended to the point where "each circuit [of the federal appeals court system] seems content to go its own way, without attempting to reconcile its verbal formulas with those of the other circuits."[24]

Judge Posner has gone out of his way to take up these problems. An open call for reform in a more recent case explains why. Posner uses his opinion in *United States v. Delaney* (2013) to warn against usage that complicates decisions about punishment. The noun "malice" and the adjective "malicious" belong to "archaic language" no longer viable in statutory provisions that "must be confusing to many laypersons, including jurors." Trial judges, it turns out, are similarly confused. Jury charges have contained "linguistic ineptitude," "barbarism," and intrinsic puzzles without solutions. "What does it mean," Posner asks in tracking one of several ambiguities, "to say that a person did something intentionally but without malice?"[25]

It Is What It Is, Until It Is Not

Imprecise use of legal language is always dangerous and never more so than for prisoners who lack most rights and legal means. Rights and legal means demand the clearest definition. Imprecision in the range of them has encouraged restriction on the claims of the incarcerated who make it into court, and we are left with an unfortunate conclusion. The legal language that exists does not deal with regular abuse in the prisons of the United States.

In the Supreme Court case *Farmer v. Brennan,* a prison official will be liable "for denying humane conditions of confinement . . . *only* if he knows that inmates face a *substantial* risk of serious harm and disregards that risk." "Substantial risk" actually means recognition of "*excessive* risk" to be actionable, and the harm caused must "be *objectively* '*sufficiently* serious,'" with the prison official having a "*sufficiently* culpable mind," a "state of mind" so clear that it reveals "*deliberate* indifference." Nor will the Court allow a corresponding objective gauge for the prisoner's side of the coin. "We reject petitioner's invitation to adopt an objective test for deliberate indifference" regarding behavior "*more blameworthy* than negligence" with "*more than ordinary* lack of due care."[26]

The wiggle words rendered in italics suggest that virtually no practical level of proof will be sufficient if a correction officer is the defendant. Recall that "indifference" to the misery of another is one definition of cruelty. "Deliberate indifference" edges toward the finding of malice, but it is almost impossible to prove. The Court wants that higher and vaguer level of difficulty before it will penalize a prison official. In case after case, courts have used the vagaries in punishment doctrine to protect the already empowered rather than the powerless in prison life.

The abstractions as well as the confusions in legal terminology allow courts to deny claims without consideration of the realities in the incidents described earlier in this chapter. The majority in *Farmer v. Brennan* limits its awareness of prison abuse through one more elevation in thought. Disembodied language over the treatment of human bodies carries the day. "The Eighth Amendment," says the Court, "does not outlaw cruel and unusual 'conditions'; it outlaws 'cruel and unusual punishments.'" This rationalization dismisses the essential problem. It says that someone beyond the Court, not the Court, must take responsibility for "conditions" that dictate behavior.[27]

Two other decisions verify this conclusion through careful limitation. Both seem on the surface to ease the doctrinal roadblock in "deliberate indifference," but it is telling that neither case called for the criminal discipline of a correction officer. In the first, *Estelle v. Gamble,* argued over admitted medical malpractice for a prisoner who had been injured by an accident during a work detail, the Court found that alleged omissions in treatment had to be sufficiently harmful to show "deliberate indifference" and that in this case the failure had been sufficiently "inadvertent" to reach the "cruel and unusual punishments" standards of the Eighth Amendment.[28]

The second case, *Helling v. McKinney,* involved an even more passive form of environmental concern. The Court decided that a prisoner who sued for not being moved away from a cellmate who was a five-pack-a-day smoker had an argument but would still have to go back and prove three things at trial: the scientific danger for his future health in secondhand smoke, the support of general communal standards for his plight, and once again the deliberate indifference of authority over him.[29]

Novelty frightens people, but as language hides us, so may it open us. "Words," writes Aldous Huxley in keeping with his remarks on cruelty quoted above, "are the instruments of thought; they form the channel along which thought flows; they are the molds in which thought is shaped."[30] We need to break some molds in the language of punishment and establish new ones with an applicability and direction currently lacking.

A current slogan in American parlance, one that is dangerous to all normative thought, explains what is ultimately at stake. In the twenty-first century we like to say "it is what it is" when we relent to something unpleasant. The phrase enables a shrug of complacency. "It is what it is" ignores positive situations. It supports a status quo we do not like while sustaining that status quo against fresh explanation and thought.

Is the phrase used in a penal context? Yes it is, and in defense of abuse and corruption. When Joseph Ponte, New York City's correction commissioner, appeared on October 9, 2014, before the city council to answer questions about prisoner abuse and a massive cover-up of it in New York's Rikers Island Prison, he was asked why the warden responsible for allowing such abuse was not appearing with him to speak before the council. Was it that "he didn't have the backbone to show up"? Commissioner Ponte answered, "He's on vacation. It is what it is."[31]

If we use these words to equivocate about the American penal system, more than unpleasantness is involved. Complacency about legal punishment in the United States ignores treatment of people that is impossible to defend when known. Since Aristotle, Western thought has held that a community should be measured by how it punishes, and the United States punishes more heavily than any other society that it measures itself against.[32] In words that should sting, Montesquieu adds "severity of punishment is fitter for despotic governments, whose principle is terror, than for a monarchy or a republic, whose spring is honor and virtue." The sting gets sharper when put in positive terms. "Lenity reigns in moderate governments."[33]

Against the combinations of malice, cruelty, and habit on the way to severe punishment, the place to attack is going to be habit and what habit does to language. All three characteristics are intrinsic to human nature, but the first two, malice and cruelty, are mostly episodic in nature. Habit changes everything. It blunts recognition of malice and cruelty by numbing understanding and turning bad treatment into a routine. Habit accepts that some levels of malice and cruelty cannot be avoided in the social conditions of incarceration.

The result has been a language without responsibility. Judicial avoidance and penal justification reinforce each other at linguistic levels that have little to do with what actually takes place in incarceration. Together they have made extreme punishment an American habit, a habit with far-reaching public ramifications.

2

Do Americans Like to Punish?

The Puzzle Faced

IF THE PEOPLE FAVOR HARSH PUNISHMENT, then perhaps all debate about the subject is moot. Is there reason to doubt the assumption? The question cannot be ignored. Do Americans like to punish? Leading critics of penology have said so, with support for their conclusions.

The United States clearly punishes more heavily and for longer periods than other countries with comparable social and political values. You can land in an American prison for life over minor offenses, a punishment not used for serious offenses in Western Europe. You can be locked up forever for siphoning gasoline from a truck, shoplifting small items from a department store, attempting to cash a stolen check, or possessing a crack pipe.[1]

But if the facts are in, do the comparisons prove the claim? A "politics of dignity," the leading comparativist on criminology James Whitman argues, has instilled "mercy" and "mildness" in European systems, while leveling impulses, distrust of authority, and too much power in the people is said to have left the United States with "a criminal justice system long in degradation and short on mercy." In America, it is said, "harshness and democratization go hand in hand," eliminating the prospect of leniency. "Ordinary voters are never capable of the routinized, sober, and merciful approach to punishment that is the stuff of the daily work of punishment professionals."[2]

It is certainly true that mercy is not a recognizable trait in American law.[3] Perhaps, though, we should look beyond the people for the absence of it. Consider the second factor just raised: "the daily work of punishment professionals." What are we to make of the interaction between the professionals and the people? Are the people in control of punishment in America, or does it come down to them through authority exercised from above? Much about reform depends on the answer to this question. What is it that the people do not know that makes them harsh in the face of suffering?[4]

Assumed expertise is not without its own limits. The beginning of wisdom on the subject is very basic and should be remembered throughout this book. There are no real experts on punishment, none you want to meet anyway.

In the United States presumed expertise comes from members of the legal profession, and we might pause over what they learn and how they learn it. In his excellent study of the subject, Whitman notes that "all law students are trained to think of punishment as aiming at one of five goals: deterrence, retribution, rehabilitation, incapacitation, or the expression of a society's condemnation." Here we also have an important admission: "the theories that philosophers use to justify the pursuit of these various goals generally tell us little about how and why forms of harshness and mildness can vary."[5]

Five discrepancies in the language of expertise are at work in these comments. First, the five goals mentioned might not be the best way to think effectively about punishment. Second, they operate on punishment only through unbalanced interaction with each other. Third, as stated, the philosophical theories behind them tell us nothing about the degree of punishment inflicted. Fourth, there should be some uneasiness when we find every expert being trained in the exact same way on any subject, and that is especially relevant given the dismal record of punishment in American history. Fifth, and most germane for present purposes, these typical expressions in legal thought do not reach the grime and sordidness of actual punishment in American jails and prisons. They do not reach the problems that the incarcerated experience on a daily basis.

Notice, too, that the key to each discrepancy lies in the language used. Is it possible that the language offered by experts, the emphasis assigned to given terminology, has as much to do with harshness as the often cited political orientations in state authority? The question becomes acute if we accept the possibility that language and its uses may be the best way to initiate change in the behavior patterns of institutions. Left without regular linguistic scrutiny, institutional approaches hold to established routines, and punishment regimes are no different in these tendencies.[6]

Language can take thought in many directions, and nowhere is this more accurate than in legal thought. The language of law has no physical referent, like medicine with the human body, architecture with building materials, or science with classical mechanics. Law comes closer to religion in this regard, and in religion we have curbs and directions on understanding through the hierarchical claims of orthodoxy, much stronger than legal precedent.

The language of law is more self-sufficient than other professional discourses. It controls thought as well as people's actions. It decides what is observable about events through its insistence on proper standing before a grievance or charge can be recognized. Major formulations in a rule of law must appeal to the people, but how much legal language must defer to the people in practice, and in what way?

Reverence for legality runs deep in a nation that claims to be defined by it. So when the public is asked by officialdom about its attitudes toward criminals we can expect a severe response: "Do you want serious criminals locked up?" "Well, yes." That, however, is not the same thing as reckoning desirability or proportionality in specific punishments, which is left to legal capacities.[7] Either way, American deliberative democracy accepts a passive role in questioning legal determinations.[8]

The Rubrics of Punishment

Nothing absolves the people of responsibility for severity in punishment, but the direction of thought from professional articulation to popular acceptance complicates the issue quite a bit. Think again about what the five rubrics in punishment imply: deterrence, retribution, rehabilitation, incapacitation, or the expression of a society's condemnation.

When a person commits a crime, the first rubric assumes that deterrence has failed, and behind the assumption are premises that encourage severity. The criminal, it is thought, *has not been deterred* by making a calculation between illegal gain and getting caught. This sounds well enough in theory, but the premise ignores the fact that many in prison do not choose so much as fall into a background of illegality out of communal self-protection, existing criminal connection, and the need to make a living otherwise not available.

Deterrence works in the theory of time sequence that a prosecution assigns to a criminal's choice; it works less well in real time. Environmental conditions, lack of education, peer demands, and the absence of meaningful opportunities all cut into the presumption of free will in many cases. Without free will, deterrence loses its purchase. Yet none of the extraneous pressures to commit crime stop officialdom from seeking heavy penalties in its name.

Retribution, second on the list of goals, drives criminal justice. It is the reflex in all punishment, and it is encouraged by a freewheeling adversarial process that weighs everything in argumentative terms. Self-righteousness, revenge, and even hatred lurk in the shadows of retribution. By ascribing absolute worth in the legal decision maker, the process secures a desire to punish heavily. It also targets a person by the crime committed, a besetting problem in the fixed identity given to people in prison.[9] Revenge is rarely satisfied, and severity comes naturally if you are always known by what you once did.

The impulses in retribution freeze thought about punishment. The core meaning implies a permanently fallen state in a person legally punished. The concept comes from the Latin *tributum,* to pay regularly or be taxed. In a classical understanding, it signified what the weak or conquered had to pay the strong on a continuing basis as long as they remained vulnerable or otherwise undeserving of equal respect. *Re*-tribution, the obligation to pay repeatedly, suggests unending punishment.

Although rehabilitation would seem to be a simpler term on a scale of severity, it is not. "Rehab-" invokes the world that you previously inhabited. A return to it, through the root meaning of "habit," suggests that the incarcerated person must have begun life with correct behavior. "I hate the term 'rehabilitation,'" responds one prisoner with impeccable logic. "It implies I am recovering something I used to have. But I never had it to begin with."[10]

The hopelessness of rehabilitation becomes hope in the reformer's imagination. Rehabilitation says you are responsible for yourself against every environmental temptation even if the stigma of prison keeps you from profitable engagement with society. It does not say "preparation for a better life." Nor, as worded, does it indicate process so much as completion and, by extension, the idea that if you have not completed it, perhaps you were not punished enough.[11]

Incapacitation, the fourth goal in punishment and the close companion of retribution, lends itself to a similar severity. It speaks to social fears that give priority to the protection of the fearful, and there is no end to fear. The answer to unlimited communal uneasiness is perpetual incarceration. Incapacitation puts no limits on itself as a rubric in punishment. The term now used to describe that phenomenon in the United States is "warehousing."

Pause over this language. We are not shelving items but individual human beings in a state of stillness by deeming them unusable and therefore unwanted. Just holding them makes them ever less usable, more unwanted, and, soon enough, too dangerous for a measure of freedom.[12]

All of which leads to our fifth and final rubric in punishment, "the expression of a society's condemnation." The dictionary definition of "condemnation" begins with "adverse judgment" or "judicial conviction." Both apply, but a far more expansive frame of reference attaches to the goal in American punishment. Adverse judgment makes communal denunciation a synonym. In a religious understanding, "condemnation" signifies more than legal conviction. "To condemn" is "to doom or devote to some (unkind) fate or condition," "to damn," "to be doomed by fate," or "to pronounce incurable."[13]

The condemned have no recourse against such absolute designations, and one response is "to give up." The expression of a society's condemnation lifts responsibility off of the criminal justice system and onto popular opinion with profound connotations. What poll of a community is going to approve of criminals if there is crime? Blaming punishment on the people frees the conscience of prosecutors to do what they will as "the people's lawyer."

Leniency does not exist anywhere in this five-pronged lexicon of punishment. Nor does a regularly used definition of legal punishment call for leniency. Take a look at "the seven features of punishment" stipulated by a leading criminologist, Nigel Walker, and widely accepted in legal circles. Legal punishment is:

1. The infliction of something that is assumed to be unwelcome to the recipient.
2. The infliction is intentional and done for a reason.
3. The inflictor has the right to do it.
4. The infliction is for an action or omission that infringes a law.
5. The recipient has played a voluntary part in the infringement.
6. The inflictor must offer a justification.
7. The belief or intention of the inflictor, not of the recipient, defines the act.[14]

The objectification of terms in these seven features should not disguise a lopsided feature that holds them together. As so conceived, legal infliction has no countering reciprocity. Anything beyond enforcement is external to its importance. Punishment is imposed. Agency for the punished ends with the crime committed, not in a subsequent or projected mutuality with the punisher. The punished exist in the passive act of reception.

Perhaps there is no feasible alternative, no room for mutuality. After all, what might reciprocity mean in punishment? Isn't punishment always just imposed? This book is about finding better answers to these questions. It is about the need for a new understanding of punishment. Lon Fuller, in one of the best-known analyses of normative value in law, argues that "the principle of reciprocity" requires "voluntary agreement" and "symmetry" through the possibility of "reversible exchange": "The parties must in some sense be equal in value."[15]

These things do not happen in prison. Can we see any of Fuller's possibilities for normative crossover in the relations of correction officers and prisoners? If there is a saving aspect in his comments, it comes in his buried qualifier: "the parties must *in some sense* be equal." Much depends on whether we can think of a prison as a community of mutually engaged people instead of a holding pen or warehouse.

In the Way of Reform

Why should people on the outside want to change this situation? The quick answers are that abuse of prisoners is dehumanizing for all concerned and that it gets in the way of issues that are central to the public interest. The two primary goals of incarceration are, first, the security and health of everyone there, including visitors and correction officers, and second, a path for the imprisoned to become law-abiding citizens so that the vast majority can be safely returned to society instead of being dumped back on the streets ready to hurt others. Right now, getting hurt and hurting others are what people in prison learn, as demonstrated by their predictably high recidivism rates on release.

Abuse leaves many prisoners in a state of arrested development. Short-term prisoners in particular are caught between feelings of victimization, anger, avoidance, and the desire to strike back in some way. Human beings learn by what is done to them. Mistreatment encourages more of mistreatment and increases criminal conduct. Writes one sage lifer in prison, "the temptation to adopt criminal thinking is pervasive and compelling. If you want to learn how to be a criminal, go to prison. A shoplifter might learn to become a home invader, a drug user to become a drug dealer, or a man in on simple assault may become more violent, risking a future manslaughter or murder."[16]

Don't expect any of this to change from within without pressure or what might better be termed a better environment for thought, policy, and action. Cruelty in prison begins with open contempt and dismissal of all identity in new arrivals. Names are turned into numbers; everything of value is taken away. This first step of incarceration makes you nothing at all. You must somehow establish a new identity in a savage pecking order of unsympathetic supervisors managing gradations of predators and victims under them, and you cannot succeed by being amiable and friendly. Survival techniques depend on absorbing the casual cruelty all around you. A new arrival in prison gets tested at every turn.

A major difficulty lies in the problem known but not spoken. No level of officialdom wants incidents of cruelty talked about beyond the institution. In any walk of life, you know when your behavior is inexcusable. A sure sign of an unjustified act is when you don't want to speak about it beyond those who already are aware of it.

Penal authorities resist outside investigation until they are forced to comply. Surely the implications are clear when a correction officer's guidebook declares "there are many things officers can do to burn [hurt] inmates and make their stay in jail a living hell. I won't list them because inmates may get copies of this book."[17] Prison bureaucracies rely on the interstices in their institutional levels to hide abuse when they can.

The language unspoken that needs to be spoken is just as important from the prisoner's side. To change within a culture of abuse, people in prison must struggle with a transition in thought that is as poignant as it is difficult to make. At some point, the incarcerated have to realize that they do not like what they have become equally as much as the place where they are kept. This realization, once articulated, enables another intellectual step, and it is a step that the penal system ostensibly wants everyone to make, even though it says nothing about it.

That next step is hard to make under the circumstances of incarceration. A constructive view of the self requires the ability to reach beyond whatever hatred prisoners hold for the keepers who violate them. Dislike of the place infects all thought and encourages defiance in designated culprits who are constantly reminded of that status. Prisoners must somehow begin to dislike what they see in themselves and take responsibility for it. That is what thoughtful prison narratives say over and over again.[18]

Recalculation of one's identity is no easy task in any situation, and most of what we now do in penology impedes it. Frustration over the ability to rethink an already damaged life naturally grows when the thinker absorbs further damage from aggressive handlers and other prisoners. Whenever possible, the incarcerated need encouragement instead of repression in the name of the offense that brought them there. Correction officers are all too happy to categorize their charges through the crimes they committed—often crimes committed long ago.

There is another hidden dimension in these prison problems, one rarely recognized for its pernicious impact. The stasis in prison life, the notion of time simply to be waited out, distorts every aspect of behavior in prison. It influences those who hold as much as those who are being held. When there is no sense of development in a situation, people regress. Here is one prisoner's version of those who supervise him in a federal prison: "Their main concerns and the *only* topics of conversation among them are (1) years to retirement, (2) vacation, (3) overtime opportunities, (4) exploiting the paid sick leave policy, (5) other job opportunities within the Bureau of Prisons that involve less work and a better environment. That's all they ever discuss. Inmates do all of the work while Bureau of Prisons staff sit (sleep) in their offices and 'supervise.'"[19]

No one on either side of the bars in a correctional facility really wants to be there, and the consequences are as insidious as they are persistent. The boredom that permeates prison life, the one thing that prison narratives can never fully convey, is an acid that seeps into every aspect of behavior. Prisoners quarrel and attack each other to recover some excitement to existence. Guards torment their charges to make their own lives more interesting. Brutality passes the time where benevolence doesn't compute. Idleness breeds a playground of cruelty. No one cares about caring. Prison guards call those who try to help prisoners "mud lovers."[20]

Prisons are always going to be about punishment, but they should also be communities where healthy behavior becomes possible. They are not that now. Writing the obvious, one prisoner observes, "American correction officers (COs) are not educated in rehabilitation. . . . They know only one tool: punitive treatment." A hammer always hammers. "Whether [COs] are sadistic or simply disillusioned and cynical, they cannot be convinced that inmates are redeemable, and so they justify their abusive actions."[21]

The result is a world with positive rules that don't count because they are regularly broken, and those rules have nothing to do with the claim of "good behavior." In one explanation from inside, "the profusion of lawfulness and lawlessness in such close proximity is unmatched in civilian life." Where damage is taken for granted and often enjoyed, you can be unlucky at any moment.[22] Law lives and breathes on its predictability. In the words of Lord Hardwicke, "Certainty is the Mother of repose, therefore the Law aims at Certainty."[23]

The only certainty in prison is incarceration. When left in close proximity, lawfulness and lawlessness mean no law at all. The philosopher Arthur Schopenhauer explains what happens next. "Man is at bottom a savage, horrible beast. . . . Wherever and whenever the locks and chains of law and order fall off and give place to anarchy, he shows himself for what he is."[24] But what if lawfulness tacitly condones lawless behavior?

Brutal treatment is a little different when a legal institution tolerates it on a large scale. Moreover, cruelty in a rule of law occurs only when society lends some credence to it. No one should believe that prison abuse has to happen in this country. The causes are identifiable and controllable. Official misconduct and neglect are the catalysts that turn prisons into war zones, and both are sanctioned by communal attitudes toward the imprisoned. Once again we return to the question we started with. "Do the people like to punish?"

The Role of Stigma

The impulse to condemn deserves closer scrutiny. The baseness that the prison guard assigns to everyone in prison has its corollary in the stigma that society heaps on the convicted. We need to know how these correspondences work in order to change them. Stigma is a category in human behavior. It thrives on the common desire to keep someone or some group from fitting in. Its strengths depend on language and how it is used.

Stigma, so identified by the leading expert on its manifestations, Erving Goffman, focuses on "an attribute that is deeply discrediting" where "a language of relationships, not attributes, is really needed." In something of a contradiction, stigmatization works through a stereotype even though condemnation decides that the person targeted has had the chance to avoid the condition. The condemner forgets that "the role of normal and the role of the stigmatized are parts of the same complex, cuts from the same standard cloth." Instead an assumed normality ranges itself against "an undesired differentness." That which is strange thereby becomes unacceptable and a threat to established decorum.[25]

The social points to take away from the operations of stigma are twofold. First, as in punishment itself, stigma reinforces the notion that the person differentiated is responsible for the imposed loss in consideration; second, stigma authorizes a shift to lower status. From the outside looking into prison, stigma reinforces the belief that punishment is deserved with little regard for the extent of it. Loss in status, once assigned, introduces a second belief: the likelihood that the stigmatized person will re-offend. Certainty of someone's guilt assumes the possibility of more of it and a justification for harsh treatment now.[26]

Stigma also generates fear of group deviance. Through it, a whole collectivity can be dismissed from normal relations and expectations. The explanation, in Goffman's terms, is direct. "These are the folk who are considered to be engaged in some kind of collective denial of the social order." As such, they represent a threat to "the motivational schemes of society." It follows that if normal morality tries to rescue the stigmatized, it might unwittingly endanger the social order. Control of the stigmatized represents the safer alternative.[27]

Imprisonment supplies the perfect stigmata for continuing difference. It is perfect because, once more in Goffman's calculations, "stigma symbols have the character of being continuously available for perception."[28] Nowhere are these symbols more convenient than in permanently differentiating those who have been put away.

So powerful and accepted are these hierarchical implications and shaming structures that they permeate prison life itself. The stigmatized in prison invariably create their own severe pecking order of shame. They mimic society by making some among them worse than others. Those who will not be tolerated as different include sex offenders, gay people, the sexually vulnerable, the young, and the otherwise weak, but that is not all. In their need to create their own internal hierarchy, the imprisoned stigmatize anyone who cooperates with authority.

The greatest problem in severity of punishment may well be here. There is psychological relief in not having to care about people who are understood to be wrongfully different, who continue to prey on difference among themselves, and who necessarily have been put away. Better far, the logic runs, to leave them where they can act out their own disastrous version of life so different from what society is willing to accept.

Changing the Way We Think About Punishment

But are the people to blame for all of this? If there is a silver lining for the people, it can be seen in penal authority's fear of exposure of what it does. Prison officials clearly do not want anyone on the outside to know what their frontline officers do on a daily basis. This means that criticism often comes over failures to communicate rather than over hidden episodes of actual abuse. In the canny explanation of one long-time prisoner, speaking of the fences, walls, and barbed wire around a prison, "the barrier isn't there to keep prisoners in. It's to keep the rest of you out."[29]

We must start by ending the official silence over prison abuse, and this again comes back to the integrity of language and its uses. The U.S. Department of Justice's detailed investigation of New York City's jails on Rikers Island in 2014 spoke for all attempts to end mistreatment in prison when it reported "a powerful code of silence prevents staff who witness force from reporting. . . . Officers frequently affirmatively state that they did not witness any use of force despite other evidence that suggests they were at the scene where force was used."[30] Every prison and jail has this code of silence over its treatment of prisoners. Putting people "away" is more than a figurative term.

Nothing in public understanding can be in favor of a policy where, in the Rikers report, "officers and supervisors pressure inmates not to report [after they have been hurt physically], using a phrase that is widely used and universally known at Rikers as 'hold it down.'" "Inmates who refuse to 'hold it down' risk retaliation from officers in the form of additional physical violence and disciplinary sanctions." The public has to know "that some injuries reported to be the result of alleged slip and fall accidents in fact involved unreported use of force, based on the unusual frequency of slip and fall accidents and the serious nature of the injuries that allegedly resulted from them."[31]

Whether or not the people are to blame for such abuse depends on where and how they can be responsive to it. What might public recognition do about these and other problems in American punishment? It would be a lot easier if the language of punishment actually protected the unprotected in prison. Academic abstractions and scholarly bickering over theories of punishment have been of no help here. A more concrete recognition of blatant mistreatment and unprofessional behavior is called for. The unwarranted extension of punishment in prison needs its own identifying vocabulary with legal action behind it.

Increased dialogue about prison reform and coverage of it are hopeful signs. Bipartisan political support may be possible through justice reinvestment initiatives. Governmental and nongovernmental institutions are also exhibiting better coordination on needed initiatives through the Bureau of Justice Assistance of the U.S. Department of Justice along with such private organizations as the Pew Research Center, the Council of State Governments, the Vera Institute of Justice, the Crime and Justice Institute, and the American Civil Liberties Union. Regular discussion and recommendations about penal problems can mean a better informed public.[32]

The highest levels of legal concern have come to accept that the corrections system in the country is defective. In 2015, Justice Anthony Kennedy of the Supreme Court, joined by Justice Stephen Breyer, testified in a congressional hearing, saying, "in many respects I think it's broken. . . . This idea of total incarceration just isn't working, and it's not humane."[33] The dual emphasis, in pleading for Congress to act, is important. Something not working is a pragmatic observation with utilitarian implications. Something being "not humane" demands a more philosophical recognition. Both claims are essential to addressing the difficulties over prison reform.

What, in brief, needs to be done to bring policy, politics, and public understanding together? First, trial judges must stop thinking of the sentence given as the end of their involvement in punishment. Exaggerated judicial deference given to the administrative sphere of penology is a primary cause of unaccountability in our prison systems at all levels. Those who issue sentences should take the time to see those whom they have sentenced. Prisons should not be islands sealed away from public pressure, involvement, and recourse.

Second, the people and their political leaders should do what they can to produce change in penal hierarchies as we now understand them. The typical answer to prison abuse is to suspend perpetrators, often with pay, and to move around or replace a few top prison officials. That will never bring meaningful reform. Higher authority has to be made responsible for what takes place on the prison blocks instead of looking the other way and shielding identified abusers through bureaucratic obfuscation.

Third, correctional officers should not be employed without better and different kinds of training and regular re-training. Few in this country grow up wanting to be a prison guard, but many think of becoming a fireman. We think well of firemen because they try to save people. Correction officers must be trained to want to do the same thing. More sophisticated and extended programs for correction officers should be made the highest priority. Hazing, physical threats, derogatory assertions, and profane assertions should be forbidden and punished whenever they take place in the penal workplace.

More can be done because it has been done. Candidates for the position of correction officer in Norway must obtain a two-year degree from a staff academy, they are paid while they study, and graduation yields a position of honor in the larger community. American programs must be designed for correction officers to have a similar status. Among other things, their education must include the ability to see and understand the person behind the offense.[34]

Fourth, and related, correction officers need more constructive union leaders with again more formal education than they now receive. The powerful heads of unions protect the abusive officers in their ranks through political and financial leverage over legislatures and the manipulation of corrupt penal structures.[35] Union leaders currently do everything they can to resist improvement in the treatment of prisoners. They are public officials, and they should receive political and legal censure when it is deserved, and it frequently is deserved.

Later chapters in this book take up each of these needed reforms in detail, but a key to all of them is the language we use to define and accept punishment in this country, and that is a matter of professional as well as general education. We need to reexamine the reigning theory of punishment and adjust how we proceed. No one should be treated the way the incarcerated are dealt with in the first decades of the twenty-first century, and not just because current treatment is counterproductive.

Culpability assigned is an automatic aspect of prison life. It needs to be balanced by thoughts of capability and its possibilities. We have sophisticated means to gauge the latent skills of anyone incarcerated, but we currently lack the will and hence the means to act on those capacities. The language of culpability is clear enough. A corresponding language of capability can provide that act of will. Positive development in any prisoner should temper regard for the reason the prisoner is there.

There is plenty of evidence that education and further training works in prison when properly managed. Otherwise we simply destroy the lives of those that we need to punish. The people in this country believe in education. They need to show it here, and they have another reason for doing so. Education, it turns out, is the best answer to crime.

Either law or silence hides unjustified punishment, and when law is the choice, as it often is in this country, it refuses to talk about the problem in explicit terms. Call this a special form of legal silence. When the words come they twist understandings of punishment in bizarre ways and cause language to lack meaning or application to what is actually done.

We already have seen why silence on this subject is so pervasive. Unaccountability in the punisher means that infliction soon becomes too severe to be justified. There are no exceptions to this pattern. The same thing happens again and again. Since it cannot be justified, each heightened level of infliction requires more of a cover-up of practices too shameful to be revealed and harder to stop as they become common practices.

The most important legal philosopher of recent decades may have explained it best. Ronald Dworkin, in his last book, wrote, "Our felt conviction that cruelty is wrong is a conviction that cruelty is really wrong; we cannot have that conviction without thinking that it is objectively true."[36] The objective truth is what we must bring to treatment of the incarcerated. No one can justify cruelty, and yet it thrives in our prison system. Here is the puzzle in American punishment that no one quite wants to acknowledge fully.

It is simply the case that people are at their very worst when there is no check on the power they have over others, and that describes the average correction officer in every jail and prison in America. Earlier I referred to a playground of cruelty in prison life. It endures because meaningful rules do not control it. Unaccountability is the monster hiding in American penology, and in order to proceed we must first understand how it feeds itself.

Legal punishment changes a person in some way. Cruelty in punishment does much more. It mutilates identity. The ensuing disfigurement embodies the ugly side in metamorphosis, and to see that for what it is, we must reach back to move forward.

3
Accounting for Unaccountability

The Hidden Subject in Punishment

WHAT CAN A ROMAN POET FROM THE first century of the Christian era tell us that we don't already know? The answer is plenty. The Romans were among the cruelest and most refined of punishers, but they also believed in law, and that combination encouraged an acceptable severity. They saw that law can be the mask for unaccountability in a punisher. Where do we face what we do not want to face? We do it through the lens of literature.

The ancients turned to verse to explain human drama, and Ovid used that convention to see punishment and the responses to it. *Metamorphoses,* his great epic poem composed between 2 and 9 CE, explores the variables across 250 stories of excessive retribution. The result is extraordinary for its penetration—so extraordinary that it carried into the Renaissance and still informs our own understanding of the subject today.

Much of what Western thought came to feel about the subject of punishment originates in Ovid's artistic treatment of the subject.[1] He grasped what no culture likes to think about itself until it must. Punishment, he realized, is more than itself. It provides satisfaction for the punisher and through misery designates a flawed identity for the punished. That synergy also explains why punishment invariably goes up whenever it is not watched closely.

Ovid insisted that punishment is at once an ordering device and the problem in all of order, and he struggled with this contradiction across the fifteen books of his poem. That struggle became more acute when it turned personal. In 8 CE, with the poem unfinished and Ovid at the very height of his powers, the Emperor Augustus banished him to what is now the far coast of Romania. "Relegation," the legal term used, came as a surprise, and its terms were unduly harsh for a loyal subject who had committed no known crime.[2]

The consequences for Ovid were devastating. "Cast among hostile people I suffer the ultimate ruin." The leading poet of the age spent the last nine years of his life writing in alien and uncomfortable isolation on the barbarous outskirts of the Roman Empire where his language, Latin, was not spoken. Physical hardship, intellectual alienation, and the constant threat of tribal incursion filled these forlorn last years. *Tristia,* a final collection of poems (literally of sadness), were all written in and about exile. They plead obsessively for forgiveness and return from Tomis on the bleak edge of the Black Sea.

By any account, Ovid's offenses were trivial. Banishment fell personally and ruthlessly from the all-powerful and often capricious emperor, and the cause remains vague to this day. Punishment is bearable only if it is comprehensible and in some way deserved. Ovid correctly wrote that many others received less punishment for far greater known transgressions; never mind that his own have remained a mystery.[3]

These last added poems in exile animate the philosophical tangle of punishment at the heart of *Metamorphoses.* They grovel before imperial authority in the admission of error, yet they are also an eloquent legal brief on appeal.[4] The attempt to harness punishing power to legal authority in *Tristia* reinforces what is already there in *Metamorphoses.* The silence of power is the only answer Ovid ever received. Pardon never came. Augustus seems to have chosen this punishment to display his personal hold over the Roman Empire. Banishing the greatest poet of the age proved that he could level anyone, including the most famous of his subjects, on nothing more than a whim.

To appreciate Ovid's obsession with punishment in *Metamorphoses* we must start with the precise philosophical problem that drives it. His concern is with the misfortune that comes from punishment as opposed to mere misfortune, a serious distinction. Trouble comes to us all. We try to understand it in different ways, but everyone wants it to have significance, and the easiest way to give it meaning is to believe that it has been imposed for accountable reasons or because the unfortunate one has made some mistake.

Otherwise all is chaos, and that form of dissolution threatens everywhere in *Metamorphoses*.[5] The menace in chaos is the pulse of the poem, and we must understand its implication if we are to appreciate the depth of Ovid's purposes. The poet believes that order can succeed only by forcing itself imperiously on an unruly world, and the ruthlessness required raises a serious problem. Can power alone reign or must it depend on the larger meaning that a legal order requires? Law, as understood even then, supplies a framework beyond the imposition of force for the cooperation it needs to function well.[6]

Here is where the problem of unaccountability enters. *Metamorphoses* uses transformation to argue that imposed change robs people of who and what they are. Punishment leads so frequently to a terrible loss of identity that there must be a higher purpose to it, and that purpose must come from punishers who know what they are doing if human discord is to be anything more than an appalling presence. Again and again, the poet has his doubts about that answer.

The gods are really extrapolations of the violent worst in Roman society. They are *not* accountable. The poet uses them to warn against what we must guard in ourselves. Divine reference serves as an expedient tool, and we see as much at the end of Ovid's poem when he supplies an alternative to the Olympian menagerie. There the philosopher Pythagoras—"His mind came close to the gods"—brings a more hopeful and reasonable perspective to conflict. Change is again pervasive, but the Pythagorean version of it encourages peace and harmony, values that cannot be found in the earlier hierarchical construct of gods and men (15.62, 165–179).

By operating as poetic apparatus, the gods leave Ovid unhampered by orthodoxies. He freely twists them to his own philosophical purposes in his versions of their stories, and he puts that freedom to good use. When the gods attack and when they relent in the human world are keys to distinguishing between mere imposition and an emerging concept of order under regulation. Occasional acts of leniency and limitation in punishment begin to draw readers toward justice instead of "just the way things are."

Mostly, though, the gods attack. They are punishers, and very active ones. They are capable of rage, envy, spite, torture, pleasure, and selfish satisfaction in punishment. A singular absence supports their retributive impulses. "The cheeks of the gods are never allowed to be moistened by tears" (2.622). Can there be mercy without the prospect of tears? All of the leading male gods—Jupiter, Neptune, Pluto, Apollo—are serial rapists. Rape functions as the device by which Ovid creates the animate parts of his world, but he never forgets that it is also a crime that destroys its victims or turns them into monsters.

Sexual assault in *Metamorphoses* invariably destroys the beauty and character of its victims. One example can stand for countless others in the poem. The hideous Medusa, with snakes for hair and a stare that turns men into stone, first appears as "an exceedingly beautiful maiden sought by an army of suitors" until Neptune rapes her (4.793–803). Medusa is innocent of the wrongdoing that robs her of her natural identity, and as in so many cases of abuse, the trauma twists her into an abuser herself.

Medusa's story asks how innocence should be protected in the punishment cycle. Rape has cosmogonic significance for Ovid as a birthing mechanism, but it also represents a clever use of law with a larger purpose. Rape is one of the hardest crimes to punish in every society. Evidence is easily manipulated, and more victims go unanswered than vindicated. The history of rape proves the point. Many accounts acknowledge the escape of the rapist, and so it is in Ovid.

At least in this one context, the gods find their equivalents today. Prison guards rape women with impunity in American prisons and jails despite the Prison Rape Elimination Act of 2003.[7] Power and intimidation make statistics hard to come by, but official complaints reveal a "pattern of sexual misconduct" in female correctional institutions with no one held accountable.

Numbers complicate the mistreatment of women in facilities originally made for men. "The numbers of women jumped by 646 percent between 1980 and 2012—from 25,000 to more than 200,000" without adequate protection from assault.[8] A high percentage of those women have previously suffered abuse and are afraid to resist it in prison. Is prison rape an American institution? At least one book-length study makes that claim.[9] There is a pretty good argument that all correction officers in prisons for women should be women. The Bureau of Justice Statistics indicate that 80,000 women and men a year are sexually abused in American correctional facilities, and many more cases go unreported.[10]

Metamorphoses, by revealing the pain of victims like Medusa, asks ageless questions. What is punishment for and when is it deserved? When does the power of the strong amount to more than sway over the weak and vulnerable? Is status more than a matter of power? Will understanding punishment be enough to make it legitimate? Could it be that severe punishment gives the only means to a secure order? All of these questions lead to a more precarious one. Where does law figure in an acceptable theory of punishment? Legal terminology appears in the pages of *Metamorphoses* with great regularity.[11]

Literary form allows Ovid to ask these questions in a world that otherwise might not accept them. Torment after torment in his stories of rape takes the shape of a finished performance that we want to remember, and in making us remember, the poet asks that we think about each episode in terms of a reality behind it. Grounded in myth is a world we recognize.[12]

The Punitive Web of Implication

Critics often identify one story as the model for all of *Metamorphoses* in conveying the essence of punishment. Minerva's brutal transformation of Arachne into a spider summarizes the problem of punishment as the Roman world understood it. The legend circulated as early as 600 BCE, but even though the earlier Greek word *arachnê* means spider, our knowledge of the myth comes from Ovid, and all later accounts retain his stamp about the nature of punishment.[13]

The facts are straightforward across books 5 and 6 of Ovid's poem, one of the most extended narrative sections in *Metamorphoses.* Minerva comes to earth, specifically to Mount Helicon, home of the muses of poetry and song, where she hears story after story about divine prerogative in which one god after another punishes a victim simply because power wants to impose itself in proof of itself.

Minerva, who listens with growing impatience to these stories, begins to feel that her own power as a god has not received sufficient respect in the order of things. "I also need to be praised in turn," she declares. "No mortal shall scoff at my power unpunished," and she immediately looks for an offender to prove her own might. "She therefore considered how best to dispose of a Lydian girl, called Arachne, who claims (so she heard) to equal herself in working with wool" (6.1–14).

It is telling that Arachne has risen from a "humble home." Her distinction comes entirely through her art as the best weaver of tapestries, a skill that represents creativity in women's work. Such art and ability from a low and ultimately powerless status is the crime that Minerva cannot stand, and it will be Arachne's pride in her skill and hard-earned reputation that will do her in. Significantly, Arachne does not challenge Minerva; the god challenges her! Arachne, much like Ovid himself, is art without power, a dangerous combination in a world full of punishment.

The ensuing contest over who can weave the best tapestry is really about power disguised as skill and hence as law. Minerva has already decided to destroy the rival that she has created herself, and it is easily done. The god is always more than a contestant in this story. She is controlling witness, artistic evaluator, prosecutor, sole judge, and punisher all wrapped in one. Minerva does not win a victory so much as she conquers a designated victim. Ovid's purposes have to be understood against the hopeless predicament that Arachne represents for all humanity. Punishment is Minerva's plan, the inevitable outcome of the story, and the unavoidable lot of the human race in the poet's understanding, but none of this comes without artistic protest.

The two tapestries in the contest approach the subject of punishment from opposite directions. The result is the puzzle in punishment fully rendered. Minerva's tapestry presents the Olympians sitting in formal counsel and creating the world that humankind needs to prosper. The corners of her tapestry reveal the gods guiding that world toward legal harmony. In Minerva's web, the gods punish mortals who disturb an established coherence. Transgressors are destroyed only for the good of the whole. Punishment here is law and social order.

Minerva changes anyone who threatens that stability into a familiar geographical element of nature that the Roman world knew and loved: particular mountains, birds, and temples are frequent results. She completes this positive vision of justice by wrapping it in "a border of olive branches," "symbol of peace." The border reflects the center of the tapestry in which Minerva, Athena in Greek mythology, depicts herself giving the olive tree to Athens to ensure her chosen city's prosperity in the world. Divine guidance through punishment secures human direction that would not be possible without it (6.70–102). This is law as aspiration, with punishment coming only to those who deserve it.

Arachne, the human contender, turns this conventional theory of punishment upside down. She moves from the punisher's perspective to that of the punished, a depiction reinforced by the fact that only the human beings in her tapestry appear in their own form. Her punished figures are invariably innocent victims, not the malicious transgressors previously described by Minerva. The gods in her tapestry appear in the animal forms and other disguises that they have assumed as deceivers and rapists of the blameless mortals they desire to overwhelm.

Criminal acts of bestial lust dominate in Arachne's tapestry, and since lust is not love, the sexual conquests of the gods yield new monsters of disorder rather than the peace and harmony pictured in Minerva's understanding of the world (6.103–128). This is not a panorama designed to please Minerva, although it clearly pleases Ovid. Here is a world of power without law, where the weak suffer and the strong take what they want against all rightfulness and philosophical integrity.

The poet uses the story of Arachne to recognize the pleasure principle in unaccountable punishment and its pernicious effects. Disguise, deception, and selfish infliction by the powerful control Arachne's portrayal of the world, and she cannot help but remind us that Minerva has first appeared in disguise to engineer this contest (6.26–43). Nor does Ovid allow Arachne to lose! When Minerva turns to Arachne's tapestry neither she nor Invidia, appropriately the goddess of envy, can find a way to "criticize weaving like that"; the tapestry is simply too good and accurate. How good is it? Arachne has pictured what *Metamorphoses* presents across thousands of lines of verse (6.26–43, 128–129).

Ovid confirms as much in the conclusion he gives to this contest. We have Arachne's understanding of punishment acted out on her own person in a figurative rape of her body. Resenting "Arachne's success" but with no intellectual answer to it, the enraged Minerva chooses violence instead of judgment as her response. She rips apart "the picture betraying the god's misdemeanors" and beats Arachne over the head with the hard wooden shuttle that she has used to weave her own tapestry. Violent use of the shuttle is a special stroke. Ovid turns the instrument for creating order and beauty out of chaos into a weapon of destruction that denies the art it is meant to serve. Nor is it enough to destroy the evidence and chastise Arachne for presenting the truth (6.130–133).

The story devolves into the most horrifying and memorable physical transformation in all of *Metamorphoses*. Arachne in despair tries to hang herself, an honorable recourse often granted in the Roman Empire when a presumed offender tried to avoid more excruciating imperial punishment, but Minerva will not allow it. "Live, you presumptuous creature," the goddess cries. Arachne must live without the worth that life gives. "Don't count on a happier future," Minerva warns while detailing the torments to come. "You'll hang suspended forever, my sentence applies to the whole of your kind, and to all your descendants" (6.136–138).

Under this judgment, Arachne slowly devolves into a loathsome spider weaving mechanically rather than creatively. The transformation is one of Ovid's most graphic images of metamorphosis in punishment: "her hair fell away, and so did the ears and the nose. The head now changed to a tiny ball and her whole frame shrunk in proportion. Instead of her legs there are spindly fingers attached to her sides. The rest is merely abdomen, from which she continues to spin" (6.140–144). With no restrictions on her ability to punish and no limits placed on her anger, Minerva can turn the price of Arachne's presumption into permanent torture and life imprisonment. What was "former art" in Arachne falls into the unknowing drudgery of meaningless labor, the lot of many on Earth (6.140–145).

The levels of anger that fuel this account from start to finish are instructive. Arachne, like Minerva, is defined by "anger all over her face," and Ovid knows what he is doing by focusing on this emotion (6.35). Horace, Ovid's immediate predecessor as the earlier reigning poet of the Augustan era, defined the problem: *Ira furor brevis est* (Anger is a short madness); it robs anyone under its influence of proportionality and clarity in punishment.[14] No one engages in punishment without resentment infecting the subject.

The difference between Minerva's created aspirations and Arachne's forlorn reality depicts a scene of hypocrisy found in every civilization.

Punishment dignified as a tool of social control rarely justifies the extent of its actual infliction. The excess in anger eliminates moderation *unless carefully and legally watched.* Minerva has unlimited power to do whatever she wants. Ovid lets us see that the contradictions between the abstract concept in punishment and its ugly physical manifestations are intrinsic, and no culture has ever come up with a lasting solution to the discrepancy or the means to control it.

This discrepancy signifies that all theories of punishment remain works in progress. Rome is the first advanced culture to so much as pretend to find an answer, and in recognition, the poet offers a glimpse of one. He interrupts the endless processes of punishment so central to *Metamorphoses* only once, but the interruption is as significant and memorable as it is moving.

We find it for a moment in Arachne's weaving but more appropriately in the art of song. There Ovid attacks the puzzle in punishment directly. The struggle for a full answer is not won in his poem, but the struggle is indeed there. In book 10, with a story as famous as that of Arachne, Orpheus, the greatest singer and musician of antiquity, tries to retrieve his bride, Eurydice, from Hades through the powers of song and musical craft.

In this one instance, *Metamorphoses* allows human art to forestall the punishment regime at the center of the poem. Eurydice, frolicking in a field on her wedding day, has been fatally bitten by a serpent. Typical of classical thought, too much happiness has been derailed by the misery that is always near, but Ovid insists on a pause in which everyone has to stop and think about what he or she is doing.

Orpheus risks everything, his life as well as his art, for love. He sings of his willingness to do anything for it. "If fate forbids you to show my wife any mercy, I'll never return from Hades myself." That way, he says, "you may joy in the deaths of us both." Even the Furies shed tears for the first and only time over these words, and all torment in Hell ceases. The five mythological figures who symbolize the meaning of punishment in the ancient world—Tantalus, Ixion, Tityos, the Danaids, and Sisyphus—feel no pain during this song (10.17–30).

Tantalus no longer lunges in thirst for the pool he can never reach. The wheel of crucifixion to which Ixion is tied ceases to turn; vultures no longer peck at Tityos's liver. The Danaids stop filling the useless urns that have holes in the bottom of them, and Sisyphus sits upon his gigantic boulder instead of pushing it forever up the hill only to see it always roll back down again. So powerful is Orpheus's art that Eurydice is released until he forgets and looks back for her on their path out of Hades. The love that "was too strong" for him to accept her death now confirms it (10.40–57).

Perhaps nothing has been accomplished, but what exactly has happened here? Punishment need not be perpetual and unrelenting! The punishers in Hell have seen for a moment what it means to be human. Mercy exists! Orpheus's plea reveals the full effect of mortality alongside the joy and the courage that are possible in life precisely because it is so ephemeral. Punishment falls into a void. Its inflictors lose their taste for what they do.

One may assume that this dormant state, this hiatus in punishment, is a momentary distraction, but Ovid's point seems to be greater than that. Fate and circumstance, often the explanations for continuing to punish in the way the world does, are no longer in full control. Orpheus wonders if fate forbids the gods from showing mercy. Ovid responds that nothing is forbidden, least of all mercy, and he works hard to prove his point.

The path to mercy or leniency against reflexive punishment owes everything to a combination of aesthetical, spatial, and social mechanisms.[15] Orpheus's song is beautiful. That beauty is enhanced by the place he dares to sing it, and the social relation, saving his new bride, is compelling. This triad, when taken together, creates sympathy and mutuality in the punishers of hell. Remember these mechanisms when we come to reform in our prison world of today, where aesthetic appeal is not allowed, spatial relations are insufferably cramped, and social relations are deliberately warped.

The Sisyphean Perplex

Hell is the ultimate scene of punishment. Each of the five paradigmatic figures noted above exemplifies an egregious challenge to the established order. If these ultimate offenders in *Metamorphoses* have been allowed to keep their forms, instead of being transformed, it is to better deter others through the representation of agonized human flesh. But that is not all. For deterrence to work, an observer must also know the crime that must not be committed.

Curiously then, the only figure out of the five that we remember in any detail in modern life is Sisyphus, and if we do manage to recall all five, we know far less about his crime than we do about theirs. Sisyphus is famous for his punishment, not for what he did, and the discrepancy tells us something important about the subject.

The connection between crime and punishment is easily made in the other four figures who receive such prominence. Tantalus steals ambrosia and nectar, the food of the gods, and tries to feed the gods human flesh. His punishment is intuitively obvious. He has water and food in front of him but can reach neither. Ixion foolishly tries to rape Juno, the wife of Jupiter, and is crucified on a revolving wheel for it. He has lost all hierarchical perspective. Tityos assaults the goddess Leto. The vultures eating at his liver depict eternal suffering because the liver, the seat of sensual passion, regenerates itself after each attack. After the fifty daughters of Danaus kill their husbands on their wedding night, they must perform the common domestic task of filling their urns with water, but their efforts are futile; their urns will not hold water. In killing marriage, they have made duties in the home meaningless.

These punishments fit the crime. So, in fact, does the punishment of Sisyphus, but at a philosophical level that is often ignored. Based as it is on an idea as much as an act, his offense shakes the order in things far more drastically than the other transgressions mentioned. Sisyphus cheats death itself by binding Thanatos, the keeper of the dead. No one can die as long as Thanatos is helpless! Related stories confirm what has happened by having Sisyphus avoid death in other ways.

Sisyphus has disturbed existence itself, and the alarm on Olympus is substantial. If humans become immortal, they can challenge the gods. Status, one of the criteria that justify a punisher's right over the punished, will be lost. The answer of the gods is exact. Given Sisyphus's love of existence, the gods decide to make his life as meaningless as possible. The hurt of infliction is as mental as it is physical.

Sisyphus is the smartest and most cunning of mortals. To reduce all of this intellectual power to useless hard labor is to have an Einstein dig ditches that no one needs or wants. Today common parlance makes any thankless exertion "a Sisyphean task." Perhaps we remember Sisyphus the most because pointless activity strikes so many nerves in modern life. How many people perform jobs and tedious chores that they would relinquish in a moment if they safely could? In my own childhood home, Sisyphus was known as the patron saint of housework. You clean the same dish and make the same bed knowing that you will have to do it all over again the next day.

Pushing the same rock up the hill with all of one's effort and watching it fall down again to no end trivializes more than the effort it takes; it attacks existence itself, and that is the aspect that controls modern interpretation. Albert Camus takes up the subject at length by turning Sisyphus into his absurd hero. Meaninglessness in the task frees its victim to ponder the lack of meaning in life. Writing in 1942, one of the darkest years of the twentieth century, Camus has Sisyphus ponder humanity's existential dilemma each time he walks back to begin another push up the hill. Intelligence, in this view, raises him above it all. "His scorn of the gods, his hatred of death, and his passion for life won him that unspeakable penalty in which the whole being is exerted toward accomplishing nothing."[16]

Maybe so, but no one should forget that the penalty endured by Sisyphus is indeed "unspeakable" in ways that need to be recognized. The horror in it exposes a vital problem in punishment. Sisyphus is so intelligent and cunning that he can fool even the gods, but that is not all he does. He is a confidence man, a master of fraud who loves what he does and will continue to do it every time he is given the chance in the sheer pleasure of his capacity to commit crime. He cheats everyone he meets, including death.

The problem in punishment changes under these circumstances. What is to be done with an unrepentant transgressor? Correction becomes hopeless in such a case. Sisyphus therefore presents the starkest issue in punishment. The incorrigible criminal frustrates every concept of leniency and mercy. Here is the underlying fear in penology. What if correction is futile?

Here, too, is one institutional reason for too much punishment. The fear that correction will not work leads the punisher to assume incorrigibility in all of the punished with heightened degrees of infliction as the presumed answer to it. Everyone receives severer treatment in the name of the criminal who cannot be changed. One of its modern equivalents? In American prisons a transgression by an unknown prisoner when no one will confess or reveal the perpetrator can lead to everyone being punished through a "lockdown" or removal of other privileges, such as television or a hot meal.

Ovid handles this issue in punishment by returning most recalcitrants to the natural world from which they came. The human race has evolved from stones, according to *Metamorphoses*. So when elements in it misbehave, the poet returns them to that static state, immobility through transformation. The device is a precursor of permanent incarceration in the modern prison. But Ovid also eliminates the problem of mentality in crime. The most frequent punishment in the poem has a living person changed into inanimate matter, and the worst aspect of it is the loss of an intelligible voice, which is almost always noted.

Voice is what makes us human in the poet's understanding. To remove it is to send us back into the earth where we bear "the unmistakable marks of our stony origin" (1.400–415). By the same token, we have seen that a continuing human form in the punished may correct others through the observation of its pain. That is why Sisyphus must push the stone instead of being turned into one. His unrepentant individuality is his attraction and simultaneously the reason why he is the ultimate problem in punishment.

For if Sisyphus retains his identity, he also retains his criminal nature. One reason for his punishment may be to so exhaust him that he has nothing left to communicate or offer to those whom he might involve in further crime. But if so, the punishment seems impossibly harsh. How much do we blame Sisyphus for wanting to live longer? Don't we all wish for that? We remember Sisyphus because he naturally comes closer to our situation than do Tantalus, Ixion, Tityos, or the Danaids. Their crimes are vicious physical interventions. There is nothing admirable in what they do. Sisyphus is punished for his challenge to the limits of existence, something we all struggle against at some point in our lives.

His passion for life is one reason Sisyphus remains more of himself in Hades and is intact in ways that the others who pause during Orpheus's song are not. Admittedly, we never hear Sisyphus speak again, but the gods have not taken away that capacity or interrupted his human form, and he remains as clever as he has ever been. We are told that "Sisyphus sat upon his boulder" during Orpheus's plea while the others in Hades simply pause. He alone turns his torture instrument into a resting place! Perhaps he also gets the most out of Orpheus's appeal among the punished. The others have twisted life in their pursuit of it. Sisyphus simply wants more of it in precisely the way that Orpheus is pleading for life in song.

The philosophical contradictions are acute when we think of Sisyphus. We are caught between the idea of law as a normative source of accepted meaning and law as the imposition of force.[17] Normatively we find ourselves on the side of Sisyphus; legally, perhaps we cannot be. Thoughts of the incorrigible criminal dictate legal punishment as almost nothing else does, and the typical policy across history has been to punish obduracy very hard.

This obduracy is one of Ovid's troubling premises. He presents a rebellious human race in need of chastisement, with Sisyphus as its most accomplished exponent. But how much chastisement is justified? Do we agree with Sisyphus's punishment? Do we sympathize with him? Do we agree and sympathize at the same time? With any sympathy at all, how can we condone the colossal waste of so much mental ability to all-consuming physical torment? The gods think only of retribution in their rage against Sisyphus. By fooling them, he has appeared to be their equal, and that is what the punisher can never tolerate in the punished.

The stringent hierarchy in Roman society keeps Ovid from fully understanding this part of the puzzle in punishment. For if we are really all alike and act on it, punishment must surely be moderate. Ovid sees instead that presumed superiority in a punisher will fuel unlimited severity in dealing with the punished. Punished unfairly himself, he realizes that unchecked superiority will punish the innocent as harshly as a transgressor and without the slightest qualms. Cruelty, in its unaccountability, is a matter of not caring about the difference. The point is an obsession in *Metamorphoses*. Ovid recognizes the pleasure in punishment and knows that it is a problem that must be handled, but how?

The Problem Faced

One does not have to read between the lines of Ovid's poetry to grasp how his anxieties about punishment define major problems in it then as well as now. Civilizations punish severely when they feel threatened, and the rulers over them have their own reasons for emphasizing those threats and levying the punishments that follow therefrom.

The Emperor Augustus repressed the most imaginary of oppositions. By way of comparison, the United States is one of the safest nations in history, but it imprisons more people than any other country in the world in irrational fear of crime and alien invasion. Punishment is a reflexive communal response to the presumption of peril, and it is easily played upon by those in authority against the disadvantaged in their midst.

But if the will to punish is always there, and if Ovid shows it more intensely than others, then the real problem in *Metamorphoses*—and in American punishment regimes today—exists at another level. Lack of accountability in a punisher is the main source of unwarranted severity. The gods in Ovid's poem strike without limit or control. They can even boast openly of their "excessive cruelty" (4.540). They save their greatest inflictions for those who are perceived to be different from them or for those who are too close to them and hence a threat to their existence.

The easiest answer to all of this misfortune is fatalism, but there is a side of Ovid that suggests more. Why else would the poet spend so much time depicting the innocence of so many who receive punishment? Innocence allows us to see guilt but adds an element of bewilderment when it is harmed. Innocence destroyed pleads for a sense of justice somewhere. To the extent that order is viewed through the capacity to punish, power becomes the solitary gauge of application *unless* it is checked by law.

The poet saw that law was the answer. He simply did not know how to get there. He did, however, fasten on something crucial that we miss today. He realized with special clarity that unaccountability in a punisher will make the transformation in the punished as ugly and terrible as anyone can imagine.

We overlook Ovid's problem, his puzzle in punishment, when we believe law actually stands in the way. But what if it doesn't? What if law as construed encourages unaccountability? This is what must be faced if we are to change legal punishment in America. Current policies of imprisonment *legally* destroy more lives than they save. The unchecked power of our penal systems is not that different from the control of Ovid's gods right down to the racism that intensifies punishment in both worlds.

4
Rights Talk and the Enabling of Wrongs

The Habits in Rights Talk

I HAVE SAID THAT LAW HAS MADE punishment in prison more unjust, and it is time to prove it. Civil rights have ever been the legal recourse of the downtrodden, and they are often celebrated on those grounds. Why, then, do civil rights not work for the incarcerated? There is a significant lacuna in both understanding and practice here.

Why does unaccountability in our punishment regimes, an unprecedented aspect of American institutional understanding, fail to alarm us? One of the ironies in prison abuse comes here. Rights talk, the language used to protect individual liberty in civilian life, disowns the more than 2 million people we hold in prison and jail. Communal complacency is not hard to explain or entirely at fault either. Rights talk disowns the incarcerated while seeming to do the opposite.

The typical court opinion on prisoners' rights proclaims constitutional guarantees in principle while taking them away in practice. Judges say a right is available but not in the decision before them. The rhetoric used resembles the sleight of hand in a shell game. The proverbial pea designating rights exists under one of the three cups—just not under this one!—and, as in the game, habit and hypocrisy both play roles in the deception.

We'll start with habit. The abstractions in rights talk allow many particulars to be ignored even as the stress on individual rights ignores the collective nature of prison problems. The rubrics that protect civil rights depend on balancing tests between particular redress and communal interests, and these tests invariably work against prisoner complaints through security claims. Prejudgment easily dismisses *the person complaining* through *the crime committed,* sometimes long ago.

The predisposition in American law against prisoners' rights also has historical foundations. In 1865, the Thirteenth Amendment of the Constitution abolished slavery and involuntary servitude "*except* as a punishment for crime wherever the party shall have been duly convicted." The exception has led the judiciary to adopt a hands-off policy when it comes to the legally punished. Justice Thurgood Marshall, referring to that policy in 1977, called it a "discredited conception of prisoners' rights and the role of the courts."[1]

Marshall saw the modern Supreme Court returning to a hands-off policy from the Reconstruction era, and his concern soon became the reality.[2] Judicial acceptance of sharp restrictions on prisoners' rights has formed a pattern extending into the twenty-first century. The presumed civil entitlements—freedom of religion, freedom of speech, freedom of assembly, freedom to grieve against the government, freedom from search and seizure, and the right to privacy—depend implicitly on the right to liberty, and that is what is taken away from people in prison. The result has been a discrepancy between logical explication and court doctrine. The conventional patterns in rights talk work against a prisoner's human needs when loss of freedom also eliminates freedom of choice. Citizenship is the right to have or choose to exercise rights.[3] If that right is severely diminished, so is every claim on other civil rights. The question never asked? When does diminished citizenship make a prisoner less of a person in the eyes of the law?

Prisoners cannot vote. They do not always receive the mail or books or many of the visitors they want. They are denied vocational possibility. They are deprived of the possibility of minimal physical comforts such as a good bed or chair. They cannot address each other freely. They lack minimal protection from abuse. They do not own secure property. They cannot resist a trespass. They do not receive timely medical care in most instances, and they do not receive proper nourishment much of the time. The whim of authority can take everything away from a prisoner except life itself, and life itself is often made precarious.

Leading legal critics have explained the several ways that rights talk goes amiss in judicial decision making. "Striking a balance between the rights of the accused individual and the demands of society" produces a "false model" with unrealistic balancing metaphors at "the heart of its error." This is so, argues Ronald Dworkin, because a fundamental individual right should have priority over all but the greatest of social demands.[4]

"The language of rights is the language of no compromise," adds Mary Ann Glendon in the leading work on this subject. The individualism and no compromise in rights talk get in the way of collective suffering of the kind found in prison. "Its legalistic character, its exaggerated absoluteness, its hyperindividualism, its insularity, and its silence with respect to personal, civic, and collective responsibilities" all resist "a grammar of cooperative living."[5]

It is also true that civil rights protect the fortunate more often than the unfortunate. "The language of rights is so open and indeterminate that opposing parties can use the same language to express their positions" in the adversarial system, with power dynamics winning in the end.[6] The abstractions in theories of individual rights obscure "the provisional quality of social hierarchy." They posit an abstract equality of opportunities not always found in actual conflicts and rarely apparent in conflicts where penal authority is at stake against a prisoner's claims.[7]

Judicial language as it moves up the ladder of appeal is especially prone to these abstracting tendencies. "Facts and interests can be decomposed or universalized at will, to trivialize or exaggerate the weight of the facts or interests," explains Mark Tushnet, an expert on the contingencies of constitutional law and legal history. Specificities, the kind of problem that a prisoner legitimately complains about, are frequently lost in the law's reliance on precedent and doctrinal understandings. In court, writes Tushnet, "a balancer who wants to 'recognize' a right can choose the measure of value, the necessary consequences, and the necessary level of generality. So can a balancer who wants to deny the claim that a right has been violated."[8] Appellate judicial panels approach individual cases through the general language of rights discourse. Too frequently the nature of that language lifts a dispute away from visible patterns of injustice.[9]

Larger ideological considerations are at work as well. "America's justice system suffers from a mismatch of individual rights and criminal justice machinery, between legal ideals and political institutions," writes William Stuntz in his seminal analysis of "the collapse" of the criminal justice system. In the legal shuffle of priorities, "constitutional law in the United States pays too much attention to procedure, and too little to substance."[10]

Hypocrisy follows habit. If established ideology is a controlling factor, why do we find so many narrower, even specious, stances in the decisions that limit prisoners' rights? Habit, through precedent and doctrinal repetition, is required of courts, and it explains many self-imposed judicial restrictions, but it is not enough to explain the level of restriction placed on prisoners' rights. The comfort in habit leaves room for hypocrisy to enter when habit is challenged. New ways of thinking face this problem. In the words of the cultural anthropologist Mary Douglas, "the commonest and entrenched social analogies are always there, resisting change."[11]

Habit trusts to general thought. Hypocrisy can ignore a perceived reality, obscure another intent, dismiss established policy (without saying so), or fail to acknowledge desert. All of these elements appear in Supreme Court decision making when prisoners' rights are under consideration.

The Hypocrisies in Rights Talk

The bellwether decision and still the standard on prisoners' legal complaints is *Turner v. Safley* handed down in a 5-to-4 decision on June 1, 1987.[12] *Turner* established a four-pronged test based on a standard of "reasonableness" in answering prisoner petitions (2262). The four prongs are arranged to protect the claims of prison authority and to deny most petitions out of hand. They include the following:

1. Penal authority's claim will hold if there is "a 'valid, rational connection' between the prison regulation and the legitimate governmental interest put forward to justify it."
2. Courts will also side with authority if "there are alternative means of exercising the rights that remain open to prison inmates."
3. All decisions must consider "the impact accommodation of the asserted constitutional right will have on guards and other inmates, and on the allocation of prison resources generally."

4. Then, if all else fails, judges must remember that "the absence of ready alternatives is evidence of the reasonableness of a prison regulation."

Just how fair-minded is *Turner*'s test of reasonableness? The Court's decision establishes elaborate regard for penal authority expressed as a "principle." Justice Sandra Day O'Connor, speaking for the Court, details the many reasons for judicial deference to that authority: " 'courts are ill-equipped to deal with the increasingly urgent problems of prison administration and reform' "; " 'the problems of prisons in America are complex and intractable, and . . . not readily susceptible of resolution by decree' "; and "separation of powers concerns counsel a policy of judicial restraint" (2259).

Limits placed on judicial competence in *Turner* also presume professionalism in all penal arrangements. "Running a prison is an inordinately difficult undertaking that requires expertise, planning, and the commitment of resources, all of which are peculiarly within the province of the legislative and executive branches of government." And if these strictures are not enough, other reasons for granting deference remain unnamed. "Federal courts have . . . additional reason to accord deference to the appropriate prison authorities" (2259).

Noted far less forcefully and extensively is another opening principle: "federal courts must take cognizance of the valid constitutional claims of prison inmates" (2259). The brevity and tonal reluctance in these words are palpable. Cognizance does not denote action, and the adjective "valid" set before "constitutional claims" raises a warning flag. Another warning comes in the Court's invocation of "separation of powers" against traditional understandings of that phrase. "Separation" originally signified the need to handle and balance conflicting institutional powers that naturally arise; it did not imply abdication to another branch of government's expertise. We live today in an age where the presumed "authority of experts" controls too much of thought.[13]

Consider the Court's many reasons for deference in light of the four-pronged test offered in *Turner v. Safley*. If prison authorities, under the first test, establish *any* "rational connection" between "prison regulation" and "a legitimate government interest," the other three dominoes in the test fall quickly into place on the side of authority. With a "rational connection" identified, how difficult will it be for prison authorities to claim, in prong three, the presence of a negative impact on personnel and prison resources generally? The onus in prongs two and four also shifts. It moves to the petitioning prisoner to prove the absence of other sources in exercising the right against the lack of alternatives, a difficult proposition.[14]

Consider how much the Supreme Court must change to get its result. The thin 5-to-4 majority in *Turner v. Safley* reaches its decision by denying vital facts in the case, by overturning decisions in both the trial and appellate courts, by rejecting its own earlier precedents, and by undercutting long-established doctrine on the need for strict scrutiny as the desired approach when fundamental constitutional rights are in question. The strain in these denials is telling, and it dominates the rhetoric used by the Court.

Turner v. Safley originates in a class action to determine the constitutional right of inmate-to-inmate correspondence, the right of inmates to marry, and the right to visitation privileges in former inmates. The trial court in the Western District of Missouri decided that both marriage and communication involve basic human rights. It agreed that rules prohibiting former inmates from visiting prison within six months of their release were a legitimate exercise of discretion but argued that exceptions, including some that had been offered, should be possible.[15]

In the lower court's decision, *Safley v. Turner,* discretion in authority could not mean wholesale exclusion. The "strict scrutiny test" of judicial review applied because fundamental constitutional rights in the prisoners were being challenged. To succeed, penal policy had to demonstrate a compelling government interest narrowly tailored and least restrictive to accomplish the task. The trial court thought that prison authority had failed on all three counts.

With close attention to the facts, the trial court also decided that the policies of the Renz Correctional Institution in Missouri were invalid. Prison authority's absolute prohibition of marriage by inmates was "far more restrictive than was either reasonable or essential for protection of any state security interest or any other legitimate interest," and "prison regulations and practices against inmate-to-inmate correspondence were unnecessarily sweeping." Restrictions on former inmate visitation rights were similarly rigid. "The evidence shows that exceptions to the rule should doubtless be made, as in the case of a former inmate who wished to help in the Alcoholics Anonymous program." Notably, the trial court was also swayed by evidence of retribution in the enforcement of some rules.[16]

The original decision took as its base a very detailed "Findings of Fact." A numerical listing totaling forty-five separate points of arbitrary enforcement supported the lower court's finding. Divisional regulations in the Missouri Department of Corrections allowed correspondence between inmates, but they were repeatedly violated by correction officers in Renz Prison. Many letters to and from persons not incarcerated, to other incarcerated family members, and between inmates had been "stopped without notice or explanation to either the correspondent or the recipient." Delivery had also been refused as a stated punishment. Finally, letters between inmates had been denied against "evidence that the correspondence was desired simply to maintain wholesome friendships."[17]

The trial court brusquely rejected several loose allegations by prison authorities that were not compatible with the record. It was not true that the staff lacked effective methods "to scan and control outgoing and incoming mail, including inmate-to-inmate correspondence." Nor could prison authorities come up with a shred of evidence to support their claim that mail was being used for conspiratorial purposes or escape plans. Mere conjecture was not enough to interfere with a constitutional right.

Much is at stake in these trial findings. The import of withholding mail in a prison setting, failing to deliver mail, and dismissing it without notice should never be minimized. Friendships are one of the few guides, comforts, supports, and satisfactions in prison life, and these relationships were broken—deliberately broken at Renz Prison—through frequent moves of an inmate to another institution. Mail then becomes the only way to maintain a friendship. The trial court found it to be "a basic human right."[18] Anyone familiar with prison life knows that nothing is more important to the incarcerated than mail. It conveys meaningful exchange otherwise lacking. Correspondence is priceless. It is one of the most useful sources of personal reflection and growth during incarceration.[19]

In determining marriage to be "a basic human right" the trial court observed that a number of women had been "refused permission to marry . . .

on the unexplained ground that the proposed marriage was not in their 'best interests.'" More to the point, prison authorities in Renz prevented all marriages as a matter of policy, and prisoners who sought them were "threatened with the loss of writing privileges and visitation privileges with family members."[20] Everywhere there was evidence of a heavy hand in the applications of authority.

Punitive measures did not stop there. Inmates were "threatened with loss of parole and of parole privileges for attempting to exercise their marriage, correspondence, and visitation rights." They were "harassed and threatened" for pursuing their grievances in court, "threatened with the loss of custody of their children," and subjected to "retaliation or harassment by employees of the Department of Corrections" for testimony in seeking their rights.[21]

Not surprisingly, the trial court discovered "some evidence from which a spiteful attitude could be inferred." Straining for a more generous interpretation, it agreed that the behavior of prison authorities could instead be construed as "excessively paternalistic." Either way, its decision did not split the difference. The court pointedly "ORDERED that defendants engage in no harassment of inmates for their participation in this lawsuit."[22]

It would be hard to come up with a more concrete case of prison mismanagement, violation by authority of its own rules, and administrative vindictiveness against reasonable redress. Again and again under strict scrutiny standards, the court determined that there were always less restrictive ways for the prison to maintain the security arrangements it claimed to be of paramount concern.[23]

With such a clear record before it from the trial court, the Court of Appeals for the Eighth Circuit had no trouble siding with the district court's interpretations, and it added theoretical heft to what already had been decided. On appeal, prison authorities argued that "the plaintiffs' status as prisoners" meant "the district court should have applied a rational basis or reasonableness test rather than strict scrutiny" in making its decisions. The authorities further contended "certain of the district court's findings of fact are clearly erroneous." The appellate court disagreed on both counts after conducting its own thorough examination of the record. Its perusal found "substantial evidence to support each finding of fact" in the lower court's consideration of the case.[24]

The appellate court reviewed all apposite precedents to sustain its confirmation of the trial court's application of the strict scrutiny test. Prisoners did not fall into a lower level of constitutional consideration on fundamental rights simply because of their "status" as inmates. Against the penal system's insistence on severe restrictions to prevent security breaches—"plans for escape, violent uprisings or other illegal activities"—the appellate court, like its predecessor, pointed to the lack of evidence to support such claims. "No specific incident of the realization of any of these concerns, involving these or other inmates, was alleged or shown." The appellate court also said there were clearly other ways to handle the problem. "The prison official's authority to open and read all prisoner mail is sufficient to meet the problem of illegal conspiracies."[25]

None of the level-headedness, clear view of prison life, use of court precedent, correct resort to established doctrine, attention to evidence, or common sense in both lower court decisions reaches the Supreme Court. *Turner v. Safley* denies the relevance of every point in a cascade of abstractions away from the concrete elements in the case. The Court's language, not its logic, explains an otherwise unaccountable reversal. Language, to be sure, gives coherence to thought. It is what we think with, but it also sustains subterfuge when speakers or writers wish to achieve an understanding all their own, and that is what happens here.

The kindest thing one can say about the Supreme Court's decision in *Turner v. Safley* is that it is disingenuous, a point verified in a vigorous dissent signed by four justices. The majority opinion takes what it pretends to give. It ducks the central issue of prisoners' rights by shifting attention to the discretion that penal authority must have to control a dangerous and difficult environment. It takes no notice of the facts it does not want to see. It discovers danger where none exists and forgets that the difficulty at issue flows from official restrictions imposed rather than from observed behavior in prisoners. These strange evasions are the ultimate puzzle in *Turner v. Safley*, but to understand them we must first see how deeply they are grounded in court rhetoric.

In the technical holding, the majority opinion uses the Court's new "lesser standard of scrutiny" to reject for prisoners the more basic right protected by the Constitution, the right to free speech through correspondence.

It then upholds the lesser right of a prisoner to marry but only under certain unspecified conditions (2257). The double finding achieves the appearance of balance without the substance. As Justice John Paul Stevens notes at the end of his withering dissent (one joined by Justices William Brennan, Thurgood Marshall, and Harry Blackmun), "the Court's erratic use of the record" rests "on an unarticulated assumption that the marital state is fundamentally different from the exchange of mail" although "the Constitution more clearly protects the right to communicate than the right to marry." This shot by the dissenters is a powerful one. The few inmates who might want to marry are marginally helped under certain conditions while the many who could gain "satisfaction, solace and support" from writing letters to each other are summarily denied (2274).

Justice Sandra Day O'Connor, writing for the slimmest of majorities, begins by denying an open truth. She asserts that "the regulations challenged in the complaint were in effect in all prisons within the jurisdiction of the Missouri Division of Corrections." In fact, the restrictions imposed by the Renz Correctional Institution were far more restrictive than elsewhere in the Missouri penal system as a matter of record (2257). She further conveys the impression that she is agreeing with the procedures of the lower courts when she is not. "We begin, as did the courts below, with our decision in *Procunier v. Martinez*" (2259).[26] The word "begin" is misleading. *Martinez* is effectively overruled in the Supreme Court's *Turner* opinion with other opinions in the line recast to eliminate "strict scrutiny standards" in dealing with prisoners' rights (2261).

The majority opinion merely gestures to the controlling observations in the trial court's analysis while emphasizing the conclusions that it wants to disagree with. In another evasion, Justice O'Connor ignores the appellate court's renewed attention to the facts in order to concentrate her fire on how the appellate court parses the precedents that dictate strict scrutiny on fundamental rights. (2258). "We disagree with the Court of Appeals that the reasoning in our cases subsequent to *Martinez* can be so narrowly cabined" (2258, 2259, 2261, 2262). She reaches instead for the abstract logic used by the appellate court in order to replace it with her own: "when a prison regulation impinges on inmates' constitutional rights, the regulation is valid if it is reasonably related to legitimate penological interests" (2261).

The wiggle terms in O'Connor's statement are "impinges on" and "related to." The word "impinge" refers rather vaguely "to have an effect on" rather than to "prevent." "Related to," also vague in thrust, connotes a connection more than a direct influence. Neither phrase gets to the root of the matter: the extreme vulnerability of prisoners under the absolute control of unresponsive and openly obstructive correction officers.

With such logic and terminology in place, the claim of judicial balance by the narrow majority in *Turner* looks very different. Past precedent, it turns out, "simply teaches that it is appropriate to consider the extent of this burden [of a regulation on prisoners] when 'we [are] called upon to balance First Amendment rights against governmental interests.'" So identified, "balance" tilts toward authority. The Court quietly eliminates "a tenuous basis for creating a hierarchy of standards of review," and, without that hierarchy, it can move to its own looser "reasonableness standard," based on deference to penal authority. More cover comes through the invocation of agonized decision making: "the difficult judgments concerning institutional operations" (2261).

One other sleight of hand clinches the majority's direction. In obvious reliance on retributive instincts, its creation of a new "reasonableness standard" allows every prisoner to be seen as dangerous. "Reasonableness," the Court argues, cannot "be construed as applying only to 'presumptively dangerous' inmate activities." Instead, *every* prisoner falls under suspicion and becomes worthy of restriction. "The determination that an activity is 'presumptively dangerous' appears simply to be a conclusion about the reasonableness of the prison restriction in light of the articulated security concerns" (2261). Simply?

Repeated use of the adverb "simply" masks a circular argument. The determination of danger by authority is the same thing as the restriction justified by security concerns. All penal authority has to infer to get its way is the possibility of "a significant 'ripple effect' on fellow inmates or on prison staff" (2262). "Danger," hence the justification for restriction, has come to reside in the mind of authority, not in the presentation of an actual problem.

With these rhetorical ploys in place, the Court's four-pronged test joins a rhetoric of inevitability against prisoners' rights. Pay attention in the following paragraphs to the intensifying adverbs and adjectives in the Court's clinching sentences.[27] Strict scrutiny must be rejected because "*every* administrative judgment would be subject to the possibility that *some* court *somewhere* would conclude that it had a *less* restrictive way of solving the problem at hand" (2261). "Applying our analysis of the Missouri rule barring inmate-to-inmate correspondence, we conclude that the record *clearly* demonstrates that the regulation was *reasonably* related to *legitimate* security interests" (2262).

That is not all. "*Undoubtedly,* communication with *other* felons is a *potential* spur to criminal behavior: this *sort* of contact *frequently* is prohibited *even* after an inmate has been released on parole" (2263). "The correspondence regulation does not deprive prisoners of *all* means of expression. *Rather,* it bars communication *only* with a *limited* class of *other* people with whom prison officials have *particular* cause to be concerned—inmates at other institutions within the Missouri prison system" (2263). Where, exactly, are long-term prisoners in Missouri likely to find or keep friends if not in correctional institutions?

Lost in the intensifiers of the opinion are essential realities. Why should we make judgments on "the possibility" that "some court somewhere" might make a mistake reversible by a higher court? How can a record "clearly demonstrate" when it is hardly examined? When should "potential" behavior deprive people of fundamental rights? What is the assumed spur that makes other inmates so prone to criminal behavior? Which sorts of expression remain to a jailed person seeking contact with a friend moved to another prison?

The majority in *Turner v. Safley* builds its argument on imaginative projections rather than on grounded proof about the inclinations of people in prison. Its decision has little to do with the facts of the case and everything to do with a culture of fear and the controlling rubrics in theories of retribution. The adjustment from active scrutiny to reliance on the mere attitude of penal authority changes what counts for evidence, and we need to understand how much that alters the approach in this judicial opinion and in all of the ones that follow it.

The four dissenting justices show the way. They deride the majority's airy suppositions for what they are, turn discussion back to the ignored record, and dismiss the logic of the Court's "newly minted standard" as "virtually meaningless" because it turns on "nothing more" than "a *logical* connection between the regulation and any legitimate penological concern." They also remember to denounce the Court's improper use of its own procedures and point to the absence of real knowledge in the experts to whom the Court so absolutely defers (2267–2275).

Justice John Paul Stevens writes for all four dissenters. "Application of the [Court's newly minted] standard," he begins, "would seem to permit disregard for inmates' constitutional rights whenever the imagination of the warden produces a plausible security concern" (2667–2668). Next he challenges the majority's "plainly improper appellate encroachment into the fact finding domain of the District Court" and dismisses the way it "sifts the trial testimony on its own in order to uphold a general prohibition" (2268). He returns repeatedly to the trial record to disclose the majority's evasions of fact, all part of "highly selective use of factual evidence" and "erratic use of the record" (2270).

There is, as well, obvious insincerity in the majority's decision to concentrate on the appellate court instead of the trial court to reach its decision. "The ostensible breadth of the Court of Appeals' opinion," Stevens wryly observes, "furnishes no license for this Court to reverse with another unnecessarily broad holding." Several detailed pages with careful footnotes from the trial record prove that the "experts" on which the Court depends testify based on suppositions and fears rather than on grounded facts or knowledge of events (2269–2273). The Court, in sum, reached a totally erroneous conclusion by relying on "its own selective forays into the record" (2275). Poor judging has led to an even poorer decision.

The puzzle in *Turner v. Safley* comes here. The cogency of Stevens's logic exposes the flimsy basis of the majority's decision, but it has not kept the decision from remaining the central test on prisoners' rights for three decades and counting. To answer why this decision continues to shape basic legal understanding, we must see the influence of the majority opinion on later decisions dealing with prisoners' rights. Only then do the deeper ideological considerations in control of both judicial and communal thought reveal themselves.

The Shrinking of Prisoners' Rights

The Court in *Turner v. Safley* congratulates itself with a "principle"—namely, its concern for rights—but the phraseology used offers cold comfort to anyone incarcerated. "Prison walls," it declares, "do not form a barrier separating prison inmates from the protections of the Constitution" (2259). The claim has communal appeal, but the three internal references to division in this sentence—walls, barrier, and separation—warn more than they assure, and the Court's ensuing distinctions between inmates and outsiders on available rights underline the warning. The protections listed here by the Court are also minimal. Prisoners have the right to petition the government for the redress of grievances (where they regularly lose). They are protected against invidious racial discrimination (not true in any prison or jail in the country), and they enjoy the protections of due process (sometimes).

What is left unsaid gives direction. The emphasis in *Turner* and later court decisions sides with *the problems* of officialdom against *the conditions* of prisoners, and it reaches as well to the use of force. Thus, in *Whitley v. Albers* only "obduracy and wantonness" in the use of force that causes painful injury to a prisoner is answerable by authority. There is no fault when force is merely "unreasonable" and "unnecessary in the strictest sense."[28]

Turner has removed the single most valuable source of constitutional protection. It eliminates the need for close legal attention to the behavior of those who govern prison life. Its holding says "the lower courts have erred [in] the application of a strict scrutiny standard of review for resolving respondents' constitutional complaint." Henceforth, "a lesser standard is appropriate whereby inquiry is made into whether a prison regulation that impinges on inmates' constitutional rights is 'reasonably related' to legitimate penological interests" (2256).

The negative repercussions in these positions have a devastating effect on prisoners' rights. *Procunier v. Martinez,* essentially overruled by *Turner,* had established a far more active test: "when a prison regulation or practice *offends* a fundamental constitutional guarantee, federal courts *will discharge their duty to protect constitutional rights.*"[29] Admittedly, some earlier Court denials of important prisoners' rights relate to free speech, but the four-pronged test in *Turner v. Safley* makes it so much easier to avoid prisoners' petitions. Abstract wordplay carries away from appraisal of the right involved to the restrictions imposed.[30]

Eight days after *Turner,* the Court used its new test in *O'Lone v. Estate of Shabazz* to deny a claim of freedom of religion by Muslim prisoners who were prevented from engaging in their major weekly religious ceremony by prison regulations. Here the "reasonableness" test of *Turner* gives an automatic edge to whatever established penal expertise wants to announce. An official claim is enough to find a legitimate governmental interest in prison security.[31]

Justice William Brennan, dissenting in *O'Lone,* another close 5-to-4 decision, sees the danger immediately. Checks and balances in control of power have disappeared. "If a directive that officials act 'reasonably' were deemed sufficient to check all exercises of power, the Constitution would hardly be necessary," he observes. A deeper protest identifies the radical apartness of prisoners established by *Turner* through too much reliance on the prerogatives of penal authority. "It is . . . easy to think of prisoners as members of a separate netherworld," Brennan warns. That is what the Court has done, yet "the society that these prisoners inhabit is our own . . . no act of will can sever them from the body politic."[32]

Brennan goes further. He explains the implications of *Turner* and *O'Lone* when taken together. The Court has forgotten the true basis of fundamental rights. "When prisoners emerge from the shadows to press a constitutional claim, they invoke no alien set of principles drawn from a distant culture. Rather, they speak the language of the charter upon which all of us rely to hold official power accountable." By implication, the danger to prisoners could well be everyone's down the road, and there is a deeper truth to be digested here. Retribution in control of the elemental forms of punishment remains the signifier in judicial thought, and with a larger significance. Poor decisions that last may tell us the most about ourselves.

Turner remains "the landmark case for establishing standards that other courts must use when they evaluate the constitutionality of prison and jail regulations that restrict prisoners' rights."[33] Two years later, the test in *Turner* justified a regulation that left the access of publications to prisoners to the discretion of penal authority.[34] Using the test again in 2003, the Court found no need to examine visitation or association rights of prisoners closely because, under *Turner,* the challenged regulations that reduced visiting rights had an identified rational relation to legitimate penological concerns.[35] There, in *Overton v. Bazetta,* the Court ignores that visitation supplies an important safeguard against later recidivism. It can forget the prisoners' plight because it has made *Turner* the "unitary deferential standard for reviewing prisoners' rights."[36]

The reach of *Turner* further down and throughout the legal system has been vigorous. Three elements in particular have dominated prisoners' rights adjudication at all judicial levels: first, "the seemingly ubiquitous application of the deferential, rational-basis test"; second, "the trivialization of 'legitimate' penal objectives, which are nonetheless allowed to top prisoners' rights, including those 'fundamental' to ordered liberty"; and third, "a willingness to forego empirically based 'facts' in favor of prison officials' asserted 'truths.'" Again and again, the test has worked against prisoner complaints. "*Turner* remains the most influential of all prisoners' rights cases."[37]

Malice Allowed with Forethought

The single most informative decision involving retributive instincts in judicial attitudes actually comes three years earlier, in *Hudson v. Palmer,* and it explains much of *Turner v. Safley*'s continuing importance.[38] *Hudson* makes clear what *Turner* hides: an animus and fear that make all people in prison suspect and unworthy of basic consideration. In this earlier opinion, the Supreme Court decides that the Fourth Amendment right against unreasonable searches and seizures does not apply to prisoners or grant any right of privacy or protect a right to any personal property whatsoever they might possess (517–518).

As noteworthy as the decision are the realities that the Court so grudgingly must admit in making its decision in *Hudson v. Palmer.* The basic facts are not disputed. Ted Hudson, a correction officer in the Bland Correctional Center in Virginia, ransacked the effects of prisoner Russell Palmer several days in succession, destroying legal and personal items that had nothing to do with security issues. No contraband was found in either "shakedown."

Hudson further accused Palmer of destroying state property. The property destroyed in question? It was a torn pillowcase found in a trash can "near respondent's cell bunk," not directly in Palmer's area. Found guilty of this charge, Palmer had to reimburse the state for the cost of the material destroyed, and he further received an official reprimand with the prospect of more time to be served as part of his punishment. Here it didn't matter that prison guard Hudson's punitive actions received considerable attention in the lower court record made available to the Supreme Court.

The record showed that Hudson had clearly singled out Palmer. Testimony by other prisoners corroborated Palmer's claim of harassment by Hudson. After the first shakedown of Palmer's possessions, Hudson had even been heard to say by other prisoners that "next time he'd really make a mess." Still other facts from the testimony of other prisoners support the allegations of harassment. Prisoner Palmer was housed in a dormitory, not a cell, and the trash can in question was a communal container near Palmer's bed only because of his position in the dormitory. Any prisoner could have dumped the ripped pillowcase in the trash can, if, in reality, a prisoner did the dumping. Also known? An intact pillowcase was on Palmer's bed, and prisoner testimony established that Hudson had the reputation of making "lots of false charges against inmates here in Bland [prison]."[39]

The Supreme Court could not avoid at least the momentary animosity in the behavior of the prison guard in this case. Nor could it, in common sense, evade a darker implication from the more serious charge made by Hudson against Palmer, the almost certainly false accusation of destroying state property with the punishment of both costs and further prison time for Palmer on the trivial basis of a torn pillowcase that anyone could have left in the "nearby" trash can. Hudson's added charge shows more: deliberate and lasting malice.

The Court, in deciding to find for the guard over the prisoner, had to swallow the malice by one in authority in dealing with a prisoner, and it did so in cowardly fashion. The Court hid behind a strained fatalism: "intentional acts are even more difficult to anticipate because one bent on intentionally depriving a person of his property might very well take affirmative steps to avoid signaling his intent" (533). Here the malicious intent of the prison guard is obvious, and the Court wrings its hands and shrugs: What can we do?

The majority opinion in the highly contested 5-to-4 decision for *Hudson v. Palmer* is written by Chief Justice Warren Burger, which suggests that he chose to write it himself. The anthropologist Mary Douglas, in *How Institutions Think,* tells us that favorite hierarchical analogies will win out when private conflicts are resolved in a public forum. "Then we see how each contestant musters public opinion to justify his or her actions against the other, and we observe the onlookers, who have no special interest in the case, listening to hear a general principle in which they can sympathize. The favorite analogy generalizes everyone's preferred convention."[40]

The favorite hierarchical analogy in *Hudson v. Palmer,* which Burger relied on to win his bare majority, consists in the claim that prison authorities are sincere and must be trusted to do their dangerous work while prisoners are stereotypically bad and not to be trusted. Led by Justice John Paul Stevens, the dissenters' contrasting call on the rights and dignity of prisoners falls on deaf ears. Chief Justice Burger succeeds by balancing abstractions: "the interest of society in the security of its penal institutions and the interest of the prisoner in privacy within his cell." "We strike the balance in favor of institutional security," he writes. In other words, the American people take the blame. "Society is not prepared to recognize as legitimate any subjective expectation of privacy that a prisoner might have in his prison cell" (529, 526).

The strategies by which the majority disposes of the malice of the prison guard take predictable lines. Chief Justice Burger opens his opinion with the irrelevant information that Respondent Palmer is "serving sentences for forgery, grand larceny, and bank robbery convictions" (518). In other words, forgers and larcenists are thieves who always lie. Burger's problem is that the appellate court found a "limited privacy . . . against searches conducted solely to harass or to humiliate" (522), and in a standard trope, he also has to admit that "no iron curtain" separates prisoners from the Constitution, in this case the right against unreasonable searches and seizures (523).

The curtain may not be iron, but neither does Burger want to lift it. For if "persons imprisoned for crime enjoy many protections of the Constitution, it is also clear that imprisonment carries with it the circumscription or loss of many significant rights" (524). To prove the point—keyed first to the assertion that prisoners are "persons who have a demonstrated proclivity for antisocial criminal, and often violent, conduct"—Burger offers several pages of statistics about prison violence (524–525) with the further observation that "under our system of justice, deterrence and retribution are factors in addition to correction." Each of the three general claims about punishment used by Chief Justice Burger *independently* justifies "the complete withdrawal of certain rights" (525).

The Burger opinion works through communal animus against crime with many unsubstantiated references to the negative opinions of society about the incarcerated. Prison authority's "constant fight against the proliferation of knives and guns, illicit drugs, and other contraband" in prison must be left to its own methods and policies if the violence is to be kept down there and away from society. The chief justice translates this understanding of weaponry into an accepted policy of random search by prison guards even if "there is a risk of maliciously motivated searches." "The uncertainty that attends random searches of cells renders these searches perhaps the most effective weapon of the prison administrator" (528).

At first implicitly, but then explicitly, the majority opinion turns prison life into a war of "us" against "them." Prisoners, in this battle of "weapons," have no rights because they are the enemy. Since inmate Palmer lacks *all* right of privacy, he also has no right to challenge "the reasonableness of the particular search" made by Hudson, and the more serious problem of malice by prison authority drops off the table (529).

The dissent by Justice John Paul Stevens addresses this sleight-of-hand maneuver by the majority (541). The record, against the decision, has required the Court to deal with the fact that "prison guard Hudson maliciously took and destroyed a quantity of Palmer's property, including legal materials and letters, for no reason other than harassment" (541). Failure to recognize that harassment means two things: first, the whole problem of malice in prison can be evaded and, second, "no matter how malicious, destructive, or arbitrary a cell search and seizure may be, it cannot constitute an unreasonable invasion of any privacy or possessory interest that society is prepared to recognize as reasonable." Everything a prisoner has, even the small items that "enable a prisoner to maintain contact with some part of his past and an eye to the possibility of a better future" is thereby "subject to unrestrained perusal, confiscation, or mutilation at the hands of a possibly hostile guard" (541).

Justice Stevens's dissent is one of the most prescient in the history of the Court. The failure to allow *any* right to possession marks "the difference between slavery and humanity" (541). The Court's decision does not "comport with any civilized standard of decency" (548). Much is at stake in prison policy as well. "Prisoners deprived of any sense of individuality devalue themselves and others and therefore are more prone to violence toward themselves and others" (551). The Court has said "prisoners are entitled to no measure of human dignity or individuality . . . nor anything except standard-issue prison clothing." "It declares prisoners to be little more than chattels," Stevens concludes, "—a view I thought society had outgrown long ago" (555).

Here is the vision that prison becomes in the remaining decades of the twentieth century and into the twenty-first: unchecked prison abuse, hostility on all sides, warehousing, solitary confinement, and overcrowding of human beings who are understood to be objects more than subjects. Unaccountability has been given full rein.

The Prospect of Reform

Hudson v. Palmer furnishes the low point rhetorically in prisoners' rights just as *Turner v. Safley* supplies the low point methodologically. Left unexplained are the reasons why powerful dissents by four justices in both decisions have had no real effect on the restrictions that have contributed to prison brutality and, by extension, to mass incarceration.[41]

Part of the answer lies in what reform-minded critics of our punishment regimes are willing to grant. Even helpful critics insist that punishment should be no more than loss of freedom, and there is accuracy in the claim. But accuracy aside, the hidden problem in such thinking is that it relies on retribution as its source. The emphasis in incarceration is still on *loss*. As Chief Justice Burger writes in *Hudson v. Palmer,* and it is worth repeating, "under our system of justice, deterrence and retribution are factors in addition to correction" (524). More accurately, retribution leads the parade, with deterrence next and correction lagging far behind.

Retribution is more than a contributing factor. It is the controlling force in American punishment, with uniquely visceral connotations. It tallies with reciprocal pain, an eye for an eye, and the animus in it translates theoretical hatred of the act into personal hatred of the person, which means that punishment can define a prisoner indefinitely. Primal if not primitive feelings are involved. Applications of it are so much simpler to grasp than any other idea in measuring crime. Nothing quite matches it. Missing from legal infliction is a modifying effective counterweight, a more flexible gauge of punishment.

Recent hopes for a better solution have turned to concepts of dignity borrowed from the discourse on human rights, and these hopes begin to have some purchase when the courts use the term in judicial decisions about prisoners' needs. The problem? "Dignity" is a vague term. It depends not just on one's philosophy but on the eye of the beholder. The case most often cited for help in this regard is *Brown v. Plata* (2011). There the Supreme Court used the term to step in and confirm lower court decisions to cap California's prison population, which would force the release of as many as 30,000 prisoners from the seriously overcrowded California prison system.[42] Even so, nothing in the Court's decision removed punishment from the context of retributive thinking.

Brown v. Plata is a heavily contested and qualified decision. Justice Anthony Kennedy, writing for the narrowest of majorities, has to admit that the decision is *de novo* (literally "from the beginning" or "afresh") or bound to these facts. It is true that the Court does not defer here to prison authorities in the usual way but only because those authorities have so manifestly lost control of the prison system and have failed to take steps repeatedly required by lower courts to regain effective control.[43]

The five justices supporting the decision in *Brown v. Plata* against the four who complain against it are helped by another differentiating factor. The case brings no direct charges or penalty against anyone in penal authority. Justice Kennedy carefully objectifies blame as a function of overcrowding beyond everyone's management. "Cramped conditions," writes Kennedy, "promote unrest and violence, making it difficult for prison officials to monitor and control the prison population."[44]

This and other references to unrest and violence in prison life obliquely confirm the centrality of retributive thinking in *Brown v. Plata*. The ultimate stance remains the same *unless* one makes more than Kennedy is willing to make when he writes "prisoners retain the essence of human dignity in all persons." So far so good, but how far does the essence of human dignity extend to anyone behind bars? Not far. Kennedy backs off. He reaffirms Court resistance to any possession of rights beyond life, racial discrimination, and minimal care. The party line of restriction remains the same: "prisoners may be deprived of rights that are fundamental to liberty."[45]

Conventional legal understanding of the right to rights continues to run through retributive instincts and takes its cue from the right to liberty. Loss of liberty defines the convicted in *Brown v. Plata*, a premise confirmed and reinforced by the four angry dissenters in the case. Justice Antonin Scalia weighs in here. He insists that all prisoners must be treated as less than valuable citizens. Releasing them before their time enrages him; they have not received enough punishment. Justice is not complete. Scalia foresees "inevitable murders, robberies and rapes to be committed by the released inmates."[46] All inmates are as one in his comments: they are dangerous, too dangerous, by definition, to be given their freedom.

These negative stereotypes encourage others in *Brown v. Plata*. "Many will undoubtedly be fine physical specimens who have developed intimidating muscles pumping iron in the prison gym," Scalia complains of those to be released early. Justice Samuel Alito joins Scalia, warning of a "grim roster of victims" from the planned prisoner release, again with no supporting evidence.[47] Actually, serious crime rates drop in California after the releases required by the Court, but no roll call of statistics ever seems to shift negative thinking at the core of American punishment.[48]

Anger remains the hallmark in retribution, and Justice Scalia shows no restraint in using it here. He calls *Brown v. Plata* one of the worst decisions in the Court's history. It represents "perhaps the most radical injunction issued by the Court in our Nation's history." It is an "outrageous result" and "a judicial travesty." Along the way, he taunts the majority by deciding to "heartily disagree" with "our judge-empowering 'evolving standards of decency'" as any basis for challenging the helpless and avoidable collective misery of the legally incarcerated.[49]

All of this explosive wrath and resentment comes against prisoners who are literally dying unnoticed for hours in California prisons from rampant disease and personal conflicts in severely congested living conditions—so congested that some prisoners are being left for days in narrow stand-up body cages because there is no other place to put them. The majority attaches photographs of these conditions to show how directly inhumane prison life in California has become.

How can what was then our most intemperate Supreme Court justice be so intemperate even here? First, the controlling climate of ideas in the United States makes the convicted criminal a permanent source of pejorative reference. Second, as anthropologists teach us, decisions have a cognitive dimension (the demand for order and control of uncertainty) and a transactional dimension (the need to maximize responsible activity and consequence).[50]

Law, in the hands of a precedent-minded judiciary, leans toward the first dimension: the demand for order and control of uncertainty. It is so much simpler to keep people in prison, especially if they are assumed to be permanently dangerous criminals who will revert to type as soon as they are given their freedom. Recognize, as well, an unavoidable admission in Justice Scalia's rant. The supposed institutions of correction do not correct. Scalia assumes that prison teaches no one to be law-abiding until, miraculously, their waiting time is up. Against such rigid animus the uphill battle to recognize a manageable dignity in prison life requires more than itself.

Other ways of thinking are needed. New ideas are, of course, hard to find, but sometimes they hide in plain sight, and at other times the problem to be addressed can be at least part of a solution. What hope is there in that? In 2016 the Supreme Court in a 6-to-3 majority gave an inkling of larger possibilities in *Montgomery v. Louisiana*. This decision gave the right to seek parole to juveniles sentenced to life without parole, "whose crimes reflect the transient immaturity of youth." It said life without parole could be "disproportionate when applied to juveniles" because "protection against disproportionate punishment is the central substantive guarantee of the Eighth Amendment" against "cruel and unusual punishments."[51]

In practical terms, *Montgomery v. Louisiana* gave a man who had been incarcerated when seventeen years old, in 1963, the right to seek parole now in his seventieth year, and it helped that he could claim to be "a model member of the prison community." The decision also cast a jaundiced eye on current notions of punishment, even though its holding was tied strictly to people sentenced as juveniles in consideration of a child's "diminished culpability and heightened capacity for change." In a run-through of the standard theories of punishment, Justice Anthony Kennedy's controlling opinion found that none of the traditional rationales—retribution, deterrence, incapacitation, and rehabilitation—sufficed in such instances, and without them, it meant "the penological justifications for life with parole collapse." Punishment had become disproportionate in ordering this child, now a man, to die in prison.[52]

Kennedy was careful to limit *Montgomery*. "Those prisoners who have shown an inability to reform will continue to serve life sentences." Still, the logic in this language reaches toward new possibilities. Why shouldn't *anyone* who has become a model prisoner and developed positive standards of behavior, over a considerable amount of time, have the capacity to be a good citizen? Why shouldn't that person have the right to seek parole? The desire to look beyond the standard rubrics about punishment opens the door just a crack to the feasibility of other choices in thinking about incarceration.[53]

No human being can remain inert; it is against our nature. Yet serving time represents an insistence on inertia, which makes anyone less than a person. Most of the negativity in the rights talk about prisoners depends implicitly on this impossibility. You *wait* on your release from prison. The stasis involved takes away the adventure in existence and hence the right to any real part in its opportunities. Dignity therefore has no room to demonstrate itself. What might it take to find such room?

Dignity, in addressing rights, has two possible indications. It applies to one's mere existence as a human being but also to one's further existence as a process or endeavor or form of behavior. The first, more innate, category, presence in existence, is the one generally applied to prisoners when it comes to rights talk, and it allows judgment to leave them in the most reduced of elemental states. There are psychological costs as well as value in fastening the concept so entirely to the fact of being, particularly if you are given no other access to the opportunities in life.

Recent investigation has begun to worry about this underappreciated double valence in the meaning of dignity and its relation to rights. Ronald Dworkin, in *Taking Rights Seriously*, has suggested that it is not enough to think of rights through access to liberty; he wants an additional basis in "the right to equal concern and respect." Dignity must be more fully recognized. And the means must be through reciprocity.[54]

In another take on the subject, the legal theorist Jeremy Waldron feels that for rights to have a full measure of dignity they must include responsibilities beyond the fact of one's human presence.[55] Dignity becomes more when seen as an active element in behavior. Philosopher Martha Nussbaum has argued for a capabilities emphasis in rights with a human development approach to identity. "What," she asks, "is each person able to do and to be?"[56] The economist and philosopher Amartya Sen has drawn useful distinctions between freedom and agency when it comes to an understanding of well-being; both belong if well-being is to flourish in a life with some dignity.[57]

Each of these initiatives from related disciplines has its own worked-out complications, but a common impulse drives them. That impulse points toward a theory of punishment that can qualify retributive instincts, much in the way we saw in *Montgomery v. Louisiana*. Each of these thoughts about dignity as a controlling idea relies on some degree of empathy or reciprocity. Recognition of capable behavior matters. Everyone wants her or his behavior to count in some way. It is the definition of worth. Acknowledged agency, not innate presence, is the common theme that more and more thinkers bring to the subject of dignity.

Human beings are, after all, different from other animals in what behavior portends. Other animals rest when not called on to use their natural gifts. A dog will spend most of the day sleeping if left to its own devices, and no matter what you tell it, it will always remain interested in attacking a squirrel. Human beings react endlessly to the world around them and to themselves. They decide what they will become and what they will do while developing skills and knowledge and needs beyond the common elements and practices of their species. Humans form a unique personal identity both within and beyond circumstance, and they do it through the activity that imagination gives to behavior. These are the essential ingredients in the thrust of human life.

The point should not be misunderstood. The human capacity for conscious development does not trivialize other animals or their patterns of behavior and special advantages. Accept the distinction for the point that it reveals. The single greatest problem in prison life—certainly much of its internal deviance, transgression, and defiance—comes through the high level of deprivation enforced in it. All positive development is denied its inhabitants. People in prison have been forced to the existence plane of the other animals in ways that they cannot possibly accept. Some way, somehow, they must do something about it in order to hold on to a sense of themselves, and too often this implies "doing" in a way that challenges penal authority.[58]

Denial of capability affects the keepers as well as the kept. If all you are doing is holding prisoners and watching them, your job becomes a tedious one. Nothing of positive interest occurs that you want to see. Two things happen to correction officers in this context because they are bored. First, and every prison narrative or letter confirms this behavior pattern, the watchers and holders become lazy and unhelpful in their jobs. Second, to amuse themselves, some prison guards frustrate prisoners with deliberate displays of arrogance, indifference, and open cruelty.

The behavior of correction officers devolves into these negative patterns because they have nothing to contribute to the people they are supposed to correct. Communities are built on reciprocity, mutual understanding, and some measure of trust. Across every difference in society, some communication makes conflict bearable. The code of silence in correction officer life extends to conversation with prisoners. The stark separation from any caring activity toward prisoners swiftly becomes its own problem. Everyone is held in place instead of wanting to accomplish something he or she can be proud of doing.

No one should underestimate the difficulties in promoting a theory of development in punishment. People arrive in prison with established patterns of deviance. Most of them are seriously undereducated, and many have no established patterns of vocational responsibility to call upon. The important realization has to be that most prisoners leave an institution in the same state that they entered. Recidivism rates are so high because the average person released lacks the skills to find productive employment. Unless you knew how beforehand, and even if you once did, you are probably lost when released into a computerized era of constant electronic change.

The difficulties in reform have their answer in the failures of the current criminal justice and penal system—failures that feed mass incarceration, criminal behavior, and a system too overburdened to work fairly or well. The rest of this book turns on what it might take to institute a developmental theory of punishment. In favor of it is a startling statistic. If recidivism rates are high in prison, well over 60 percent, they drop to low single digits with a proper education.

The chapters that follow claim the power of development, each in a different way. They also wrestle with the dilemma of how virtually every past program of reform has been twisted into the negative practices of punishment. How do we guard against the natural tendency and expectation of pain in punishment?

A theory of development can work because most people, though certainly not all, prefer a positive frame of reference. Everyone connected with criminal justice would have to be willing to do more and to think differently about how to proceed from initial indictments, plea bargains, trials, and then the treatment of prisoners all the way up the chain of command in authority.

Responsibility should not just rest on the experts either. Prisoners should be *required* to learn a skill that they can use on release or given an education that they can take pride in if release is not coming. Too many penal institutions currently prevent prisoners with long sentences from receiving any kind of formal education. Programs for developing relevant skills have to be created. The carrot in this economic stick is that the right programs could send more people out of the prison system permanently. Studies show that the costs might average out.[59]

Where might such a metamorphosis begin? For many reasons, it probably makes sense to start with the top. Those who have the most ability to think

5
Sentencing the Disappearing Convict

The Decision to Punish as a Form of Speech

WITHOUT RIGHTS, PEOPLE IN PRISON are left to the mercy of a grudging criminal justice system, and that lack of mercy began long before they were convicted. Any real change in theories of punishment must begin earlier in the process and extend into the reform of incarceration.

Judges are the most accountable figures in the criminal justice system. They are the ones who actually send people to prison, and because of that they need to be even more accountable if there is to be meaningful penal reform. Yes, judges have limited powers in this regard. They preside hemmed in by mandatory sentencing guidelines, prosecutorial discretion, plea bargaining, overloaded dockets, communal suspicion, institutional deference, and, in state jurisdictions, vulnerability to popular vote. Still, judges *do* punish. They gauge and deliver the sentence. They are the last to deal with the convicted before incarceration, and their powers in that moment reach beyond a term of years to be served.

Too many discussions turn on the length of a sentence assigned and the crime that justifies it. Fixation on these elements is certainly understandable. Loss of freedom—how *much* loss of freedom?—is crucial but not the only issue to be addressed. Other aspects should not be ignored, and judges do not help perception when they withhold or minimize publication of the sentences they hand down. Publicity over sending a person to prison is not the way most judges want to be remembered.

Media sources add to the problem. They pick out the censorious statements in a judicial sentence along with the years to be served and the reasons for it. A full account of what was said rarely reaches beyond the courtroom unless a mistake encourages grounds for appeal. Everyone in court must listen to the judge in respectful silence, but the number of years and the reasons for it are what auditors remember.

All of these elements have merit. Inveighing against crime is a judicial obligation, and it will always be part of the sentence. It should not, however, be the only part we remember or value. The two main questions in this chapter grow out of that qualification. First, what is properly said in the delivered sentence? Second, what has been left out that might also be useful?

Is there room to adjust the modes of judicial address to encourage fairer punishment regimes in the United States? The judge who sends to prison is creating a helpless ward of the state. The state carries out that sentence. Officially, the state punishes by taking away the freedom of a person. Unofficially, it does much more. The inflicted pain and humiliations in prison go far beyond the legal fact of serving time, and every judge should be fully aware of that discrepancy in rendering judgment.

Coming to grips with the judicial sentence has its difficulties. Complexity, divided roles, distinctions between federal and state courts, overcriminalization, and retributive instincts have created a mess in the sentencing procedures of the United States. "After a quarter of century of changes, there is no longer anything that can be called 'the American system' of sentencing and corrections." Fragmentation and judicial frustration over variations flourish across jurisdictions, and even within jurisdictions.[1]

These frustrations extend to the highest in the land. Consider the leading Supreme Court case on judicial sentencing: *United States v. Booker* (2005). In it, the justices fight to a standstill over the range of discretion, sentencing guidelines, and the province of juries. They puzzle and then quarrel over who should decide, what should be decided, when it should be decided, and how it should be decided.

Booker is the poster child that proves the mess in sentencing. The Court's decision contains two controlling opinions in tacit conflict with each other, each based on a different 5-to-4 vote. Trailing after are four compounded and compounding dissenting opinions. Justices on both sides of the controlling opinions agree in part and disagree in part.[2] What can one conclude from so much difference? Many have tried to answer that question, but only one thing stands out. Judges have more discretion, but certainty in sentencing will have to wait for another day, and that day is yet to come.[3]

The court kerfuffle in *Booker* is as arcane as it is unsatisfactory. All sides bemoan the further confusion their decision foists on the criminal justice system. Justice Antonin Scalia said it most vividly at the time. He called the Court "a black-robed Alexander cutting the Gordian knot." His colleagues had engaged in a simplification that ignored the complexity in sentencing while generating more of it. "This," he decided, upset enough to mix the metaphor, "is rather like deleting the ingredients portion of a recipe and telling the cook to proceed with the preparation portion."[4] His distress grows across his own contribution to three separate opinions in the case.

The question of how much to punish raises a hidden dilemma in sentencing. The length of time to be assigned to prison differs across highly variable philosophical beliefs about human nature. Many of those beliefs are voiced by judges without real explanation. Even the supposedly expert United States Sentencing Commission admits that its guidelines are modeled on no particular philosophy.[5]

Without philosophical underpinning, suspicion over the scope of judicial discretion triggers much of the confusion over sentencing. Nevertheless, the voice from the bench speaks for itself in this situation. Personalities emerge in a declared sentence. Judges are free to embellish on the punishment they exact. They speak as the voice of gathered wisdom on the situation. A sentence pronounced is also an opinion in both senses of the noun: legal and more generally attitudinal. What that sentence can mean holds possibilities beyond statutory and doctrinal limitations, and it has special implications for the recipient of it.

License has been part of the sentencing practice from the beginning. The Latin origin of the term, *sententia,* had a double legal meaning. It referred to "an authoritative decision, decree; (esp. a judicial pronouncement, sentence, judgement)." But along with this precision it raised the prospect of speculative analysis ("the spirit as opposed to the letter of a law"). Public sentencing in Roman antiquity encouraged both, coming as it did out of court procedures involving public outrage.[6] Traditionally and in current practice, normative concerns coexist with the formulaic announcement of punishment.

Less certain is the acceptable range of normative address in the sentencing moment. Precision and objectivity, the hallmarks of fairness, represent the cardinal virtues in a judge presiding over the legal system. But these virtues have minimal effect if the system beneath them is broken.[7] Caught in that predicament, judges have the right and even the duty to call attention to the normative aspects of their role, especially when they face prescribed court action that does not match the situation before them.

The major distinction, the one we work with in this chapter, involves what judges *must* say against what they optimally *can* say, and since the obligatory aspects establish rhetorical bench marks, we start with them.[8]

There are always three audiences in a judicial sentence: the recipient, appellate courts, and the public at large, with tonal needs that apply to each. The voice for the first is corrective; for the second, protective of the speaker. The voice for the third must be calibrated to public explanation and common sense. All three registers must demonstrate power exercised and certitude about what has been done, and each depends on a personal as well as corporate (judicially embodied) identity.

In any extended speech, the clue to analysis begins with a question. What really troubles the speaker? Judges fear getting sentencing wrong (adding to an unjust result), getting overturned on appeal (an embarrassment), and being misunderstood and criticized for it (a peculiar public vulnerability when the freedom of a person is the subject). Sincerity invoked is the most obvious safeguard. Without quite realizing it, the truly candid judge applies J. L. Austin's theory of performative utterance. The sentence requires a locutionary act (the words accurately expressed), an illocutionary act (the words connected to a meaningful context), and a perlocutionary act (the words received and accepted with full understanding).[9]

Difficulties come with these needs. The words accurately expressed in a judicial sentence are going to be complicated and not easily understood by all present. Each intended audience receives it in a different way. The immediate recipient, the person convicted, is now held silent in unhappy compliance. The second audience, the appellate courts, are technically suspicious, even disapproving, if they decide to examine a trial judge's sentence. The third audience, public onlookers, fracture in reaction between those who exalt, those who protest, those who sympathize, and a larger group of voyeurs. These differences can become intense. Among the voyeurs are media sources who seek to make as much as possible of the conflicts played out before them.

For our purposes, the second aspect of J. L. Austin's performative audience, the illocutionary act (words connected to a meaningful context), is most crucial. Almost always left out is the context of prison: the thing promised and being delivered, the main subject as the convicted defendant's destination and the reason for everyone being in court. The experience of forthcoming incarceration is where current judicial sentences customarily have nothing to say, although judges will occasionally admit that American prisons "are an awful place to be."[10] The structure of the judicial sentence is vexed in this regard, and we must turn to it next.

The Words That Send Someone to Prison

Judicial sentences stand out for a simplicity within immeasurable complexity. Everything said has been previously arranged except for the sentence itself. Predictability controls the unfolding narrative. Clarity, a hallmark in simplicity, dictates tone. The countervailing complexities come through sentencing guidelines, and the detailed calculations required trouble the official decider, the judge who must come up with an exact right number by the end of a sentencing statement.[11]

Judges begin by asking all of the active participants—prosecutors, defense counsel, probation officers, and the defendant—to identify themselves. The next step lists all relevant documents: presentencing reports (PSR), written objections, governmental responses, probationary recommendations, and any letters or other material in support of or against the defendant. Each participant must then acknowledge having read and mastered these documents. Primal understanding is the key to sentencing statements.

Throughout these introductory portions, judges repeatedly ask a defendant if everything has been comprehended with or through available counsel. Translators are provided when necessary. In either order, the prosecution and the defense present additional arguments over the nature and length of a sentence to be proposed. Victims in many jurisdictions, including the federal, get a chance to speak. Defendants are allowed to address the court, and sentence is then imposed, often with a relevant homily from the presiding judge.

These procedures are clear. Conviction has already taken place. It is the sentencing guidelines that create a separate intensity to otherwise transparent proceedings. The basic variables in sentencing guidelines are threefold: first, the offense level taken from the conduct identified (there are forty-three levels); second, the defendant's criminal history (with problematic assessments for any previous convictions); and third, graduated sentencing zones (four in number, with expanding lengths of required time to be served). The combinations can escalate quickly into draconian levels. Twenty years or longer in prison, half of an adult lifetime, is not an unusual phenomenon.

Many other factors can influence these gradations through what are called "departures" up or down or "enhancements," always up. A sentence can change dramatically through degree of involvement in a joint crime; through early cooperation with authority; through obstruction of authority; through the likelihood of serious harm; through manifest harm; through the presence or use of a weapon; through the degree, nature, and extent of criminal intent; and through connections to any other crime. Amazingly, everything must be given a set point total.

Many judges prove reluctant to impose the amount of time imposed through the seemingly objective calculation of a cumulative point total. Sentences can therefore turn into elaborate justifications for a variation up or down from what is generally required. A side effect is worth mentioning. Arguing the technicalities through objectified point totals becomes its own blood sport between counsel and judge, and it leads to less attention given to the defendant's situation, prospects, and plight.[12]

Haggling over the point totals in guidelines tests a judge's knowledge, ingenuity, and craft. Worried about making a mistake, many have to pause and ask counsel "Is this right?" The obsession with points turns a convicted offender into an instrument of policy. Relief over an agreed-on number of months to be served has another effect, too. Months, the unit called for in sentencing, disguises the length of time to be allotted. Does sixty months sound the same to you as five years in prison? How about ninety-six months instead of eight years? That number has a prisoner going in when his daughter is twelve and coming out when she is an adult at twenty and maybe married and in her own separate home.

The sentencing judge who has spoken at length against sentencing guidelines is Jed Rakoff, now on senior status for the Southern District of New York. In the high-profile sentence of Rajat Gupta, a well-known businessman and philanthropist convicted on four counts of insider trading charges from which he drew no direct profit, Judge Rakoff attacked "the arbitrary world of the Guidelines." He said "the notion that . . . responsibility can be reduced to the mechanical adding-up of a small set of numbers artificially assigned to a few arbitrarily-selected variables wars with common sense" and goes against "just punishment."[13]

The government wanted the uncooperative and unrepentant Gupta to receive a sentence of between eight and ten years. The probation office asked for six to eight, and the defense wanted assignment to community service. Against this wide spread, Judge Rakoff assigned a two-year sentence with a $5 million fine tacked on. On several occasions, he has urged that sentencing guidelines be scrapped altogether.

Many other leading judges on both the state and federal level have agreed with Rakoff, and on more than one issue. They often carry their criticisms of the guidelines into protests against the enlarged role of prosecutors in the sentencing process. "What really puts the prosecutor in the driver's seat," writes Rakoff, "is the fact that he—because of mandatory minimums, sentencing guidelines . . . and simply his ability to shape whatever charges are brought—can effectively dictate the sentence by how he publicly describes the offense. . . . It is the prosecutor, not the judge, who effectively exercises the sentencing power."[14]

The shift in power from judges to prosecutors at sentencing bothers those who must take official responsibility for the sentence. Judge Alex Kozinsky of the Ninth Federal Circuit adds: "any prosecutor worth his salt can get a grand jury to indict a ham sandwich. It may be that a decent prosecutor could get a petit jury to convict a eunuch of rape." New and overwhelming prosecutorial powers come from "the trend of bringing multiple counts for a single incident—thereby vastly increasing the risk of a life-shattering sentence in a case of conviction—as well as the creativity of prosecutors in hatching up criminal cases where no crime exists." The guidelines encourage such practices, and as a result, in Judge Kozinsky's words, "prosecutors hold tremendous power, more than anyone other than jurors, and often much more than jurors because most cases don't go to trial."[15]

Time and again, this imbalance in official roles comes up in sentencing hearings. Judges regularly confuse point totals in complex guideline possibilities that can mean years of difference in prison. They must constantly query prosecutors over the policies behind given point totals.[16] So much confusion exists that a judge at the last moment will sometimes ask, "Counsel, is there any legal reason not already argued to me why I cannot impose the sentence I have described as stated?"[17]

Thus, in an open-and-shut case of a terrorist openly boasting about his crimes in court and facing many counts of life in prison, is it any wonder that an exasperated and very experienced judge would respond testily to the many interruptions from a prosecutor? Judge Miriam Goldman Cedarbaum had been sitting on the federal district bench for twenty-four years, when, on October 5, 2010, in response to too much guidance, she leveled her prosecutorial interrupter by saying "a long time ago when I was an assistant United States Attorney, we did not think it was the function of the prosecutor to be heavily involved in sentence."[18]

The tensions in give-and-take over guidelines between the professionals are now routine fare in sentencing hearings, and they push the defendant to one side through displaced tensions, worries, and disagreements. Judge Rakoff's protests against the guidelines in *United States v. Gupta* are again relevant. Coming in well below the government's request in sentencing the philanthropist Gupta to two years, Rakoff claimed that "the Guidelines virtually ignore this measure of the man." Missing in the government's charge was the living person in front of the bench. "For on this day of judgment, must not one judge the man as a whole?" Less rhetorically, he declared the means by which the judiciary can always reassert itself. "The Guidelines," he insisted, "must take second place to section 3553(a) [of the federal criminal code]."[19]

Section 3553a, under "Title 18: Crimes and Criminal Procedure," restores the normative dimension in sentencing. (Similar variations appear in many state codes.) The section requires "a *sentence* sufficient, but not greater than necessary." It recognizes, along with the guidelines, "the nature and circumstance of the offense and the history and characteristics of the defendant," but subsequent passages in the statute implicitly come back to the stipulation "not greater than necessary." Under a subheading, "the need for *the sentence* imposed," section 3553a supplies four categories to be considered in any sentence:

(A) To reflect the seriousness of the offense, to promote respect for law, and to provide just punishment for the offense;
(B) To afford adequate deterrence to criminal conduct;
(C) To protect the public from further crimes of the defendant, and;
(D) To provide the defendant with needed educational or vocational training, medical care, or other correctional treatment in the most effective manner.[20]

Judge Rakoff in *Gupta* summarizes the normative implications for imposing a lesser sentence than one required by the guidelines: "First, 'the need for the sentence to be imposed' to afford specific deterrence, general deterrence, 'just punishment,' and the like, and second, the requirement that any sentence imposed be 'sufficient, but not greater than necessary, to comply with [these] purposes.'"[21] There is adroit insistence on flexibility in Rakoff's offhand phrase "and the like," and he cleverly couples it to a shift in the order of stipulations in the statute by finishing with the phrase "no greater than necessary."

Not indicated in Judge Rakoff's summary are the duties of care to be provided a prisoner noted in section D, and there is the rub. Preoccupation and debate in justifying the proper number of years in a sentence overlooks an implied duty of care for the prisoner to come. Frequently, judges don't know enough about prison, and when they do, they seem embarrassed.

Several examples of stumbling judicial commentary on prison life should suffice. While delivering a two-year sentence to a defendant convicted of attempted burglary, a state judge recently concluded, "You are not going up for very long, although, don't misunderstand, it's a tremendous thing to go to State prison, meaning, it's a horrible—it can't be good. I don't mean horrible meaning unsafe, although it might be, not particularly safe, but just make use of the time, try to read, try to learn a craft. I don't know what type of options you'll have in State prison."[22] Take another instance on a receiver's dubious prospects in prison as a sex offender. "Stay with good people you know and they will help you," advised the judge. "Good luck to you. I'll keep my fingers crossed for your life."[23]

Sometimes judicial references appear so fanciful as to defy belief, given what American prisons have become today. Choosing uncertainly between six, fifteen, eighteen, and twenty-one months for the wildly overcrowded prisons of California and pondering a longer sentence, one judge recently asked all present, "Why isn't it better to think of it just from a vocational-training point of view, the longer he's in prison—it's like going to college, almost—he's got more of an opportunity to get into programs and learn something and better himself." The appalled public defender boldly responded, "I don't think it's true that the longer in prison, the more opportunity you have to better yourself."[24]

Guess who is right here. When asked about vocational options in prison, much less college, the embarrassed probation officer in this sentencing hearing could not come up with a single example "off the top of my head." We might better trust the word of two long-time lifers in the California prison system. "Prison isn't a university, it's a breeding ground for blind conformity to some of humankind's lowest philosophies." Adds another, "the prison system [in California] allots a mere two percent of its annual $9 billion budget toward rehabilitation programs."[25] Yet nothing stopped this judge from concluding that he is close to right. Going to prison, he concludes in finally delivering sentence, "would be kind of like going to college, except a little different."

Some judges will recommend assignment to a specified prison, and some will not at the request of defense counsel. The difference is largely immaterial. Judges sentence, but they do not determine where the convicted serve their time. When sentencing Bernie Madoff to 1,800 months in prison (that's 150 years!) on eleven federal felony fraud counts for the greatest Ponzi scheme in history, then federal district court judge Denny Chin was asked by defense counsel to recommend the Federal Correctional Institution in Otisville (seventy miles from Manhattan), but no judge can designate a prison. Knowing that, Judge Chin recommended "an appropriate facility in the northeast region of the United States." It didn't happen. The Bureau of Prisons assigned Madoff to the Butner Federal Correctional Complex in North Carolina (five hundred miles from New York City). The length of a sentence, not judicial determination, controls an assignment, and the decision is left entirely to the Bureau of Prisons.[26]

Which brings us back to what judges can and cannot do about prison life. A remaining area of control over sentencing lies in what a defendant says during a sentencing hearing. Expressions of remorse do not automatically reduce a sentence, although they can. "The deepest remorse" and "tears" from a leading senior partner in the prestigious law firm of Kirkland & Ellis LLP over failure to report $2.4 million in taxable income over five years to the Internal Revenue Service, "a crime of greed, not need," led to a sentence of just one year, well below guidelines and also below the prosecution's request for a two-to-three-year sentence, even though the defendant had still to pay back taxes and was granted three months before surrendering to serve his term.[27]

On the other hand, a defendant who shows no remorse can expect a longer sentence than others. Expressing remorse before the court gives minimal acknowledgment of continuing membership in a moral community held together by mutual obligations. A judge who sentences will condemn the apparent selfishness and total disregard that failure to speak in these terms can indicate.[28]

Take the case of the person who stands up and announces, "I'm a good person, Judge. As a matter of fact, I'm probably a lot better than a lot of other people in this world. My mother and father [the father also convicted of the same crime] always used to tell me, you worry about everybody else, but you don't worry about yourself. . . . All I did was help people." The defendant had nothing to say, as the judge pointedly noted, about the harm caused to others through a long-running union extortion and money-laundering scheme. Finding these "remarks to be among the most extraordinary remarks I have heard" and concluding "you have not taken any responsibility for engaging in a single criminal act," the judge sentenced at the high end of the guidelines, 135 months in prison (11 years).[29]

Despite flexibility and real power in deciding how long someone should be incarcerated, judges know far less than they should about incarceration, and court doctrine helps to explain why. The Supreme Court has repeatedly deferred to "substantive penological judgment" when problems in punishment come before it. Deference, in this sense, has accepted "the primacy of the legislature, the variety of legitimate penological schemes, the nature of our federal system, and the requirement that proportionality review be guided by objective factors."[30]

The principles, as just articulated, are valid in themselves. They do not, however, read as well in the context in which they were given. Justice Anthony Kennedy delivers these principles in *Harmelin v. Michigan.* Ronald Harmelin, without a record of any prior felony convictions, had been sentenced to life without parole for the possession of 672 grams of cocaine, and the Court decided that the "cruel and unusual punishments" clause of the Eighth Amendment did not prevent such a draconian sentence. "Severe, mandatory penalties," wrote Justice Antonin Scalia for the majority, "may be cruel but they are not unusual in the constitutional sense."[31] Not unusual in the constitutional sense? How cruel must prison be before it is understood to be unusual?

Who thinks about life without parole as a practical experience? Prisoners do. Maybe only prisoners do. In the essay collection *Too Cruel, Not Unusual Enough,* those living life without parole write about its physical and psychological torments instead of parsing its constitutional niceties. More than 41,000 are serving life without parole in America today, so Justice Scalia was technically if cynically correct when he said the sentence is "not unusual." It is, just the same, "capital punishment on the installment plan." It turns a prisoner into "dead man walking, only in slow motion." Another writes of "the horror in my life," "no one who hasn't been sentenced to die in prison can truly understand this experience." Explains one more, "life without the possibility of parole is nearly unthinkable in other civilized nations."[32]

Partly responsible for these torments and mass incarceration itself has been "extreme deference in reviewing prison sentences" by the judicial branch of government. Studies show that deference has produced "political paralysis" when reform has been needed. The courts have left all authority to "administrators' 'discretion' over prison operations." Judicial decisions have created "a punitive power limited by no democratic or professional restraints."[33]

The consequence of penal unaccountability has been severity in the practice of punishment everywhere, as we saw time and again in Ovid's *Metamorphoses*. Human nature will be cruel given the chance. The more tactical consequence has been an oblivious judiciary. In deciding "to put on one side" or "to set aside"—the first and main definitions of the word "defer"—judges have absolved themselves of the need to know the literal implications of their sentences.[34]

To Defer or Not to Defer, That Is the Question

What exactly *is* judicial deference? *Black's Law Dictionary* does not bother to enter the separate terms "deference" or "deferential review" until its tenth edition in 2014, where its designation reads "conduct showing respect for somebody or something; courteous or complaisant regard for another"; also "a polite and respectful attitude or approach, esp. toward an important person or venerable institution whose action, proposal, opinion, or judgment should be presumptively accepted."[35]

"Complaisant regard" certainly characterizes the attitude of the Supreme Court when it comes to petitions from the incarcerated, and the *Oxford English Dictionary* does a better job of defining the Court's overall policy. Deference, according to the *OED*, means "submission to the acknowledged superior claims, skill, judgement, or other qualities of another."[36] Close enough, but a decision *not* to act, to defer, is harder to analyze than an action taken, and who is to define the "superior skill" that must be acknowledged?

Legal scholars turn the question of judicial deference into the equivalent of the blindfolded child's parlor game: pinning the tail on the donkey. In this case, quixotically, the donkey is alive and moving.[37] Actually, the Supreme Court defers only when it wants to defer. A prime witness and instigator of this open policy is also easy to find. Observe the chief justice of the United States writing one of the landmark opinions that decided the fate of the Affordable Care Act, known popularly as Obamacare, in 2015.[38]

Judicial discretion, not judicial deference, rules the roost in *King v. Burwell*. In 1984, the Supreme Court used *Chevron v. Natural Resources* to set its standards for granting deference to a government agency's interpretation of a statute it administers.[39] The easiest way for Chief Justice Roberts to affirm the Affordable Care Act would have been to defer under *Chevron* to the Internal Revenue Service through its administration of the requirement that citizens maintain health insurance or make a payment to the IRS.

Roberts, in writing his opinion, had to admit, "The Affordable Care Act addresses tax credits in what is now Section 36B of the Internal Revenue Code." He, nonetheless, hides behind the lack of an exact stipulation giving the Internal Revenue Service precise control, circumventing *Chevron* altogether by declaring "this is not a case for the IRS. It is instead our task to determine the correct reading of Section 36B." Roberts's language cloaks willful discretion in the guise of burden. "Anyway, we must do our best, bearing in mind the fundamental canon of statutory construction." "Our duty, after all, is 'to construe statutes, not isolated provisions.'"[40]

Without saying so, Chief Justice Roberts decided *King v. Burwell* by ignoring deference and embracing discretion in a raw exercise of judicial power. He excused his evasion of *Chevron* by arguing that the Affordable Care Act had serious economic consequences for everyone, "involving billions of dollars in spending each year and affecting the price of health insurance for millions of people."[41] Of course, the same logic could be applied just as well to the more than $80 billion spent on American punishment regimes.

Deference, an exercised negative, is thus a matter of choice and consistently the choice when exercised on prisoner petitions to sustain penal authority. Used again and again, it has defeated prisoners' expressed needs and qualified their rights at just about every turn. Case after case reveals a shocking level of judicial indifference to the conditions and problems of prison life.

Even a partial list is telling on this score. In 1974, *Pell v. Procunier* upheld a prison regulation prohibiting face-to-face media interviews, which cut off the major source of public information about prison conditions.[42] Three years later, *Jones v. North Carolina Prisoners' Labor Union* upheld prison regulations prohibiting unions and bulk mailings, which eliminated all possibility of a safe collective voice in complaints about prison conditions.[43] In 1981, well on the way to mass incarceration, *Rhodes v. Chapman* placed no limits on double-celling.[44] *Hewitt v. Helms* in 1983 found no due process limits on assigning a prisoner to solitary confinement.[45] Pretrial detainees presumed innocent lost the right to observe officials search their cells in *Block v. Rutherford* in 1984, a carryover from *Hudson v. Palmer,* which took away all rights to privacy and property from prisoners.[46] *Farmer v. Brennan* in 1994 ignored even deliberate indifference to a serious risk of harm in an inmate without conclusive proof that the officials were subjectively aware of the risk.[47] *Lockyear v. Andrade* upheld three-strikes-and-you're-out laws with life sentences for repeat felons in 2003.[48] In the same year prison regulations restricting visitation rights remained valid if related to legitimate penological interests.[49] In each of these cases, deference to penal authority controlled the decision.

What might be done about these imbalances, all of which leave the incarcerated helpless in the hands of keepers free to wield severe levels of enforcement and unwarranted extensions of punishment? Has the Supreme Court boxed itself in with now entrenched levels of deference to penal authority? Arguably not. Much depends on what the choices in deference signify. Even more turns on what judges know about conditions that are now producing prison scandals on a regular basis and on how closely those handing down sentences hew to a strict retributive theory of punishment.

Two leading judges have openly discussed the significance of choice in deference. Minimizing the absolutes in deference, Harold Baer Jr., a long-time federal district court judge for the Southern District of New York, wrote in 2007 that "judicial intervention has been and should continue to be a viable solution" in cases "when the legislative and the executive are unable or unwilling to insure minimal constitutional rights" for detainees in New York City jails.[50]

Judge Baer explained his position in great detail. Pointing to the danger that legislatures and executives "can and have been influenced by special interests," Baer reasoned that "the federal judiciary . . . is properly insulated to protect the interests of the vulnerable and powerless, such as the men and women who populate our prisons." He was unwilling to let the abstract rubrics in "separation of powers," which are often misunderstood and misapplied, stand in the way. "In the last analysis the Judiciary is the only entity that can adequately enforce constitutional protections."

More recently Judge Richard A. Posner, sitting on the Federal Appeals Court for the Seventh Circuit, has argued "a strong norm of deference to the decisions of administrative agencies is the fossil remnant of an era in which judges were excessively hostile to agencies and in which 'progressives' had boundless faith in the potential of agencies as agents of reform." Discussing the variables, Posner answers his own question. "Must we ignore the differences and accord equal deference to all administrative decisions?" The realist judge thinks not. The realist judge thinks "deference is earned, not bestowed."[51]

What Judges Can Do

A prison sentence claims to be time served with whatever fines and financial restitution a judge sets. Plenty of evidence suggests that loss of freedom is sufficient punishment for anyone, even in the best of prisons. Nonetheless, incarceration as we now know it in the United States goes well beyond time served and beyond what every judge sentences.

Prison horrifies anyone who knows a person in prison because of its collateral effects: physical danger, unaddressed violence, utter loss of privacy, mistreatment from staff, intimidation by peer groups, poor medical help, unhealthy food, overly severe forms of confinement, separation from a family that suffers from its missing incarcerated member, the loss of commonly available minimal comforts, and the elimination of all meaningful individuality and personal dignity. The list of horrors could be much longer, but none of these basic ones gets addressed in the moment of sentencing. Judges cannot prevent these problems from occurring, but they can be part of a solution to them.

As we have seen, a federal judge is required by statutory law to consider section 3553a of the criminal code, part of which expects incarceration "to provide the defendant with needed educational or vocational training, medical care, or other correctional treatment in the most effective manner."[52] There are no direct equivalents in other statutory sentencing regimes except for the District of Columbia and Hawaii, but most state jurisdictions do require a quality level of rehabilitation for the incarcerated and some raise other concerns about conditions there.[53] Providing education and care *in the most effective manner* clearly reaches beyond the question of custody. If the words mean anything at all, they confront the failure of correctional treatment in American prisons today.

That failure should be met at each stage of criminal justice. Protection from the system is one of law's most sacred responsibilities. The most familiar public form of admonition comes in the moment someone is arrested and interrogated. The "Miranda Warning," with minor variations in different jurisdictions, runs like this:

> You have the right to remain silent. Anything you say can and will be used against you in a court of law. You have the right to talk to a lawyer and have him or her present with you while you are being questioned. If you cannot afford to hire a lawyer, one will be appointed to represent you before any questioning if you wish. You can decide at any time to exercise these rights and not answer any questions or make any statements. Do you understand each of these rights that I have explained to you?[54]

Aspects of the *Miranda* decision have been whittled away in subsequent consideration, but the decision holds in the public imagination and retains some of its original efficacy.[55] A parallel statement should be given to every person sentenced to correctional treatment. If anything, someone facing prison needs more warnings and protection from the system than a person under arrest, and the warning should have the same goals of rectification when the duties taken on by the law through its admonitions are not met. Call it "Obligations and Rights of the Incarcerated." Applying it, a judge would end delivery of a sentence to be served in prison with the following words:

Obligations and Rights of the Incarcerated

I. Incarceration brings both obligations and rights:

1. You have the obligation while under an incarceration order to obey promptly all instructions given to you by law enforcement and correction officers.

2. You must maintain civil behavior at all times toward those in authority and those incarcerated with you.

3. If you harm another while incarcerated, you can expect your time in prison to be measurably increased with other sanctions imposed.

II. Good behavior will help to ensure the following protections:

1. You have the right and obligation to improve yourself through education during your time in prison.

2. You have the right to be free of intimidation, physical abuse, and harassment.

3. You have the right to proper medical care and nourishment.

4. You have the right to report any abuse and the right to have that report considered in an open and timely fashion through all proper channels.

5. Anyone who violates these rights can be brought into this court or a court named for redress if timely consideration of your report has not been met by penal authorities.

III. Do you understand these obligations and rights as I have read them to you? A copy of them will be available to you in prison.

Statutory reconsideration may be necessary for some but not all of these provisions. The Prison Litigation Reform Act (PLRA) of 1996, passed twenty years ago during the punitive impulse of the 1990s, hampers such enforcement in court at the federal level involving any defendant, state, local, or federal, and some variants reach the state level, where prison abuse is greatest.[56] But this set of Obligations and Rights of the Incarcerated can still be a barometer of concern for measuring the pressures in a given situation. It can tell judges to look at what is done in our jails and prisons, and it can provide better access for redress when its protections are willfully denied.

Margo Schlanger, a leading authority on criminal detention, in a study from 2015 shows how the PLRA makes it hard for a prisoner to file a lawsuit in federal court by restricting almost every attempt to the formal grievance procedures set up by penal authority. In effect, grievance procedures turn into barriers. Every prison grievance must be exhausted first, and every possibility has intricate appeal levels with hidden deadlines, hard-to-follow and buried statutes of limitation at each stage of the process. The PLRA has "increased filing fees, decreased attorneys' fees, and limited damages" even though "litigation remains one of the few avenues for prisoners to seek redress for adverse conditions or other affronts to their rights."[57]

The threat of formal litigation is a key to relief. Why should prison authorities cooperate actively with a grievance procedure against their own personnel? In fact, they do not. The history of stalled or ignored or poorly acknowledged or quickly dismissed prisoner petitions through penal bureaucracies and on to courts is a long one. The proposed Obligations and Rights of the Incarcerated can begin to play a corrective role where obfuscation has been a frequent resort and where the difficulties in reaching court by imprisoned petitioners have grown.

Judges cannot stop the brutal practices of our punishment regimes just by warning against them, but they are the voices of justice in the system. Think of Obligations and Rights of the Incarcerated as one of many steps toward a more flexible understanding of punishment. Rights and warnings like the ones indicated tell everyone what prison is supposed to be and what it cannot become.

The warnings put penal officials on notice of redress through a court's statutory and stated interest in protecting the minimal rights of people that it sentences to prison. Misconduct flourishes with impunity because penal authority and the bureaucracies under it protect a closed terrain of unaccountability. The consequences are direct. Intolerable levels of abuse go unchecked every day in our prisons and jails.

The people in prison are our people, and they have the right to the minimal dignity to which all people are entitled. We have the choice of repairing lives by making prisoners more cognizant of their positive capabilities and hence more useful to themselves and others than they have been, or we can continue to destroy lives through punishment regimes too repressive to make corrections anything but a name.

Leading the way should be the country's judges. They remain the most respected professionals in public life, uniquely registered in formal address

6
The Technology of Confinement

The Institutional Basis

IN METAMORPHOSIS, ENVIRONMENTAL backgrounds shape human action just as they condition the feasibility of change, and nowhere is this truer than in the impact of institutional settings on the theories and practices of incarceration. We turn to those institutional settings, with technological wherewithal at the head of the list. Mass incarceration and current levels of punishment could not exist without the technological means to enforce them.

Jacques Ellul and others have argued that technical mastery ("technopoly") can narrow thought and make it less sensitive to human dimensions and needs. Criminologists call this level of total technological imposition "a habitus of subjection." In "total institutions," prison theorists agree that current modes of technical use have led to "mortification of the self."[1]

Prison technology is especially one-sided and imposed because it is not shared. In the absence of mutuality, it moves in only one direction. Does this have to be so? Technology may have a momentum of its own, but it is what you make of it, especially when you have complete control of its dimensions as you can in prison with the right sophistication in know-how. Can it be turned to mutual advantage between keepers and kept? Can the technological setting make for better thought on both sides?

The bad aspects of prison technology are indeed bad. The United States has so many people in prison and jail and many more under legal surveillance because technology has made it possible. Fewer people with less personal attention can guard larger numbers than ever before in buildings technologically designed to sustain poor personnel ratios. But guard them well? Lopsided numbers are their own problem. They increase the likelihood of prison revolt in a total institution geared to repression.

Electronic data sets also mean no one's crime or behavior in prison is ever lost, even after it has been paid for. Some of the details are worse. Military equipment designed for open spaces—stun grenades, shock sticks, electrified shields, tear gas, mace, and laser lighting—cause untold injuries, especially when employed in tight quarters. Prisons have invented tasteless food. Enforced medications of all kinds are used to pacify instead of heal. Any and all developments in mechanisms of control may be called upon and used as long as they do not actually kill or physically mutilate.

Retributive thought justifies all of these developments, and it twists the resourcefulness in technological advance. In commercial and political settings automation demands greater efficiency of everyone—anything to gain an edge through more speed, quicker responses to demands, and faster decisions. It normally hurries things up. In prison, the repressive side of technology slows them down.

In society, the method in technological practice has internalizing traits that are checked somewhat by externalizing validation. Prison encloses the technique in new forms of mastery without moral calculation of their external impact. Everywhere, but particularly in incarceration, "certain widely accepted reasons of practical necessity—especially the need to maintain crucial technological systems as smoothly working entities—have tended to eclipse other sorts of moral and political reasoning."[2]

A deeper point should not be missed. Technological breakthroughs can be monitored in public life, but no one really bothers to check them in prison culture. This chapter responds to that indifference. How can the uses of technology and the techniques behind them be arranged to help instead of hurting people in prison? Can advances in technology do anything except increase the hostile atmosphere of incarceration?

One of the leading philosophers of our time, Jürgen Habermas, warns that "a technocracy without democratic roots" is not equipped to maintain "social justice." "The lure of technocracy" will fulfill its own systemic logic and ignore other calculations.[3] There is no democracy anywhere in prison. Without careful preparation and forethought, new initiatives are far more likely to reinforce pejorative routines.

Anyone who urges penal change has to be aware of the sad history of reform in this area. Almost every new technological idea adopted in penology has been twisted into a form of negative interaction at the expense of the imprisoned. Marion, the first federal prison to be turned into a technological "supermax" or "level six penitentiary," began in 1964 as an institution based on "liberal humanitarian lines" built away from all major cities and presumed negative influences in southern Illinois. In 1979, just fifteen years later, that separate location became attractive in another way. It encouraged the Federal Bureau of Prisons to concentrate all of its worst offenders there with predictable results. With the worst remaining that way, authorities soon adjusted Marion into an isolating lockdown. By 1983 the model prison became a technological horror where no one wanted to go or be.[4]

For a more recent example of technological reform gone awry, look at the use of electronic monitoring through ankle bracelets. The bracelets have been celebrated as a means of keeping people out of jail. That is the theory. In practice, the wearer must bear the exorbitant cost of the bracelet, meaning that the impoverished end up in jail anyway with an additional debt to pay. "The alternative to incarceration" is not one if you have little or no money. The ankle bracelet duplicates the problem of high bail charges. It leaves people who cannot pay in jail.[5] In a similar travesty, the potential advent of Skype video phone messaging has led a providing company to ask that it replace the possibility of actual visitation so that it can continue to extract enormous profits from phone services for the incarcerated.[6]

Even the best of technological intentions can go awry. "Telemedicine," contact with prisoners by doctors through an audio console, is being used in more and more prisons. But whom does it really help? "Telemedicine is perfectly designed for prisons," if you ask correction officials in health services. It cuts some costs, increases efficiency, and allows doctors to feel safer in dealing with the incarcerated. Of course, when looked at from a prisoner's perspective "it is never going to be as good as having an on-site physician who can perform hands-on diagnosis and treatment." Substituting an electronic visual for a doctor in the room adds one more level of affectless interaction and anomie to prison life.[7]

These proposals warn against whatever one suggests about technological innovation. The negative twists in mechanism increase in prison because the psychological desire to punish remains strong, and the first sign of real disorder leads quickly to more technological intrusion. Machine culture objectifies repression. No one has to think directly about its consequences, and few who use it do. Think about the consequences. Correction rarely works without meaningful person-to-person contact of some kind. Mechanical apparatus and thought get in the way of the personal influences needed.

Parsing technology, instead of just accepting its impact, can help us to distinguish alternative options from mere imposition. Technology and the know-how that goes with it have five basic effects on circumstance, process, and human behavior. Naming them in familiar terms, they are *structure, size, ambiance, production,* and *social relations.* If these five basic influences overlap, each illuminates a discrete aspect of technological reliance. Taken up in order, each facet can illustrate hidden dimensions and functions of prison culture as they currently exist and suggest how they might be changed.

Structure

The preferred form of technical construction and architecture in modern incarceration comes from Jeremy Bentham's eighteenth-century book *Panopticon.* Bentham's idea was simple: place the keeper where he could see the kept without being seen. That way, the imprisoned would assume they were always under observation and would behave to avoid added punishment. A circular building with the keeper at the hub would fulfill this plan through windows and shades properly placed.[8] Video cameras trained on cells and prison halls have taken the place of architectural design. Television now provides the unseen seer: the electronic panopticon.

Are cameras an adequate adjustment? The underlying complications in Bentham's idea have been lost in current planners' total reliance on modern applications. Most of the purposes of the panopticon have been obscured in the practice of contemporary prison facilities, and trust in technology has been a major part of the problem.

The first to scrutinize penal systems empirically and objectively, Bentham grasped the essential predicament in all prison organizations. Borrowing from the Romans, he summarized "one of the most puzzling of all political questions": "Quis custodiet ipsos custodies?" (Who will watch the watchman?).[9]

Ironically, with all of its technological power, current prison culture fails to watch closely enough. Surveillance is extreme on the kept but not their keepers. Unobserved custodians on the front lines in prisons receive little or no scrutiny and enjoy absolute sway in their positions from the moment they enter a facility. Much of illegal contraband and many incidents of abuse come from prison guards who, when they know they are not watched, smuggle in drugs and weapons and attack prisoners on the slightest provocation or with no provocation at all.[10]

Bentham answered the problem of "control upon subordinate power" with an architectural design that subjected both "under keepers" and prisoners to the same plan of one-way surveillance. He made a totally perceiving "head keeper or inspector" the mechanism "for redress against the neglect or oppression of subordinates." He knew that abuse would occur in "that rigid sphere . . . a crowded prison" unless prevented.[11]

That was not all to Bentham's plan. He wanted spacious, clean cells open to public scrutiny. He thought no prison unit should be larger than one hundred or, under special conditions, two hundred people for safe and personal management. He wanted architectural attention given to "the prevailing ideas of beauty and local convenience" in the construction of his rotundas. He urged procedures for safe custody with meaningful vocational opportunities, not forced labor. For work to reform someone, he believed, it had better be profitable.[12]

Bentham was a man of pragmatic details. Prisoners were to return to society with some money they had earned while incarcerated. He insisted on no beatings, no chains or other restraints. The slightest punishment inflicted and not recorded had to be censured as "a lawless injury." Leniency and coercion were to be carefully balanced. It was necessary to please "the malefactors themselves" as much as "those for whose sake they are consigned to punishment." Cooperation defined operations as much as possible.

All of these worthy balances have been forgotten. Bentham knew that his admittedly idealistic theory amounted to standing an egg on end, but he also wrote "my wonder is, not only that this plan should never have hitherto been put in practice, but how any other should ever have been thought of."[13] A good, practical idea usually has a simple logic to it, and Bentham was right on both counts. Bentham used the story of placing an egg upright (ascribed to Columbus) as a challenge to prison planners over innovation and the need for imagination. New technique had to answer the tyranny of too much conformity in thought and narrow belief. (After others could not do it, Columbus simply squashed the tip of the egg to set it on end.)

Seemingly impossible quandaries can be solved! Bentham intuited that his innovative design would dominate subsequent penal practice, and it has, but people lose the pith in wisdom when it becomes routinized understanding. Despite general recognition of Bentham's "simple idea," penology has ignored the complexity and spirit of change that informs the underlying purposes of *Panopticon*.

Where did all of this go wrong? Merely duplicating a previous effect rarely fulfills the original idea. The differences between personal observation in a prison setting and electronic surveillance are actually great. Technologically, the video screen creates its own reality, and it is not that of the world. It can "starve our other senses—touch, smell, taste." You watch an actual person differently than you receive a televised image. An order delivered over an intercom gets a different reaction than a command given in person. There is no substitute for human interaction. Bentham, despite all of his stress on technique, saw that technology could never replace "embodied cognition."[14]

Instead of aiding, telecommunication has intensified the alienation in prison life. Video transmission does not keep Bentham's "under keepers" in view as the panopticon planned. Prison guards know and use the blind spots in camera coverage, called "the desert," when they want to inflict illegal discipline. Is it any wonder that a federal judge would order more comprehensive coverage in a North Carolina state prison full of abuse?[15] Cameras do not expose the unsanitary conditions of cell life or convey the tension in a growing crisis. Nor do they capture the full span of activity in a disturbance. Reaction times are also going to be slower than what Bentham imagined from his physical watcher.[16]

On the positive side of technology, video identification as evidence can be more reliable than personal recall, and a videotape studied over and over again will counter the standard fabrications that correction officers will tell about what happened. Take a typical correction officer joke. "How many CO's did it take to push the inmate down the stairs? None—he fell by himself."[17] Statistical studies using databases cut through the humor. They reveal that "slip and fall" accidents are a leading source of injury reports in jails and far outnumber those in the general community. The conclusion that prison authorities resist? "Many injuries go misreported out of fear for reprisal."[18]

The joke became stark reality for a prisoner in New York state's Fishkill Correctional Facility on April 21, 2015. Lucas Renfrow inadvertently witnessed guards push another prisoner down a flight of steps, and that prisoner died from the beating he had received. For days after, Renfrow was harassed, abused, singled out for retribution, placed in solitary confinement, and set up for a manufactured infraction that he narrowly avoided only when warned by another prisoner. "You didn't see nothing," Renfrow was told with an officer's grip around his neck. "If I hear you say anything, you'll be in the same condition that he is. You'll never go home."[19]

When such vicious events take place in a medium-security prison like Fishkill, they confirm, in the words of one correction officer, that "a current of brutality in corrections work is hard to deny."[20] One provisional solution, as the federal judge in North Carolina insisted, would make electronic surveillance absolute on both a visual and auditory basis: no hidden areas for unseen or unheard behavior. Prisoners in trouble will try to stay where cameras can record what happens.

Better technology than what prisons now have is needed for these purposes. If the observation of illegal treatment is left entirely to prisoners to identify, officers avoid censure through codes of silence and the ability to intimidate witnesses under their control. Threats, deprivation of privileges, and disguised retribution keep all but the most tragic events under wraps. Casual abuse, really anything below horrifying multiple injuries, rarely gets to a report, much less to an investigation.

The evidence is in on these problems. Investigations prove that "keeping its dirty laundry in-house is an administrative priority." They show that guards who attack prisoners away from cameras "huddle with other guards to get their stories straight and write reports with bogus scenarios to justify their brutality," particularly if the consequences on the victim cannot be hidden. Abuse is a closed system. "Line officers who commit these acts," studies of abuse reveal, "are supported by their administrators, by their lieutenants, by the major, they're all either condoning the activity, or they're covering it up."[21]

Difficulties in the innovation of total surveillance have to be met, and there are some. Absolute technological intrusion will lend itself to further misuse if not properly managed.[22] But prisoners already lack meaningful privacy, and they need more protection, from each other as well as from staff, than they now get. The move to total surveillance would keep an electronic eye on Bentham's "under keepers," the subordinate custodians on the front line, and it certainly would make it harder to lie about an incident.

Add two other differences in total surveillance with real meaning. Outside viewers, not just keepers of the kept, should regulate the ever watchful electronic eye. They should also be able to hear the audio report of an unfolding incident to ascertain its true import. Correction officers fabricate language to hide what they are doing. A helpless prisoner who is being beaten will typically be told over and over "stop resisting me!" The covering language becomes ridiculous if heard in conjunction with a video. The words reveal that punishers know their behavior is reprehensible and subject to accusation if not disguised.

Bentham's basic conception of the purpose in imprisonment dictates everything about the architectural structure he wanted. "Punishment," he wrote, "whatever shape it may assume, is an evil" and "necessarily odious." The least of it had to make do. The panopticon was to be aesthetically pleasing, as comfortable as possible, sanitary, and carefully ventilated; its residents would be provided with proper nourishment to ensure health. Extended solitary confinement was not allowed. True, the imprisoned were to live alone in "more or less spacious" cells. But Bentham's use of solitude never forgot the human need for interaction, and he gave it through vocational placement. Association with plenty of human contact would make profitable work a pleasurable experience.[23]

Central to everything in Bentham? If people could be made physically comfortable and liked what they did, they would have a better chance to reflect on how to build a better life when they returned to society. Comfort in the modern world is technologically based, and Bentham made the connection a priority—a priority now lost. His added directives get no attention in current incarceration. Mattresses are paper thin. Small chairs have no give or padding in them. Prisoners frequently complain about the lack of minimal comfort in their environment, and since the lack is easily dealt with by better and easily available furniture, it says no one really cares about who prisoners are or what they would like to do and become.[24]

The circular arrangement in Bentham's design included what would later be called structural proxemics, the theory of how space allotment affects human relationships. The comfort zones for olfaction (smell), kinesthetics (movement), feel or touch (sensation), and sight depend on how close we are to other people in the area we inhabit. Reaction to an elevated temperature depends on how many people surround us. Small unchosen space, most of prison space, is an intrinsic irritation.[25]

Feelings about proximity come close to instinct. Wherever we are, "we dislike cramped" and seek "ample." The distinction is an important one in establishing ordinary comfort levels. Between two and four feet sustains the "personal distance" or "satisfied space" we need to preserve public presentation against the self we hide behind it. Studies in "the pathology of crowding" also tell us that hierarchy and spacing determine whether a group will be aggressive or defensive in its reactions to stimuli.

Anyone remotely aware of close human interaction in anything like these terms should grasp why American prisons have become violent places. Their crowded and restricting structures spawn conflict. When President Obama visited El Reno Federal Correctional Institution on July 16, 2015, and worried over crowded prison cells, he was observing a general phenomenon. If you pile already dysfunctional prisoners on top of each other in small spaces, they will have problems coping with each other.[26]

Overcrowding turns especially volatile through the technically based institutional arrangements that manage it. Penal hierarchies—structurally detached by electronics above a packed horizontal population of prisoners—leave the incarcerated to construct their own parallel pecking order through physical intimidation and their own parallel code of silence. No one on any side of prison involvement wants to identify a source of violence when it occurs. The kept imitate their keepers with their own policies of intimidation. Again, the right technology can be part of an answer here.

It may be that misery loves company, but not too much company. Prisons smell bad in a close fetid atmosphere compounded by high noise levels and either too much heat or too much cold, depending on the season. Poorly ventilated metal corridors are filled to overflowing with prisoners who cannot wash frequently enough in disease-ridden and sometimes dangerous shower rooms. Nor is there any urgency to handle these issues despite growing discomfort levels from climate change.[27]

The detachment allowed through centralized technological oversight keeps most of these problems at a distance from higher officialdom. People, especially large numbers of people, can be thought of collectively and dismissed that way. Correction officers are taught in training school to look at the truth through objectifying terminology and mass considerations. "The truth of it is that we are warehousers of human beings." The lesson? Accept what you find. Prisoners exist as the overflow in mechanical surplus.[28]

The current objectifications in prison technology extend from the seemingly mundane to the very serious. The front office can cancel a computerized palm print or face recognition smart card and thereby avoid explaining why someone has lost access to a prison library or elsewhere. Gates that open and close automatically from an unobserved operator restrict movement by prisoners in a more convenient fashion than having guards man the gates, particularly when the central order is to keep those gates closed and when failure of a prisoner to be in the right place after a work detail can lead to demerits beyond the prisoner's control.

More serious detaching mechanisms? A deputy using a joystick and computer monitor from an office can now transmit an invisible millimeter heat wave to stop an altercation or an individual who acts up. The wave causes immediate, intolerable, paralyzing skin pain. This weapon, more euphemistically named the "assault intervention device" (AID), allows correction officers to break up a conflict without being there. It doesn't take much imagination to realize that the device could also be used to punish too abruptly or arbitrarily.[29]

Many of the recent technological tools used to suppress recalcitrant prisoners also allow prison authorities to circumvent the law. To sustain a complaint through the prison and judicial system, a prisoner must prove physical injury before mental or emotional injury can count. A paralyzing shock from a guard's electrified shield or an electrified belt around a prisoner's waist can deliver devastating pain, but it leaves no physical mark to claim a physical injury. Correction officers like to call this form of enforced submission "a 'clean' form of coercion." The phrase indicates that the officer's assault has left no *apparent* physical damage.[30]

Caring comes from knowing. Not caring grows with the numbers considered and the calculations that distance allows. Technological detachment keeps authority from having to think more positively about what it is doing. How negative can such thinking become? "If they are happy," runs another lesson about prisoners in correction officer training, "you're not doing your job."[31] The word that counts in this tutorial lesson is "they." Use of the disembodied plural pronominal form denies individuality in the name of an undesirable collectivity. Would even the toughest correction officer in a training academy actually say the following? "If *he* is happy or if *she* is happy, *you* are not doing your job"?

Poor comparative numbers aided by technology and collective numbers really matter in prison. That is why "us against them" is a winning formulation in correction office thought. Among other things, it registers fear in the knowledge that prisoners always outnumber staff with dangerous implications. For whether or not officials want it, technology is always willing to increase prison numbers through more efficient management.

Size

"Big tech" alters the size of everything. It changes the scope of all major organizations by giving them the ability to exercise centralized power over very large numbers all at once, and authority has learned to cloak itself within the interstices of institutional layers.[32] The force of these technological imperatives applies to the size and organization of most state and federal prisons with an important difference. The downwardly directed, middle-level bureaucracies found in most effective big companies form more of a barrier in penal hierarchies, and the peculiar nature of institutional size encourages it to happen.

Prisons participate in these growth patterns in singular ways because of the crowding at the lowest echelon of organizational purpose. The size of institutions that hold about 75 percent of the incarcerated bear no relation in spirit or purpose to Bentham's maximal correctional facility of 200 people under personal management. Sing Sing Maximum Security Prison in New York state holds approximately 1,700 prisoners. San Quentin in California confines 4,200, well above designed capacity. Pelican Bay State Prison in northern California has 2,900, also well above designed capacity. Stateville Correctional Center in Illinois imprisons 1,648. More than 7,500 are housed at any one time in Curran-Fromhold Correctional Facility in northeast Philadelphia.

The numbers mean that prisons in the United States have grown into small cities, except they are not cities in organizational and bureaucratic demeanor. They are ruled instead by unelected officials that lack municipal profiles. Little about their activities is known or responsive to the outside world. No public check or company board restrains prison authority, and in consequence, the power of penal authority surpasses that of leaders in municipalities and commercial corporations. Some would say that is the way it should be, but unlimited power means that the spirit of cooperation fostered in public organizations does not exist here.

If, however, the power is greater, it is also unsettled. The high ratios technologically generated between prisoners and their correction officers have created a precarious situation, and organizational compulsions must cope with the imbalance. Anxiety over the possibility of uprisings runs high in prisons, and it causes staffs to use crushing authority to curb even minimal disturbances. Experience shows that the smallest of incidents can burgeon into a riot in a repressed population that so completely outnumbers its managers and resents the methods used to keep it down. Everyone, including the incarcerated, knows there are never enough officers to deal with an incident that spreads.

More than imagination is at work here. On March 11, 2016, an extended riot with injuries occurred in the William C. Holman Correctional Facility in Alabama. There were only 17 correctional officers to hold down 900 prisoners in a facility designed to accommodate 581 people. Similar riots with fatalities in understaffed and overcrowded prisons took place in Nebraska prisons in May 2015 and in a Delaware prison in 2017.[33] Occasional hostage taking in uprisings brings humiliation, injury, and sometimes death to captured correction officers. The threat is always there.

Semi-official uses of spontaneous brutality are therefore condoned to keep order, and not just by the rank and file on the front lines of prison corridors. Higher authority gives tacit approval to the use of sudden and ruthless force for almost any reason. By looking the other way, it accepts such force as a necessary evil. It basically agrees that systemic brutality is necessary to minimize trouble.

A vicious circle compounds this problem of size management. American prisons exist full of fear on all sides. Prisoners fear arbitrary mistreatment from officers and from peers who imitate staff abuse. Frontline officers fear retaliation, spreading disobedience, sudden injury, censure from fellow officers, and explosive situations. Higher authority fears exposure of the methods it allows. Repression, secrecy, and security form a triad in control of these fears, but they also fuel them. Limited communication and its product, mistrust, add to an atmosphere of perpetual anxiety.

Prison management must keep this fear from becoming intolerable, and the solution it chooses takes one other form: intransigent bureaucratic routine and a near worship of apparatus. There is a relative calm that rote regulation can instill. Everywhere bureaucracies "dehumanize" and thereby freeze feeling through prescribed technique. They are the breathing body of the technological imperative, and prison administrations apply that imperative with special intensity.[34]

The sociologist Max Weber first coined the now popular phrase that describes bureaucratic restriction, and it bears directly on the nature of prison culture. He saw bureaucracies as "iron cages," in which "the rigidity of hierarchical subordination" by unelected experts could impose its will over an otherwise unwieldy or unresponsive organization.[35] In penal institutions, these techniques preserve a terrain of unaccountability in the lowest levels of management. The iron cage mirrors the prison cell in more ways than one.

Prison administrations make use of the indifference in bureaucratic tendencies. The problem of unruly size can be contained if all possibilities are reduced to limited practices and expectations through rigid form, the very essence of prison culture. The extended grasp of bureaucracy, in Weber's terms, "has always been its purely *technical* superiority over any other form of organization. The fully developed bureaucratic apparatus compares with other organizations exactly as does the machine with nonmechanical modes of production."

The deadening mechanics in bureaucracy map directly onto prison practices. Intransigence occurs in all bureaucracies, but it flourishes as a virtue in penal administration by protecting frontline misbehavior. Unlike in public or commercial life, efficiency means nothing and regulation of the incarcerated needs only to control them. Prison does not create, sell, or distribute a product or reward a constituency. The implications of these differences are vast. Expertise in prison management never needs to improve the quality or the completion of the product it ostensibly serves. The whole purpose is to keep a population unchanging and at rest.

It follows that obfuscation rules against any request for change or rectification. Just as correction officers instinctively hide what they do, so prison bureaucracies allow that to happen through the patterns of secrecy that define all bureaucracies. Technical manipulations flourish without restraint here. Criminologists agree that "*a bureaucracy's most basic instinct is to survive and grow.*" The goal is power held and defended with the purpose of keeping everything under wraps.[36] In the vernacular of prison culture, administrative priorities translate into "keep it down," a mantra that extends far beyond keeping a prisoner from complaining.

The members of a bureaucracy work to protect internal expertise from outside intrusion, a pattern of withholding that is especially strong in prison culture.[37] Concealment at all levels becomes a motivational and behavioral syndrome beyond anything found in civil administrative settings. Nothing stands in the way of control mechanisms. No higher authority bothers to question the independent viability that prison bureaucracies reserve to themselves.[38]

How sick do these patterns of both external and internal administrative levels of secrecy and concealment become? A prisoner who dares to talk to senior prison officials—in those infrequent moments when high authority makes rounds—faces the prospect of an unprovoked beating from front-line officers or another inmate who will be offered special privileges by guards if he instigates an attack while the guards watch. In one such instance, the inmate called in to mete out discipline reported that the prison guards promised to "take care of me," and shortly after his planned and unprovoked attack on another prisoner he received a coveted work position as a porter, "a privilege you get when you're good." Internal investigations routinely fail in such instances, and when action is taken the consequences for the officers are minimal.[39]

As before, but now in the administrative interstices, unaccountability corrodes all of the purposes in corrections. While most bureaucracies are designed to facilitate practice, prison bureaucracies render them indolent. Prison "request forms" bury inmate complaints under arcane processes. The typical request never quite fits procedural requirements. Even correction officers learn that filing a form will be frowned on up the line. Faceless obduracy is a penal art form.[40] Prisoners have every right to be skeptical about the bureaucracies over them. What is a prisoner to make of receiving notification for a hearing the day after the hearing has taken place?[41]

All of this means that prisoners, the subjects of bureaucratic intent, have no leverage to challenge the misuse of rules that hold them in place. Most complaints are stopped at the ground level through casual intimidation. When one federal prisoner finally stepped out of procedural lines and complained by writing directly to the cooking staff about food that was too rotten to eat, the rejoinder came with a veiled but openly insulting threat. The complainer was told by a CO to stay in line. "Have the courage to make your complaint directly to a correction officer standing in front of you."[42] Translation? Be afraid and stay afraid even if the food is inedible.[43]

How can such practices occur in good conscience? Procedure for the sake of procedure paves the way to personal indifference. Regulations protect prison administrators from any impulse to think in proactive terms by defining "duty" through the rules to be applied. Duty everywhere is the weathervane that distinguishes courage from cowardice. You either did your duty despite personal sacrifice or risk (courage), or you failed to do your duty when the wind blew in your direction (cowardice).[44] Bureaucracies evade this normative distinction. They do it by defining duty narrowly and away from the will to originate. Staying within the system smooths the escape from personal involvement.[45]

By reducing duty to form, bureaucracies narrow the responsibilities of correction officers. They eliminate informed consideration by moving staff from one part of a prison to another and prisoners from one facility to another, the latter at considerable expense. Both policies claim to be strategies for dealing with size and security problems, but they have a more direct purpose. Shifting keepers and the kept prevents communal feelings from developing in the scene of punishment.[46] Not knowing is again not caring.

Intransigence rules this roost. Nonetheless, the problems that size forces on penal issues have another side. Hierarchies can benefit as well as harm. New techniques can be assets against the momentums that push technology in negative directions. Bureaucracies will always survive—that is their first purpose—but with a will you can adjust them. Difficulties identified can be eased. Fatalism is the complication here, and it has to be resisted at each stage of our analysis. Many in penology recognize the problem of size but accept its ramifications with resignation instead of looking for the answers that are available.

Again total surveillance could target misbehavior now missed or falsely interpreted. Large numbers also give flexibility in organizational terms. They lend themselves to a reorganization within the problem of size into smaller, more manageable groups. Accountability can be built into any system with the right composition and deployment of units. Technology can streamline bureaucracies and make information available to large numbers. A similar transparency can take on the relationship between the two main organizational units in control of penal governance.

For underneath the penal bureaucracy is another entire institutional arrangement in need of attention: penal militarism. As the next section shows in greater detail, military postures dictate much of prison work, yet the work done in prisons ignores the strongest structural foundations of military endeavor. Penology takes only the most rudimentary aspects of military training and practice—so rudimentary that truisms over the connection between armed forces and correctional officers are less important than constructive parallels now ignored that could ease the problem of size.

The use of manpower should regard technical efficiency for the task performed. The U.S. Army functions through squads (three to fourteen soldiers, depending on assignments), platoons (three or four squads combine to give approximately thirty soldiers), and companies (three or four platoons of perhaps 100 soldiers in all), then up the personnel ladder to battalions (three or four companies), regiments sometimes called brigades (a total of 1,000 people made up from up to three battalions), and on to larger components (divisions and corps).

The relevant units for prison culture—cohesive squads, platoons, and companies—could work that way, but they do not because the task assigned is not sufficiently trusting or cooperative. Through those first three organizational levels, everyone in the army can know everyone else in units that perform with the same skill sets. Above that level, anonymity and differentiation in function take over. The significance of the distinction is where prison administration should take a stand. The efficiency of more carefully arranged numbers can improve work in corrections, perhaps decisively.

Put as a general principle, units of up to 100 people can know each other well enough and in a sufficiently integral fashion to function at heightened levels in conflict through organizationally instilled cooperation. Cooperation, in turn, forms friendships, alliances, heightened functionality, and a comfort zone for mutual endeavor. Anthropologists put this number as high as 150, with some support for that estimate coming from commercial enterprises.[47]

The ramifications for dealing with the size and anonymity issues in prisons should be clear. Nothing can be done about the long corridors in today's large maximum- and medium-security prisons, but surveillance of them can be broken down into squads that remain intact and that get to know themselves and the people on a corridor well.

A platoon of three established squads with four or five members each should be appropriate to handle a corridor of 100 prisoners in three shifts of eight hours apiece. Yes, this increases the ratio of correction officers to prisoners, but that must happen if communal reciprocity in carceral relations is to improve. Correction officer unions will surely welcome the increases in their numbers. Another desired aspect of such a plan? It would never leave a single officer alone on duty. It should assist watchers watching the watchers, and as in the military, we should expect a fixed squad of regulars to be more interested in its professional identity and record.

A better ratio between keeper and kept would have another purpose. The people who guard prisoners must learn to be *correction* officers in more than name. Will more stability in better guard units merely reinforce a staff's code of silence in the desire to protect renegade officers? The danger is real. Incidents of guard brutality that go unpunished are frequent and serious, and that is why the earlier recommendation of total video and sonar surveillance with outside viewers is necessary.[48]

Some will object to these possibilities on the grounds of expense, but the $80 billion spent on punishment regimes can be reconfigured in a more cooperative and better organized system. Overly repressive surveillance is a major and hidden part of that $80 billion expenditure. A greater difficulty involves the training and temperament of correction officers. A corrosive brand of militarism dominates the work force in American prisons, which is not to say that a military model can be avoided in a penal system. Arguably, it is the brand of militarism, not the military model itself, that needs adjustment, and issues of technique are again at the root of the problem.

Ambiance

Militarism gave the world its first "megamachines." It initiated group technique over personal activity.[49] The model is not perfect, but it may be unavoidable in the management of American prison culture. Can we take only the best from it? Basic training of troops demands a cog mentality by eliminating personal choice, ingenuity, and separate identity. Army recruits must learn to obey every command instantly, together, and without question. They must sacrifice in the name of the unit and respond to danger over their own safety.[50] They are taught to destroy where it would otherwise be a crime. Former governor Michael Huckabee gave perhaps the bluntest appraisal of these negative traits while seeking the presidency in national debate on August 6, 2015. "The purpose of the military," he said then, "is kill people and break things."[51]

Much more is at stake than these negative purposes in a proper military understanding, but for the starkest military commands to be met—doing what you ordinarily would be unwilling to do and risking your life to do it—a soldier must believe in an identified enemy that deserves to be killed. Manufactured hatred thus forms a prominent passion in the military temperament, one nurtured at some cost to the working model. How do you control such a volatile passion after inducing it in training? Hatred knows few limits and feeds other vices. Of all the emotions, it is the one that most directly dehumanizes others by turning them into objects. If not checked, it distorts perceptions of reality and prevents the capacity to change one's ideas and focus.[52]

Armed services are able to curb these problems through promoting patriotism, appealing to love of the larger unit, and keeping thought of the enemy at an imaginative distance most of the time. Those ameliorating options do not reach the penal brand of militarism, and their absence explains some of the brutality that occurs in prison. In corrections, the enemy is a fellow citizen already under control and living right next to the officer. Enmity in such proximity, "us" against "them," allows almost anything to be done to the enemy, in this case a prisoner. The desire to attack before being attacked dismisses thoughts of humanity. What do some prison guards say? "They're animals." "The lowest of the low, the scum of the earth." "I wouldn't piss on them if they was on fire."[53]

The other, more subtle, difference if the enemy lives in such proximity with you? Close quarters in daily operations forces a recognition that rarely troubles a member of the armed services. Sooner or later, a teacher in correction officer schools peeks through a door officially kept closed. "We rule," one drill instructor quietly admits late in a course of instruction, "with the inmates' consent." Prison can be managed *only* with the cooperation of the incarcerated, and the implications in the admission are twofold.[54]

On the negative side, correction officers do not carry firearms in prison corridors. Just a night stick. They are badly outnumbered, and more serious weapons could be taken from them in a crisis. COs are vulnerable on the corridors, outnumbered by as many as forty to one. "What would the average citizen say," reports one correction officer, "if it were proposed that police officers be assigned to a neighborhood which was inhabited by no one but criminals and those officers would be unarmed, patrol on foot, and be heavily outnumbered?" This is the correction officer's plight. The police norm includes fully armed personnel patrolling in pairs. Adds this correction officer in his admission of fear, "my neck is on the line every minute of every day."[55]

From the positive side, the drill instructor's admission exposes unplumbed depths. The governors in prison do indeed require the consent of the governed in order to rule, and real consent requires some reciprocity, the primal condition for any community to grow. What would it take to build that inchoate quality into a better reality in American prisons?

As a first step, the technological brand of militarism in penal thought must be reevaluated, and penal differences from the traditional military model can furnish some insight. Lost to the prison guard is love of the unit. Soldiers wear uniforms in public and proudly march in ceremonial parades. They put identifying insignia on their automobiles and maintain lifelong friendships during and after service—all of this occurs in the knowledge that they serve as the single most respected institution in the federal or state government by a nation grateful for the security they afford.

Although correction officers also deliver security of a sort, they receive no gratitude for it. Nor do the ceremonial traits of togetherness and pride apply to them. Those who work on the front lines in prisons hide their identities in public except when protecting their own. They lack the camaraderie of the soldiers and policemen they accept as a model. No other governmental figure receives so little respect for what it does, and the emotional effects on personnel are direct.[56]

Think about the differences from a true military model. Correction officers do not hang together after hours or in later social life. They retire as soon as they can. They divorce more frequently, commit suicide more often, and die earlier than in most other vocations. They are *isolatos* infused with a military temperament that lives on togetherness in every other instance.[57] Mutuality comes primarily through their code of silence, which protects them from their own misbehavior—hardly a basis for lasting camaraderie.

What can be done about this? Soldiers, firemen, and police receive admiration because in dealing with conflict they also assist the vulnerable. The route to a more positive stance in corrections is not simple, but it is obvious. Correction officers have to be trained to be caretakers and not just guards. The hatred that corrodes the guard function must be dealt with. Lost in all of that animosity is a truer vocational purpose.

To correct is to set someone straight. It seeks to improve. Hatred in the penal brand of militarism contradicts this fundamental premise, and the contradiction is there for all to see. The contradiction appears in the very nomenclature used: corrections. Says one drill instructor who trains correction officers, "rehabilitation is not our job."[58] On the face of it, correcting *is* their job. Acceptance of that positive obligation would carry toward a more honored role. Of concern is the value of the product they serve. Looked at through higher purposes, change might be possible, and technical thought can be as important as normative considerations in showing the way.

Production

Production is the lodestone in technological understanding. Commercial enterprise worships the increase in value of what it creates, while technical imperatives ensure orthodoxy in the process. The central dogma is everywhere the same. Technology, explains one leading expert on business practices, confirms "the processes by which an organization transforms labor, capital, materials, and information into products and services of greater value."[59] This search for greater value forces everyone into a competitive race against time. The technical possibilities in speed and reliability demand constant advances in operations. "No producer can afford to stay behind in the innovation race."[60]

The bywords in production are thus "transformation," "greater value," "speed," "reliability," "competition," and "innovation." None of these processes apply in the business of incarceration. In corrections, information is withheld, rigid routine replaces innovation, speed becomes stasis, and value in a product, if it is understood at all, remains the same or becomes less. The exception proves the rule. Private prisons, in which investors make money on the largest number of prisoners that can be shoved into a full facility, are abominations that should be abandoned in penal policy. Making a profit off of the convicted has no place in justice.[61]

Leading theorists of commercial and industrial production have two main things to say about successful operations. First, "capabilities are forged within value networks."[62] Second, treating people as objects hurts both cooperation and production, and it generates "accountability transformation," which means "the one thing that every party in conflict is sure of is that conflict is someone else's fault."[63] Prisons lack a positive value network. Capabilities languish in them instead of developing. Personnel treat everyone held in them as objects. Prisons are scenes of bitter conflict where the problem is always someone else's fault.

At the root of these problems is a failure in meaningful production. Prisons make nothing, not even new lives, so the value that technology can help to create is missing with foreboding consequences. It is not necessarily true that "technology destroys the vital sources of our humanity," but in "technopoly" it does mean "that technique of any kind can do our thinking for us." We tolerate that partial loss of intellectual control in regular life because of the convenience mechanism gives us in "comfort, speed, hygiene, and abundance."[64] When technology supplies none of those conveniences, the loss of intellectual initiative represses new thought and creativity, and that has been the consequence in penal understandings.

Technological imposition without an increase in value has profound institutional effects. Where no one is seeking to improve a product, less attractive motivations dictate performance. Idleness is one of them. In prison, idleness is enforced on the kept and, in mirror imaging, readily adopted by the keepers who have nothing to prove in the positions they hold. So when one prisoner in a federal institution made a minor recommendation against unnecessary waste, the correction officer shot back, "Why should you care? The Government has plenty of money."[65] Mischief and outright malice follow this kind of indifference. Left in enforced idleness, people find other ways to amuse themselves, and none of them contribute to productive behavior patterns.

A more indirect but very powerful element in technological imposition also influences prison culture in a negative way. Interest in the value of a product privileges the object. Many in society are now defined by what they have. Evolution into what is now a consumer culture has made possession of the thing itself a primary source of identity with an endless need for more things to satisfy that need for identity.

Students of consumer culture and its technological basis turn this problem of wanting into a psychological question. "Does our essence still lie in what we know, or are we now content to be defined by what we want?"[66] The constant flow of objects and other stimuli temper the question in society but not in the impoverished environment of prison where everything is limited to what people want and can get. The circumstances of the incarcerated dictate a peculiarly vivid consumer culture. Higher knowledge has little value. Prized is the lower avidity of how to get something that differentiates the holder of it.

Uniformity in attire, circumstance, and cell décor renders the smallest possession important in prison identity and satisfaction: a radio, earphones, eyeglasses, a smuggled cellphone, an extra blanket, another pillow, drugs, and, yes, weapons are major concerns. So valuable are these products in the all-important search for minimal comfort and control that all of them encourage theft, smuggling, bribery, and blackmail. Possession and the ability to get it or take it mean a lot. The objectification of people allows further objectification through objects held or passed along. A black market flourishes in every prison, adding to a world kept hidden and available for unrestrained abuse.[67]

Technical production as a value has been twisted on its head for the incarcerated. In the external world of consumerism, value networks mirror product architecture. In prison the mirror reflects product limitation and subterfuge. The result is a warped understanding of value that produces crime over the littlest things. This has to change. The way groups work together over products affects how they can change for the better.

Nothing gets better in prison. Everything gets worse because all group interactions are covert, embattled, and work on the negative side of sanctioned behavioral guidelines and production.[68] The two groups in prisons—officialdom and the incarcerated—work against each other except when illegal consumption is to the advantage of both. As entrenched as these multifaceted difficulties are, one resolution in response can be simple and direct. Positive production with a recognition of value added should help change the stultifying atmosphere that infects everyone and everything in prison culture.

Three prongs of productive management can combine to have an enormous effect on the war zone that dominates many prisons today. First, meaningful educational requirements and opportunities on all sides must replace confrontation and animus. People make up the actual product in prison, and many of them on both sides of the bars are poorly educated. Education provides the wherewithal for change. Second, a large number of people land in prison because of extensive mental health problems and learning disabilities, and we now have the means to make these identifications more rapidly. Faster diagnosis and treatment of these disorders can reduce the disruption in prison life. Third, people in prison need to develop skills that will make them viable in a service economy or other field of endeavor on their release.

All three prongs of productive management depend on technical skills readily available in the culture at large. Technological know-how can contribute if properly based in educational relationships. Television can teach if supported by a combination of online and physically present teachers with the proper training. We need programs at all levels for this to work.

With more educated personnel, we can identify and deal with problems much more rapidly than before. A basic understanding of computer technology and its programming will better prepare people in prison for life on the outside. The backwardness of technical knowledge at all levels of prison culture reflects stunted educational levels. Learning and expertise in technology could cure the idleness and boredom at the root of at least some of current mistreatment and misbehavior.

Social Relations

As just indicated, nothing can be accomplished without a change in understanding between keeper and kept and among the kept themselves. We have learned how technology and routinized technique, the modern machinery of punishment, have made everything worse. Can recognition of the problems let us see how relations in prison culture can be improved?

To summarize the problems briefly, technology unchecked and imposed is a cool medium that isolates people, and the incarcerated in prison are already terribly alone by institutional arrangement. Technique and mechanized perspectives narrow personal concern. Lost in prison is the intimacy of "embodied cognition" and face-to-face connection.[69] We have also seen that technical obfuscation in bureaucratic intransigence brings its own level of alienation to prison culture. Something is badly wrong when corrections personnel actively talk of warehousing prisoners as a form of commercial inventory.

Many of these problems seem to be intrinsic when they may not be, deep as they are. Certainly they remain real. A rooted and debased militarism with its own war mentality contributes to an already embattled environment. Prisoners, if not commercial inventory, are dismissed as opponents ranged in enemy lines. Adding to hostility is the crowding allowed by postmodern technology. Dangerous ratios between correction officers and the incarcerated have shaped a psychology of fear on all sides. Finally, production without value or development stultifies all initiative and creativity.

All of the technical influences on corrections are daunting when listed in this way, and yet we can only think of negatives as negatives if we understand that positive alternatives apply as possibilities. Otherwise, everything is as it must be. Not for the first or the last time, the fatalism so prevalent over prison reform must be met head on.

What are the positives from so many negatives? There is plenty of self-interest supporting stark incarceration, but no one would keep matters the way they are if those interests could be satisfied another way. A more important recognition whispered in prison culture but openly noted by criminologists is also crucial in this regard. To the extent that penal authority depends on the cooperation of prisoners to function, we are on the threshold of communal reciprocities.[70]

The legal theorist of social relations Roberto Mangabeira Unger notes two sets of balances that must obtain for communal norms to develop. First, hierarchical and egalitarian impulses must somehow mesh. "Community begins with sympathy." Feelings of reciprocity can reduce the vertical "spiral of dominance" that overwhelms horizontal participation. "Sympathy means that people encounter each other in such a way that their sense of separateness from one another varies in direct rather than inverse proportion to their sense of social union."[71]

The second and related balance in forming community, this time from the philosopher Michael Oakeshott, depends on the coordination of "two powerful and contrary dispositions, neither strong enough to defeat or to put to flight the other": namely, "self-determination" and "a disposition to identify oneself as a partner with others in a common enterprise."[72] Community at its best works through creative tensions.

How can these values develop in the domineering, isolating, splintered, and hostile environment of incarceration? Technology may well be the most important answer if managed carefully. The biggest problem, the source of greatest isolation and despair, comes from lack of meaningful communication between levels and on a prisoner's own terms. Cellphones, tablets, and computers can be programmed to address limited recipients. Families, libraries, legal counsel, a correction officer squad leader, and a badly needed help line could be the numbers available to dial. Devices can also be monitored. Items can also be programmed against theft so that only an assigned holder can use them.

A number of states and the federal government have begun to experiment in these areas of communication. Ohio, Florida, Louisiana, Virginia, Michigan, North Dakota, Washington, Georgia, Iowa, Oklahoma, and Minnesota currently have pilot programs of one kind or another. Refinements and close surveillance are needed to prevent threatening and criminal use of access, but the advantages for a sense of productive value and community in prison are too great to ignore.[73]

There are other possibilities. Computer access with limited and very strictly supervised access to email and the Internet can help to prepare a person in prison for the pace of life online following release. It can keep a prisoner in contact with family members at very low cost. It can provide preliminary skills for vocational searches. It would give a prisoner a voice to the outside world about conditions in prison. It would supply a powerful engine and incentive for educational training among those without preliminary skills. Not least, it would allow prisoners to record harm done to themselves and others while in prison. There is no reason why prisoners cannot participate in a surveillance program for their own protection.

Half of being a human being is having a voice that can and will be heard. We saw the importance of this in chapter 3 through Ovid's definition of a human being under the pressures of punishment. It follows that the impact on even a frail sense of community could be very significant with better telecommunications. Prisoners are routinely kept within an isolating cell mentality. The ability to be heard from that cell as an individual would supply a primitive but valued level of self-determination, one of the core values in community. The capacity to monitor illegal activity should also stimulate cooperative social union or a sense of joint enterprise in people left so completely separate from each other. And all of this strengthening of communal norms might be accomplished without disturbing the necessary dominance that authority must have to run a prison.

Resourcefulness and carefully restricted programs will be necessary. If use of strictly programmed tablets, cellphones, and computers remains a privilege based on good behavior, the incentive of the incarcerated to cooperate increases geometrically. Legal prison cellphones could undoubtedly be programmed to be differentiated from the many illegal cellphones smuggled into prisons today.[74] Any and every prisoner will want to reach the outside world to maintain contact with a family suffering from feelings of desertion by one of its members. Prisoners who run educational classes would also have the ability to coordinate programs far more effectively.

We have the know-how and computer skills to make this work. The only question is whether or not there is the will to accomplish it against the fear of change. Where must that will come from? Many other aspects of prison life deserve attention if introduced forms of computerization are to be safe tools. Bottom line? We can only accomplish what we are capable of thinking, and the current language of prison inhibits cooperative thought. That language—its uses, its misuses, its problems, and its possibilities—comes next. We need to find out what a language of serious cooperation in prison might look and sound like.

7
Prison Talk

Words Without Communication

COOPERATION IS THE KEY TO A NEW theory of punishment, and it depends on the quality of exchange possible. The singular metamorphosis that we all accomplish across a lifetime comes through the mastery of language. It is what makes us human, the talking animal. It is also the one thing we expand and improve on to become a different person with the capacity for new thought, expression, and eloquence. Ovid is remembered not just for his poetic themes but for his emphasis on a new voice—the beauty of an evolving Latin style that he made his own. Language changes us, and the real hope for prison reform will lie here.

Originality in language is an attempt at new thought, but the attempt can quickly falter in the conventional understandings that surround its new meaning. Then there is the matter of exchange. A working sincerity in language requires a respect for truth and the desire to convey it without loss. A language that can change thought requires sincere speakers and attentive listeners who are also allowed to speak. Only together can they come up with a new approach.

The world of conflict in prison naturally has its own language, and saturated as it now is with retributive instincts, it is in need of help. Every institution has a lingua franca that informs its behavior, and prisons are no exception. We have said that all institutions depend on a zone of "vocal silence," the things not talked about on the edges of understood behavior.[1] This zone plays an encompassing role in correctional facilities. Penal inhibitions turn silence into a force field, one that arranges everything done there in negative ways.

Three contradictions in penal punishment, as we now know it, cut across meaningful exchange in prison life. First, the military model explored in chapter 6, with its insistence on "us against them." Second, repression leads to resistance. Prisoners dislike confinement and protest when the level of it goes up as occasionally happens in a "lockdown." The desire for total control by authority threatens the spirit and identity of those under control. Says one correction officer of the need for obedience, "it has to work like a machine." People are not machines. One prisoner's reaction? "I kept my humanity through anger."[2] Lost is all facility in communication. No one trusts what the other side says.

Third, and in an institutional paradox beyond contradiction, prison culture has no answer to questions at the core of its purpose. How can total control of a person for years on end instill the ability to exercise a life on one's own upon release? How can personal responsibility take hold when it is perpetually denied in prison? Blame and pessimism feed on this universal frustration. People evade the questions they cannot answer, and again language suffers. Prisons are adrift in meaning.

Seeing these three contradictions at work can clarify their significance. A pervading code of silence, the first characteristic noted, reaches pathological proportions in prison culture. The worst offender is the informer across boundary lines. Punishment comes swiftly and without explanation or mercy. It comes violently for a prisoner and through the shunning of peers in the case of a correction officer.[3] Condemnation for informing reflects another implosion in language. "The snitch," in prison lingo, can make no acceptable plea. Yet in one of the unspoken corruptions of the system, correction officers "always have an informant." A useful snitch must therefore receive linguistic camouflage—all part of the general misdirection and distrust in communication.[4]

Repression, with resistance against it, our second contradiction in penal punishment, seals language within factions and prevents meaningful dialogue. Take prison use of the word "blood." From the perspective of authority, the term identifies a dangerous gang member who deserves solitary confinement on that count alone. The word has other meanings for those who live by it. "Blood" forms an acronym in gang lexicon: "Brotherly Love Overrides Oppression and Distraction." Internally, the word reaches for personal worth, identity, and a cohesion that gang members could not find earlier in fractured families and broken communities, or now in prison.[5]

Basic identities, negative and positive, are at stake. Punitive reaction to "blood" ignores the internal meaning and fortifies gang solidarity in ever more twisted ways. Gang usage asks its members to thrive on hostility, but why feed that hostility? What might it take to recognize "brotherly love" and "distraction" not through punishment but through a plan of education off of those terms? Gangs are like Antaeus, the mythological figure who gains strength when thrown to the ground.

Pause for a moment over one of the most difficult dilemmas in prison life today: gang control of the incarcerated. Think about what our second contradiction in punishment actually produces through repression: resistance and failure to communicate across the divide. The most recent in-depth study shows conclusively that clampdowns on gangs and segregation of their leaders do not work. In policies dealing with gangs, authorities need "to alter the conditions that give rise to inmate demands for them." Frank communication across the hostile barriers in safer prisons based on smaller units offers a much better chance of providing the protection and eliminating the contraband that allows prison gangs to flourish.[6]

Our third identified contradiction in punishment—the absence of positive foundations in correction—speaks to similar but ultimately more profound difficulties. Refusal and denial constitute the main threats for keeping prisoners in line. Prisons lack a system of rewards for instilling positive behavior. More restriction on top of already extreme deprivation has little practical effect on many prisoners, and, not surprisingly, the terms describing deprivation are rarely the same for punisher and punished.

In punishment, language changes depending on who acts and who is acted upon. The harshest additional penalty available in prison, solitary confinement, has many synonyms. Listen to some of the differences across boundary lines. Known officially and euphemistically as "Ad-Seg" (administrative segregation) or SHU (special housing unit), the phrases are self-explanatory only when spelled out, and authority doesn't really want you to spell them out. "Bing," another more abrupt and obscure word for solitary, comes from the ancient understanding of "a heap or pile for storage," or as a verb "go you hence." The incarcerated hear a more modern exclamation instead. "Bing!" says "they've hit you with something!"[7]

Solitary confinement maximizes punishment in a world already saturated with it. It means loss of all other basic entitlements: proper food, decent bedding, visitation rights, human association, cell seniority, mail, change of clothing, regular bathing, decent light, and personal effects (often stolen by staff after extraction from a regular cell). Prisoners know it by how it is felt. They speak of "the box," "the hole," "23/1" (a reference to being allowed out of a tiny cell for one hour out of the twenty-four), and "soul breaker."[8] Official terminology refers to "policy"; prisoners register the suffocation and pain in that policy.

The protests of the incarcerated in solitary confinement are to the mark. Says one in understatement, "not very much good grows inside of cold concrete." Everyone breaks under it in some way. Writes another, "I've had neighbors who came to SHU normal men, and I've seen them leave broken and not anything resembling normal any more." The perpetual loneliness forces "internal destruction" and a loss of humanity. Crucial to that loss? Every account says no one cares about us.[9]

Social interaction is enlivened by language that bridges.[10] Lack of transparency and sincerity in expression may be the most depressing and destructive aspect of the status quo in prison culture. How bad does this get in prison? Says one long-term prisoner, "Some officials don't believe anything an inmate says, or they believe the opposite of whatever inmates tell them. In response, some inmates intentionally tell the truth in situations where they know they won't be trusted, perpetuating a cycle of deceit that makes communication almost impossible in prison."[11]

The positive moments that prisoners point to, when asked, are illuminating. They note when someone in authority spoke to them with common courtesy or consideration. Take a simple incident. Serving Christmas dinner in a federal security prison, one staff lieutenant announced that each set of prisoners would receive a full half hour to enjoy the special meal instead of demanding the usual practice of wolfing down the food in minutes in order to make room for the next group. Some of those served thanked him for it. A small matter? Yes, but as Pascal says, "little things comfort us because little things upset us."[12] How hard is it to let someone feel a little better about himself or herself?

It is very hard to find that minimal degree of concern without some trust in language exchange. Charles Taylor, a philosopher of the meaning in conversation, explains why: "Language involves sensitivity to rightness." Rightness, how to treat others within a recognized circle, depends on "a range of [linguistic] footings we can be on with each other." Without those footings, there is no bond when we speak to each other. Only through conversation does it become clear that "what we are talking about is 'mutually manifest.'" Real exchange creates "not just for me, and for you, but for *us* undivided." It says we are persons together.[13]

Prisons are dead to community because they have no "us" across the basic lines. They operate on divisions, never an "us," and those divisions made to speak to each other devolve into a "them" without the shred of mutuality that might lead to the compassion that correct behavior requires under stress. Prisons don't kill "the language animal," but they twist and warp it until the prospect of mutuality turns into hatred. It is all so sad because so unnecessary.

The Guarded Speech of the Correction Officer

Prison narratives from the incarcerated abound. You can find them in many published sources. Corresponding explanations from correction officers are rare, and there is an explanation for the absence. The frontline officer believes "what goes on in corrections should stay in corrections."[14] We need to understand why that stance is held with such passionate conviction and willed insularity.

Information withheld governs official policy everywhere in corrections.[15] It starts on the front lines. Correction officers engage in behavior that would not be tolerated anywhere else, and they believe, correctly, that the outside world and many of their own superiors do not understand or care about the circumstances under which they must perform. The result is linguistic enclosure without solidarity in the ranks, as well as suspicion across levels of authority. Knowledge of misbehavior by COs dictates a mode of exchange "largely unintelligible to outsiders." Hermetic speech with nothing written down protects a major goal: "fencing out the stranger."[16]

There are, to be sure, exceptions to most rules, and one of the most interesting in corrections can be found in a remarkable document, the *Correction Officer's Guide to Understanding Inmates,* written in 2012 by a retired government worker who, to all intents and purposes, was an outstanding CO in the difficult world of New York City corrections for almost twenty years between 1985 and 2007. The *Guide* tells new officers how to navigate the many problems in corrections, and, along the way, it conveys those difficulties in detail and without evasion.[17]

What makes the *Guide* so remarkable is its exposure of a prison system so corrupt that the integrity of the average correction officer must meet stiff tests at every turn. As honestly and simply as the author writes, the customary incentives for knowledge withheld remain a part of the subtitle: *The 44 Keys to Power, Control, and Respect.* Early on we learn that it is "a dirty business" and that if officers do not believe in what they are doing, they will be corrupted (10–11). A little later, in a passage quoted above but worth repeating in more detail, we get some of what must be withheld even in the *Guide.* "There are many things officers can do to burn inmates and make their stay in jail a living hell. I won't list them because inmates may get copies of this book" (53).

Ponder these sentences for a moment. No prisoner is actually burned, unless invisibly through some kind of electronic device. Still, the term "burn" is arresting. It says to the incarcerated I can give you serious pain in many ways that will surprise and aggravate you, and I like it that way. A longer section, "On the Burn," details the complications in a method "necessary to maintain control." The wise correction officer has to worry that things will get out of control in "a continuous burn." In the words of the *Guide,* "if you burn them too often, it loses its effectiveness" (54–55). Burning thus becomes a tool that can be abused. Or is it a concept that is inherently abusive?

The *Guide* quietly describes the parameters of this fallen world, and they are collectively devastating. The average correction officer will discover "we all have differences with our supervisors," which means that small problems "grow and fester into larger problems that jeopardize your safety and the safety of the institution" (135–136). One of the longest chapters in the book answers this danger with a winning acronym: CYA, "cover your ass" (89–90).

How do you cover? "If you get involved in an incident and your fellow officer or supervisor acts recklessly, maliciously, or unlawfully, do not lie for him or attempt to cover up his actions." This sounds like good policy, but it comes with the caveat that many COs work "champing at the bit and eager to rush in to do battle." The desire to hit someone goes with the job, so there are qualifications for circumstance. "It is commendable to be loyal to your fellow officers, but your greatest loyalty should be to yourself, your family, and the law." The real answer? "Cover your ass" first (94–95, 69).

Where does the embattled correction officer draw the line when the price is high? The *Guide* has another long section on how correction officers mistreat their own (156–159). We learn that "what one officer does may cause problems for you" (47). Physical conflict is part of the job, and some officers never know when to stop. "You will have to use force from time to time" (70–73).

What kind of force will be necessary? The *Guide* reports, "There's No Such Thing as a Fair Fight" (111–113). The wise guard will therefore "strike first, strike hard, and strike fast" (72). Of course, you must be careful about where you strike. Why? "It is not uncommon to receive a cut or laceration on your fist by punching someone in the mouth" (69). A fair fight? "In corrections, we call five officers against one inmate a fair fight because with five officers the officer will never lose" (112). Stop here for a moment. How much damage will come to a prisoner with five well-protected attackers striking "first, hard, and fast"?

Often advice in the *Guide* comes with the adverb "sometimes" or the adjective "some" in front of the explanation. We never quite know how often some nasty problems will occur. Sometimes an officer has too much of "an iron fist" (25). "Sometimes officers do get carried away and go way past the point where physical force is justified"; "sometimes officers use excessive force on inmates that results in serious injury or death" (158). Sometimes "officers and other civilian staff . . . bring drugs and other contraband into jail" (100). "Some officers adopt the same negative attitudes that prisoners have" (125). "In every group you have [some] bad apples . . . there are supervisors who abuse their authority and take advantage of officers" (141).

Reading this litany of ills and wrongs in the *Guide* can take you to Herman Melville's famous maxim. "It's a wicked world in all meridians."[18] But that does not cover the whole situation. In order to know what is wrong one must know and believe in what is right, and this manual for new officers emphasizes what should be done correctly. Central to its mission is clarity, accuracy, truthfulness, working as a team, and above all, forthright communication between and across all levels. These aspirations dominate the *Guide,* but they are not the reality that a new correction officer must cope with. In fact, doing the right thing may get that newcomer in trouble.

A last limitation gets in the way. There is a clock-watching temperament in frontline officers based on the unpleasantness of their work. "I'm going home in eight hours" is a prevalent mentality and slogan (36). Says the *Guide,* "go home . . . when you have the choice" (84–85). Any situation is the next guy's problem. Another attitude might keep one on the job until a problem has been solved or at least moved along, but that level of professionalism does not exist here, nor apparently can it. In the tangled evolution of current corrections, a waiting game without initiatives, no solution comes to mind. The criminologist Barbara Owen explains this one commonality. Everyone bends to "time served." It applies to keeper as well as kept. All belongs to "an equally captive world."[19]

Crosscurrents of Anxiety

Explaining breakdowns in communication may seem futile except for the saving value and volatility it suggests in all of language. Words lose some of their original meaning through habit and repetition, but those meanings are never completely lost, and the words themselves survive in use because of an original resonance still faintly present. Many of the words in prison, particularly those shared across boundary lines, cloak a pervasive culture of anxiety and instability.

Correction officers and prisoners both speak of "taking a bid." For the CO it represents assignment to a particular prison, frequently not where the worker wants to be. For the incarcerated, it indicates the length of time to be served. "A nickel bid" indicates five years in prison. The original meaning refers to risk or "taking a chance." When you bid at auction you compete with others and might not succeed. A bid in cards may lose money to another player's hand.

The word "bug" has similarly universal applications in prison culture. It describes the mentally ill with the tinges of abhorrence that you would expect from connecting the term to human beings. Entomophobia, a helpless fear of bugs, is a prevalent human disorder, and it informs many horror movies. Mental illness horrifies many too, and it presents problems beyond solution for all sides in corrections.

There are no current answers to dumping the disturbed into prisons and jails. They are there because under current law there is no other place to put them when they engage in disruptive behavior. There is also a physical parallel. Bugs—roaches, spiders, and other insects—proliferate in unstoppable numbers in prison buildings. "Bug" bespeaks a shared helplessness and, through it, fear.

Confinement runs on the capacity to threaten, but it works only on those who realize the consequences of their actions. When the mentally ill do not gauge those consequences, their uncontrolled behavior becomes a danger to all and a source of general breakdown. Many go mad in prison. Everyone quietly dreads the phenomenon without knowing what to do about it. The unease over "bugs" extends quickly to all personal relationships.

"Juice" is another word used frequently on all sides. Someone with juice "has power," a capacity found in prisoners as well as officers. The literal meaning has some leverage, too. Real juice, the fruit drink, is a vexed commodity and a source of tension in prison. Most prisoners want more of it. People coming out fantasize about real orange juice. Fights in the dining hall often break out over dispensation of what passes for the same thing. A second meaning should not be forgotten either. Electricity, or "juice," is a weapon that authority can inflict to restrain a recalcitrant prisoner. Whenever the word "juice" is used, it refers to some kind of power. It is what everyone desires to have in prison to guard against attack.

Some concepts seem innocuous enough until fully recognized. "Po-po" indicates the policing function of the correction officer, but realize what is missing from the phrase: "po-*lice*" The phrase is pejorative. "Screw" is another term for correction officer. It refers to turning the key but also relates to such vulgarisms as "I'm screwed" or "screw you!" with both passive and active significance. Deeper is the mechanical act of turning up pressure and potentially the pain from a correction officer's actions. These differences extend to everything. The special tactical anti-riot (STAR) gear that COs proudly wear in emergencies or in dealing with a resisting prisoner becomes "goon armor" in the nomenclature of the incarcerated.[20] Only terms that are printable are included here.

Personal relationships between holder and held take on further significance in light of another bland term. Correction officers live figuratively and literally in "the bubble," technically the observation booth at one end of a cellblock. Most officers stay there as much as possible. Much goes wrong in prison because the correctors do not come out, patrol, and try to correct. They don't know what is going on outside of the bubble and don't want to know until it is unavoidable, and often too late. Real contact for a CO is a risk to be avoided. In the words of one long-time prisoner, observing why prison corridors are "an extremely dangerous place to be": "I was more likely to see a stabbing than a guard on duty."[21]

Other phrases hide reservoirs of dread. "A buck fifty" refers to a cut across the face leaving you "unrecognizable" with 150 stitches after someone slices you with a can lid or razor out of revenge, or an imagined slight, or just envy. Correction officers know the term, too, and have to worry about such an attack. "Diesel therapy," only a little less pedestrian, describes how prison authorities can, with impunity, ship you out "on a six month multicity tour of squalid jails and holding facilities, thereby rendering contact with loved ones impossible." Dieseled, you live mostly in the back of prison vans where handcuffed and chained you are thrown around by every quick brake or pothole a driver decides to find.[22]

Three more poignant expressions reach the more general plight of people in prison and can prepare us for their commentary in the next section. "Kite" or to "kite out" refers to a message or request sent out of the cellblocks, which may or may not be received or honored. If you have ever flown a kite, success depends on circumstance—the wind, the weight, the balance of the item sent up, the space in which to sail, and enough freedom from obstruction. A kite is easily lost. The attempt in prison signifies a risk taken. The message might be lost, only this time without one knowing about it.

A second expression, "fly" or "you looking all fly," also used in ghetto street slang, means to dress up, possibly to receive a visitor, not that frequent an occasion for many in prison but one in which recipients try to look their very best. The underlying registers of "kite" and "fly" reach for the sky, the only part of freedom that a prisoner gets to see. Prisoners envy the birds that fly over and talk about them. In the words of one prisoner when asked what he wants most when free, "I want to see a sunset without an ugly building in the way of it."[23]

The third expression delves into twisted verities. Prisoners speak of their "upside-down kingdom." The phrase invokes the inversion of common values that controls prison life with an underlying sense of residual power in that lower kingdom. In the realm of the incarcerated the violent are esteemed, friendship is suspect (trust no one), kindness is taken for weakness, initiative is dangerous, violence can be casual, lust replaces love, and time stands still. Simple mistakes can be much more than that; they can be fatal. There are many reasons why speech from the "upside-down kingdom" has its own voice, and the grip of that strangled voice has appeal fathoms deep.

The Prisoners Talk

When you first enter prison, they strip you naked, check out all of your body cavities, and leave you that way for a while. They have taken away all of your possessions, and, after you are given an ill-fitting uniform with your number on it, the number you will now be known by, they shear off your hair or, for women, they cut it short. Your immediate problem is a stark one. Dispossessed of everything, you must manufacture a new identity against the vulnerabilities of the "tank," where, as a new arrival, you are "a fish," prey for the seasoned who await you. You are no one in the fish tank unless you make yourself someone. In just a few days of total derision, writes one prisoner, "I became a fragile shell of who I used to be."[24]

The state of mind thus instilled is one of total deprivation, and it explains why going to prison is called "falling" or "going down." "I fell three years ago" or "I've been down for five." You can keep falling too if not careful. The accusation "trippin" or "you trippin" is one of contempt, and it means you have been wrong or foolish with a corresponding loss of credibility. "Wilyin' out" or "acting up" adds wildness or craziness to "trippin." Keep it up, and you turn into one of the "crash dummies" or "ball busters," out of control and trouble for everyone.

In having been made less, in constantly being told that you are less, the prisoner must respond in some way. Self-projection in search of dignity can take a person in prison either way. Bullying others can make you "a gorilla" until you encounter one stronger or meaner than yourself. Other prisoners learn to draw, carve (especially soap), exercise, or, most important, to write in search of expression and understanding. "So with pen and pad," notes one, "I clung to my sanity . . . I redeemed my soul."[25] If you don't seek a positive outlet, a negative one will find you.

Expression in the form of writing to the outside world is almost always about loss, and its tones are ones of anger, despair, and protest coupled to levels of realization about what is happening to the speaker or writer. "Prison is 'life without,' as any prisoner would tell a civilian willing to listen."[26] But who is willing to listen? How do the powerless find power in voice, Ovid's definition of a human being?

There are two dynamics in all of communicated perception. Objectively, the effort to describe and tell a story depicts place or a sense of reality within a meaningful group, "the image of one's position in social space." Subjectively, the same effort tries to change or reorder "the categories of perception and evaluation of the social world" (i.e., what happened here will interest you for itself).[27] In prison narratives, these writerly goals divide narrative into reality claimed and reform needed: "here is the reality you do not know" and "here, as well, is the reform that could give meaning to my plight." The spirit of reform can be crystal clear. "If you start dealing [with] people from a human position, you start eliminating frustration," explains one long-timer. "If you start providing people with things to do, you start occupying people's time where people don't have to sit up in a cell and focus their attention on . . . building up their anger."[28]

A storyteller from the fallen world of prison implicitly speaks for everyone there. In this one instance, a solidarity of the lost reaches to the outside world with a frightening message for every reader. Sooner or later, given the mortal condition, we all lose our freedom and ability to function as we desire. Prison writers have fallen into that state before us. They attract the reader through another fear as well. They record, as Ovid did more than twenty centuries ago, what human beings are capable of doing to each other when given the chance without restraint.

In more reformist terms, the prison narrative declares, "look what *you* have done to *me*." This second major impulse concentrates on the unfair aspects of incarceration beyond what an outside reader is likely to have known and, implicitly, should have been in a position to stop. The power of the genre in this register is indirect but formidable. Injustice recognized asks for a sense of justice in order for reception to take place.

Universals apply here. Remember the common expression "even a dog knows the difference between being stepped on and being kicked." Somewhere in a prison narrative the writer will draw that distinction in vivid terms. "Society has stepped on me, but now I am being kicked." At issue are told levels of unfairness that must be recognized and questioned to assume integrity in society at large.

Despair cannot be avoided in a sentence of extraordinary length served under terrible conditions. Life without parole, mercifully shortened in prison parlance to LWOP, gives no possibility of release from terrible conditions as long as you exist. For those under its infliction, LWOP "freezes someone into their worst moment forever. It denies the hope of positive growth and change that's oxygen for the spirit of all human beings." It says "we will never give you the chance to do better than you were." Deprivation in this state is also total. The length of a sentence determines the severity level in assignment to an institution.[29]

To say LWOP as a word, as happens in prison culture, conveys that you have been "whopped" for good. This, "the other death penalty," adds particular power to the prison narrative. We are talking about more than 41,000 individuals in the United States serving life without parole, a penalty not contemplated elsewhere. Those sentenced grapple with what it means while claiming that no one else can begin to understand it. "It is capital punishment on the installment plan." "How do you measure something that doesn't end." "I am alive, and I don't want to be." "My roots have outgrown this pot, and I am slowly strangling myself." "On and on even when on becomes off." "I can't concentrate on rewinding the clock." "I'm just a number that will eventually expire." "Family and friends run out of patience, out of hope, and out of our lives."[30]

The truth in these scattered statements about life without parole has another significance. Taken collectively, they tell us that even the sentenced can barely surround the concept. The impact of LWOP on human life defies stable meaning. The best that might be said has been said by those under it. "I do not agree that a life devoid of any possibility of restoration is a reasonable or humane alternative."[31] Often called the liberal alternative to the death penalty, permanent incarceration denies the human need for change and growth under existing arrangements. Total inertia in eternal confinement defeats the very purpose in being, and it infects the rest of the system.

People break under hopeless conditions. Suicide rates among the incarcerated are a serious problem.[32] In the mordant humor of prison, "the fifth floor is four flights up." Jumpers are said to take "the broken elevator." The details matter. "You can always tell which are the most committed, they're the ones who don't scream on the way down. . . . instinctively, you turn from the smacking thump that follows."[33]

So ingrained is the desire of the miserably confined to die on their own terms that the most careful of correction officers do not prevent suicides from happening on their beat. COs are trained to watch for it but without too much personal anxiety. "So if an inmate commits suicide in your assigned area during your tour of duty, don't be too hard on yourself. It happens even to the best officers."[34]

There may be no more fatalistic acknowledgment of the inhuman conditions that the incarcerated endure in America. Think for a moment about the dehumanizing analogy used to handle the emotional aspect of suicide. "The inmates in your housing area are similar to fish in an aquarium. . . . It won't be long before you will be able to tell when a fish is sick by the way he looks and acts."

Compounding such misery is also possible. A prisoner serving life for armed robbery in the most severe federal prison in the country, the United States Penitentiary Administrative Maximum Facility in Florence, Colorado, the ADX, had to be rushed to a hospital after slashing his own throat with a razor. Returned soon after to the same solitary cell, waiting prison guards gave him a mop and bucket and ordered him to clean up the mess left by his own spilled blood. Given no other outlet against such wanton cruelty, prisoners in extended solitary confinement attack the only thing left under their control: they mutilate and destroy their own bodies. Said one reformist warden of the ADX, "this place is not designed for humanity."[35]

Over and over again, prison narratives say "most of the correctional staff despise us." Some guards act out this contempt in staged scenes of degradation. "Drawn to this work by the allure of dominating the weak and crushing the already broken," they like to humiliate one prisoner while others watch. The goal is to diminish all prisoners through enforced helplessness. "I had no power to remove myself from witnessing this inhumanity," writes one prisoner, of a guard making sport of a new Asian-American prisoner in racist terms. "There was nothing I could do without jeopardizing my safety. We all stood there silent. Then I began to feel like a coward, and that brought the bile into my throat; I was sure I was going to vomit."[36]

How deliberate and frequent are these demonstrations? Says the observer in the racial put-down just described, "This is a situation so common, one comes to ignore (or tries to ignore) it. Ritual humiliation leaves nothing out of bounds: race, sexual orientation, physical stature, parentage. They'll say anything to get the reaction they want from us." The hidden reaction? "In a fantasy, I grabbed the big ugly guard by the collar, pulled him close and held him" with a personal challenge.

Veiled hostility is a saving stance, and the ensuing alienation of each against all has no bottom. The perception of the imprisoned is that no one cares, and it has consequences for anyone who tries to care. "There is a stigma associated with compliance with the system." Deriding any attempt to cooperate turns into social etiquette. "If an inmate attends programs without some degree of contempt, he is perceived as weak-minded." These required antagonisms reinforce every negative quality. "The temptation to adopt criminal thinking is pervasive and compelling."[37]

No one should think this is the whole story. A select few rise above every circumstance. There are people who manage to educate themselves in prison, mostly as autodidacts or through small self-protected groups who get outside help from pitifully limited programs.

The mark of these unusual people comes through their equanimity in a world of stress. One self-educated prisoner in Sing Sing, call him "Larson," has "an aura of beatific calm . . . clearly, a sort of spiritual figure, and one with a head on his shoulders." Others in prison want to be near him. Larson's nicknames prove this attraction. He is known as "Powerful, Powwow, and PW," and it is not because he seeks company. "I'm like family to them," Larson observes in a telling explanation of why others seek him out. "They can't love me like I love them because they don't love themselves. They don't know who they are."[38] Even in prison, especially in prison, knowing oneself is a matter of education.

So it can happen. Some people grow in any situation, and prison is among the worst that this country offers. Think what might be accomplished if corrections could break through the sadism, hostility, alienation, and scorn that currently dictate behavior in prison. If institutional help could really be help and be perceived as help, how many prisoners could find a new or at least better self? Standing in the way is the institution that is supposed to make a difference: our existing parole system.

Speaking but Not Heard

The part of the legal system that should be most responsive to the development of a prisoner is the least receptive. Parole boards, used in a majority of states but not all, regularly fail to recognize reform in people who no longer need to be in prison by any reasonable gauge until long after the reasons for release become obvious.[39] These failures in performance have been documented with care since as early as 1975 and confirmed as late as 2013, with detailed accounts of the institutional reasons for those failures along with recommendations for modifications that could make a difference.[40] Yet little changes.

This intransigence has many causes, and it hinges on a set institutional posture. Failure rarely counts in the administration of corrections. Remember that we are dealing with a passive holding operation. Poor performance in penal institutions has no public purchase except in five isolated instances: someone escapes, someone released runs amuck, someone in authority is seriously hurt, someone causes a riot, or someone gets killed. These are rare occasions, but they control penal thought, and nowhere do they have a greater impact than when a prisoner deserves a second chance for freedom.

Parole, the early release of a prisoner under conditional supervision, has two guiding principles, public security and rehabilitation of the parolee. In practice, these goals receive very unequal weight. Parole board members are political appointees under pressure to conform to a punitive environment. Many are former enforcement personnel. Priority goes to public security over rehabilitation in the decisions they make.

A recurring nightmare controls most of parole board thought. Commissioner positions are coveted sinecures with high salaries, secure governmental benefits, easy work, and little to no oversight. The exception, the only thing that can really go wrong in proceedings that are hardly ever public, occurs when media sources complain about a crime committed by a parolee. Whole boards have been asked to resign by state governors after someone on parole commits a violent crime.[41] Why should a member of a parole board take the risk? Official self-interest wants incarceration in full when the situation allows it, and large numbers of prisoners serve indeterminate sentences with no magic moment when release should happen.[42]

Negativity therefore reigns in parole board hearings. The many disguised aspects of this negativity and what might be done about them are our subjects in this section. First and foremost, there are almost no restrictions on the discretion and power of a parole board.[43] It bases its decisions on personal interviews completely under its own control, and personal affect in a petitioner is frequently dimmed through the medium of a video hook-up. By law, the board investigates the personality, social history, adjustment in prison, criminal record, medical evidence, and all information submitted by the prisoner, available attorneys, original victims, and any other source thought to be relevant by the board. Any one of these elements can receive decisive emphasis without explanation.[44]

There are dozens of veiled ways to deny a prisoner's petition under any system. Opposition to early release also follows communal attitudes. Most Americans think of parole and "early release" as unwarranted leniency. Eighty percent look on such mechanisms with suspicion and would abolish them or make them more difficult to obtain. Fifteen states and the federal government have no parole boards. Some have alternative "good behavior" provisions for time off of a sentence.[45] Even so, truth in sentencing guidelines (insistence that a convicted person serve at least 85 percent of a term) and mandatory minimum sentencing policies complete an atmosphere of disapproval on the early release of prisoners against evidence of reformation in a petitioner.

If you take all of these elements together—emphasis on public security, political appointees subject to political approval, parole boards stocked with enforcement personnel, unlimited discretion in decision making, fear of a mistake, grudging public acceptance, and severity in sentencing—you find little regard for a prisoner's claim of rehabilitation. Parole policies, like the rest of the system, are geared to retributive instincts. The presumption is that a sentence should be served, and the logic behind it defies any real interest in correction.

There is, after all, no particular rationale to the length of a sentence except in rote legal insistence on it. The length of a term in prison depends not on an absolute standard but on its relative position on a grid containing other sentences for other crimes. If a sentence for a lesser crime, say assault, is three years in prison, logic requires a much more severe sentence for armed robbery and burglary. Every length of a sentence grows out of that first arbitrary baseline, and if that first base is severe, all others will be correspondingly harsh.

Reliance on proportionality to establish the time to be spent in prison depends on a ratchet effect. The basis is one of arbitrary but specified gradation. The comfort level in negative decision making for a parole board relies on this gradation to find a prisoner's worst place on the sentencing grid in the ladder of crime. Other grids in other punishment regimes will come up with different levels in sentencing, which is why other cultures, and even different states in America, assign wildly different sentencing standards for the same crime.[46]

As long as the focus of a hearing remains fixed on the original crime, severity makes sense. The crime is the one element that a parole board can claim as certain and beyond its personal fear of risk. The sentencing grid, an internalized reality, therefore becomes its basis for decision making.

A stipulation in law enforcement—the same sentence for the same crime—confirms board fixation on the original offense. The claim is one of equal treatment before the law, but the same stipulation ignores all differentiating development in a prisoner who seeks early release, and that is where parole systems fail in current conception. The word "parole" comes from the French *parole,* meaning "the word offered." It refers to a meeting of the minds, the exchange of language required when a reformed prisoner indicates recognition and acceptance of the conditions set for release and that prisoner promises to honor them. The word offered in prison talk is supposed to become the word accepted by a parole board.[47]

The deliberative nature of the parole process claims to honor this spirit of reciprocity. You are supposed to gauge what the prisoner who has won the right to a parole hearing says in a positive light. In practice, parole boards prove reluctant to make that effort. Current comportment and development continue to count for less than the original crime. Prisoners before a board are held frozen in time. Has the prisoner shown enough to be considered a law-abiding person on release? When is no amount of ongoing law-abidingness enough against board focus on original unlawfulness? "The word offered" turns into a simpler order beyond the meaning of parole: "stay where you are." Prisoners have their own humor about the situation. When denied parole you join a very large "deuce club," and that club, as well as the nomenclature, expands with each later denial.[48]

A parole case from October 1, 2013, in the New York state system, can establish how retributive instincts so easily overwhelm the developmental program of a prisoner before a parole board. The petitioner in question had committed a horrible crime twenty-five years earlier. She was convicted of second-degree murder. The gravity of the crime, for which she is serving an indeterminate sentence of from twenty-five years to life, was also measured by its impact on a family of victims.

Twenty-five years ago, the petitioner was caught between a seriously abusive husband who beat her frequently and another man who secretly lent her money to take care of her family. On February 4, 1989, in a panic because she could not repay the loan, she killed the lender when he threatened to tell the husband, who would have reacted with new levels of violence based on unwarranted suspicions. The woman who killed had less than a high school education and faced constant trouble and injury to the point of hopelessness in trying to make ends meet for a large family of six daughters where the husband was not the father and refused to contribute to household needs. The crime was her first and only legal offense.[49]

By law, on October 1, 2013, twenty-five years after her incarceration, the petitioner had served her minimal sentence, her "limited credit time allowance" (LCTA), and she made a second appearance before her parole board, after being denied release on May 2, 2013, in a properly scheduled LCTA hearing. She had the right to speak to the board at this time. Long ago she had divorced her abusive husband.

There is much more on the positive side of this ledger. This prisoner seeking parole had given herself a high school education, attained a bachelor's degree, and achieved a master's degree in organizational management while beginning to work toward a Ph.D. in social services. In all things, she had been a model prisoner throughout her prison term. She had no disciplinary infractions in all of those years, and she had repented and taken responsibility over and over again for the crime she committed.

The petitioner also presented a full record of additional civic achievements that minimized the risk that her parole board would take on her release. Many prison programs to help others were part of her record, as well as more indications of personal mentorship to prisoners who acknowledged the importance of her assistance. She had developed a range of vocational skills that would allow her to find work on her release, including programs in animal training for the blind, clerical services, and computer skills. She ran numerous special events for prisoners and many clearly relied on her for advice and comfort. Periodic institutional evaluations had always given her "the highest possible rating in every category."

Employment options had been arranged for this prisoner on release. In every way the petitioner had become a different person except for the sentence that held her in place, a fact confirmed by many letters from volunteer workers, prison authorities, and other prisoners urging her release. After so much time in prison and with health problems, she appeared before the board as a sixty-eight-year-old admired grandmother and great-grandmother in a family that had kept in regular touch with her. Supporting her petition for release were 200 pages of testimonials from prison staff.

Even so, the parole board denied her petition on bleak statutory grounds: "There is a reasonable probability that you would not live and remain at liberty without again violating the law, and your release would be incompatible with the welfare of social [*sic*] and would so deprecate the serious nature of crime as to undermine respect for law." The board panel of three officers said that it "*remains* concerned about your callous indifference to human life in committing a preplanned killing and engaged in a course of conduct in doing so. Accordingly, this panel concludes the discretionary release at this time is not warranted."[50]

Twenty-one of the twenty-three pages of the transcript of this parole hearing rehearse the original crime, in which the petitioner again and again was forced to acknowledge with every remorse and understanding in response to question after question about the worst details of when she killed. A member of the three-person review, one who had held a position on the board for seventeen years and should have known better through the experience, trivialized the domestic violence that the petitioner had endured as a motivation for her crime. Her excellent record in prison over twenty-five years was passed over quickly as "a good thing." Ignored as well was the evaluation of the parole board's own "Risk Department," which determined that the petitioner "was extremely unlikely to reoffend."[51]

What happened here happens over and over again in hearing after hearing, many of which are held in the impersonal, desensitizing forum, like this one, of teleconferencing. Parole boards hold prisoners as long as possible, and the self-justifying mechanisms are censorious rhetoric, open mistrust of everything a petitioner says, and reiteration in graphic detail of the original crime so as to reawaken and restore all of the animus and condemnation surrounding that event.

In the parole hearing described here, another board examiner reached back twenty-five years to quote the judge's sentence for pages on end. It amounted to an empty rhetorical exercise in order to ask whether or not the petitioner remembered those words, which she did and had already indicated in more ways than one during the hearing. The purpose of the rhetorical question could only be self-justification. It kept the commissioners focused on the crime. Parole hearings turn into retrials of the crime. Disdain for the act gives a parole board all of the righteous momentum it needs to ignore whatever progress a petitioner has made.

Consider briefly a second case, that of Dempsey Hawkins, who murdered his ex-girlfriend in 1976 when he was just sixteen years of age. His ninth parole hearing, in 2014, led to another denial after thirty-seven years in prison. Needless to say, this ninth hearing of the now fifty-five-year-old Hawkins concentrated on another rehash of the crime, with each question from the board geared to an admission of what had been confessed to many years ago and in hearing after hearing. It did not matter that this member of "the novenary club," Hawkins, was a "model candidate for parole." Or that he had constantly expressed remorse for his crime.[52]

Cases like these two have encouraged the Model Penal Code to declare parole boards "failed institutions."[53] A draft of this report gave even more devastating commentary. It indicated that "no one has documented an example in contemporary practice, or from any historical era, of a parole-release system that has performed reasonably well in discharging its goals."[54] Leading criminologists, including Joan Petersilia and Jeremy Travis, have also identified parole policy as a significant yet hidden driver of mass incarceration.[55]

By 2000, over a third of prison admissions nationwide were the result of parole revocations by parole officers, not new criminal convictions. Scores of these revocations occurred on the pettiest of grounds. By law, in *Samson v. California,* a parolee can be "subject to search or seizure by a parole or other peace officer at any time of the day or night with or without a search warrant and with or without cause."[56] The license available for unnecessary intrusion is great here. Most parole officers watching over the released come from the enforcement side of the law. Their retributive instincts are looking for violations. By way of contrast, in some other countries, the person who monitors a person released from prison is also responsible for helping to find that person meaningful, permanent employment. Not here.

So serious have been parole shortcomings that the chief judge in the New York state system, along with the State Permanent Commission on Sentencing, initiated calls for legislation in 2015 that would call for fixed as opposed to indeterminate sentences, which fall under parole sway. A central goal of such legislation would be to reduce the role of parole boards in deciding the length of prison terms. "As we know," Chief Judge Jonathan Lippman asserted in a clear understatement, "the parole board process has come under considerable criticism in recent years." Parole boards, he added in a public lecture, were not judges and were not supposed to act as judges. Fixed sentences, by eliminating parole board discretion, "will return judging to judges, where it properly belongs."[57]

Another answer, a too easy one, would ask for a more flexible range in personnel from the criminal justice system. Two of the three commissioners denying release to the sixty-eight-year-old grandmother with her perfect prison record came to parole board practice from law enforcement and criminal prosecution.[58] Balance from the other side of advocacy would certainly help.

Cronyism in easy appointments also infects the system. Parole commissioners hold their positions through state governors with minimal public scrutiny or later accountability. The mechanism of selection is a long-established political perk, and it is unlikely to change in the politics of our time. However, the problems go well beyond the personnel to the philosophical basis of parole investigations. Parole commissioners, no matter how selected, need to change how they think about their jobs.

Nothing that a prisoner now says affects the entrenched spirit of retribution that controls the parole system. Rehabilitative guidelines such as "a second chance," "successful therapy," "trauma recovery," "mentoring initiatives," and "character reform" are not defective in themselves, and they do measure progress. Nonetheless, they are shopworn token phrases in a broken system, and they fall on deaf ears when it counts. Conventional thinking, established routine, and institutional limitations all get in the way of words meant to mean something.

Long ago the philosopher John Dewey saw the nature of this intractability and what must occur to change it. "No one is ever forced by just the collection of facts to accept a particular theory of their meaning, so long as one retains intact some other doctrine by which he can marshal them." Parole commissioners hold slavishly to a doctrine of retention. "Only when the facts are allowed free play for the suggestion of new points of view," Dewey explained, "is any significant conversion of conviction as to meaning possible."[59]

Current rehabilitative expressions, the programs behind them, and even the central term itself—shortened to "rehab" in the penal industry—do not stop parole commissioners from assuming that "convicts" game the system. "Despite the best efforts of parole authorities," runs a recent report by the New York State Sentencing Commission, "there is little empirical evidence to support the proposition that we can effectively distinguish those offenders who are truly rehabilitated from those who merely 'talk the talk.'"[60]

Why, one might ask, is there so "little empirical evidence" on which to decide who is "truly rehabilitated," and why is there so much fatalism against the possibility of a sincere response? Parole commissioners do not believe in the reform-minded mechanisms that they themselves have established. Prisoners lack the means of giving the concrete evidence desired in an arrangement not set up for demonstration. They can only deal with the system by "talking the talk" assigned to them. They must speak, but they are not heard.

There is, to return to the words of John Dewey, no free play in the facts during a parole hearing. The passivity of prison life furnishes a board its negative answers. How can a person held in prison as irresponsible and still called "an offender" prove responsible activity? Just possibly, realization of the frustrations on all sides of this conundrum—suspects dismissed because they are under unavoidable suspicion—can be the opening we need to rethink this situation.

To develop in a way that will satisfy authority there must be a way to progress beyond the caged reasoning that mirrors the cell mentality on which it is based. As it is, parole boards deny through "assertive incompleteness." Lacking the evidence they want, they fall back on preconceived opinions and reject petitions on the unavailability of enough information. They handle the substantive issue—whether or not to release the petitioner—by agreeing that further search for the unavailable would be pointless. A prisoner who has been responsible can demonstrate proper growth and integrity only by connecting personal well-being to a role in agency that parole boards are unwilling to accept as genuine.[61]

New language, with the possibility of new kinds of thought and action, is called for. Hannah Arendt once referred to the spirit of innovation in answering intellectual stalemate as "the tact of natality": "the newcomer possesses the capacity of beginning something anew, that is, of acting."

A difference in perspective finds another way in the same circumstances.[62] Think about what a different language from newcomers might mean for the incarcerated. It would say, "If you change, we can get you out of here. If you don't change, here you remain." The incentives for change must be realistic ones as well as aspirations.

All of us can find fulfillment in acceptable performance, and there is no reason why that sense of fulfillment does not lead to an appreciation of a responsible life through what one has become. Many prison letters illustrate the writer's evolution toward an accountable outlook, and they just as often express a wish to demonstrate control over a renewed life in proof of what the writer has accomplished while in prison. "Prison has a way of disturbing one's sensibilities. I realized that if I ever wanted to experience happiness in my life, I had to get to work on fixing myself." That writer got to work.[63]

The grandmother who has given herself a high school education, a college education, and higher degrees in subjects of social relevance while maintaining a responsible record in prison across twenty-five years should be recognized for what she has become. If authorities do not trust their current means of measuring those results, they need to change the means, and the language for approaching those means, until they do believe in them. A spirit of change should be the assignment of every prison superintendent in the country. There have to be better ways for prisoners to speak for what they have become, and for that to happen we need a new language of punishment.[64]

8
Education in Prison Reform

The Learned Helpless

CHANGES IN ASPECTS OF THE LEGAL PROCESS as well as technological innovations, structural improvements, and a new terminology of mutual respect within the corrections system are all important to penal reform, but advances in education are the ultimate source of improvement, and it will require a many-tiered coordinated program. The facts are long in. Empirical study after empirical study shows that education makes all the difference in reducing recidivism in prisoners.

Recidivism rates vary depending on the quality and the level of educational programs, and quality is notoriously hard to gauge in a prison setting. Even so, all such programs have an impact, and some have a decisive one. If recidivism rates remain at an unacceptably high peak, well over 60 percent, the percentages drop with some education and reach single digits if a person in prison completes a college program.[1]

Why does even a limited program improve a prisoner's chances of successful reentry? Prisons are cesspools of negation. Ignorance rules, and those with knowledge fear to answer or challenge its dominion. Really good advanced educational programs are few in number, small in scope, and privately funded. When they do exist, they shelter enclaves of learning for the select few who enter them, and in that way they turn individual lives around. Fortunately, their ultimate social value may be larger. If nourished and expanded, good educational programs could produce more than the inklings of community that now exist in prison.[2]

There is, in fact, a partial exception with possibilities that might be expanded. Prisons for women have more hopeful educational patterns. Female prisoners have their own problems, including trauma from previous and often present abuse, heavier familial pressures, high levels of mental illness, and specific medical needs not met well.[3] And everything is complicated by having to cope with the enormous rise in confinement rates of women. Size in numbers is always a negative factor in education. Today the top twenty-six confiners of women in the world are separate states in this country. The United States has 5 percent of the world's female population but nearly 30 percent of its incarcerated women.[4]

Still, educational potentials are greater in prisons for women and might, with a realization of what works, be carried into prisons for men. Most women incarcerated are not violent offenders and do not privilege a pecking order based on physical advantages. Perhaps in consequence, they encourage each other in classrooms and maintain group discipline and solidarity there. Many of them have special incentives to do well. They have been separated from children who depend on them.[5] There is, as well, a singular institutional advantage on the side of education. Instead of the walls of silence that exist in male prisons, prisons for women have recognized that "a talkative ship is better than a tight one." The presence of real exchange promotes communal norms against corrosive isolationist impulses.[6]

Are these strictly characterological gender distinctions, or are they translatable? It may depend on levels. The incarcerated in prisons for men who have attained postsecondary educational levels are just as eager to learn. Unlike most students on the outside, they ask for more reading rather than less. The story, though, is far more alarming at basic levels and particularly bad in all large prisons for both genders. Roughly 18 percent in public life do not get a high school diploma. Compare that with the 68 percent of state prisoners who do not receive one, almost four times the number, and this discrepancy does not touch the worst facts.[7]

Educational proficiency in prison often ends in elementary grades and not high in them either. "The average reading level of incarcerated offenders is at or below the fifth grade level. Using sixth-grade achievement as a cutoff . . . half of America's inmates are illiterate." Without a high school education, one's chances for employment become slim, and they drop to near zero if you have been a convicted felon. Wherever you look, "the link between the crime rate and educational level is well established."[8]

What educational attainment level should we assign when a prisoner does not know a sentence ends in a period, or when another prisoner must ask a friend to spell the names of his own children in order to send them birthday cards? What grade in school has someone attained who knows the North Pole is cold and so the South Pole must surely then be hot? Think of the prisoner who must learn that the word "and" is spelled with a "d" on the end of it? What of the one who cannot add a short column of single digit numbers?[9] We are close to a zero-sum game with these questions.[10]

There is an important distinction between those who *cannot* learn and those who *do not* or *will not* learn, just as there is a difference between arrested development and development that has been arrested. Prisoners who cannot learn belong in a separate location where mental illness and handicaps can be diagnosed, treated, and assigned to whatever pace is possible in educational advance. Leaving them in a general prison population is disruptive for all concerned.

Those who can learn but who are unwilling to make the effort fall into another category, best known as "learned helplessness," and this is where prison programs fail over and over again. Here we find the majority of prisoners who return to a life of crime when released. Without a minimal education, they find no other way to cope with vocational life on the outside.[11]

These recalcitrant prisoners are the former children who sat passively in the back of class and were passed through anyway until unable to compete with others in higher grades. In reaction, they quit, disrupted classes, committed crimes that put them in juvenile institutions, or threatened authority in ways that had the same effect as quitting early. In the words of one such prisoner against educational programs in prison, now in his thirties, "I ain't come here to be no slave."[12] Never mind that this angry speaker was "sent" rather than deciding to come to prison.

The ignorant who refuse to learn in prison find themselves again in the back of the classroom, disrupting procedures when they can or chatting among themselves. They are there to avoid work details or lockdown. When excused, they while away their hours watching daytime television, in aimless conversation about sports (something they know), or in less idle discussion of crimes committed or the ones they will commit more cleverly when they are released. A lot of talk goes to why they will not get caught next time. These negative behavioral patterns flourish at every state and federal institution in the country.

Return for a moment to the example of learned helplessness just offered: "I ain't come here to be no slave." The danger identified, while real, is misinformed. Mistreatment to the point of enslavement of ethnic minorities exists in the criminal justice system.[13] The speaker may even have been first targeted in this way. Nonetheless, he serves time in prison because he is without the education that he failed to attain in order to live a civil life free of crime.

If ignorance has landed you in prison do you retain the right to remain that way? Arguably you do not. Statistics show that academic achievement in prison at basic levels works as well when made mandatory as when left to voluntary participation, and the logic in making it compulsory thus becomes a simple one.[14] You have been unable to manage your life on the outside without the marginal compulsory education required there. That failure has led you to crime, and the result has made you a danger to others. In the hope of preventing further crime on your release, a correctional facility has the right to demand the education you are expected to have and that you currently lack.

The penal system has the control and the rationale it needs to obligate you to learn, and even if it penalizes your lack of cooperation, this degree of enforcement cannot be called enslavement. But if not enslavement, what intellectually justifies the obligation placed on "the learned helpless," and why should it persuade them to cooperate?

Slavery, first and foremost, represents a denial of the dignity entitled to every human being. Of course, "dignity" is a loose term, but it applies precisely in education. Francis Bacon, in 1605 and again in 1623, made it clear. *De dignitate et augmentis scientiarum*, a Latin extension of the earlier *Advancement of Learning*, defines *dignitas* as learning. You establish your worth or value by discovering who you are and what you are capable of becoming through learning. In ignorance, you really don't know who you are. Left in that state, one has no ability to ascertain the value in correct action, and that ignorance can lead a person astray.[15]

Our resentful abolitionist may not be done though. In refusing to be a slave to the educational system offered him in prison, he may, with some judgment, have recognized the education offered as unworthy of having, and that decision may not be entirely his fault. The first rule in teaching comes when still a student. It is discovered through poor performances from the other side of the desk, and the corresponding rule runs like this: "whatever you do as a teacher, do not turn off the student." Our abolitionist has been turned off by too many teachers, and the prison system has not changed his mind.

The Pedagogical Fallacy

The problem with many pedagogical plans is that they produce pedants, teachers who claim authority through a template that they enforce indiscriminately on minds under their control. One of the other rules of teaching? "You must deal with what is actually in front of you." Prisoners might not know much, but they know they hate the symbols of authority that caused them to lose control of their lives, and the pedant enforcing a template is one of those symbols. It is also true that mere lecturing may inform but it does not educate. Every teacher should remember it is not an idea unless it is coming back at you. Exchange, meaningful exchange, the voicing of an idea, is the key to education.

The primary purpose in all beginning cases should be through interests already held. Instructional handbooks tend to get in the way of such a practical contextual approach through abstract regulations. One of the most interesting manuals that I have seen in prison culture has been an *Inmate Tutor Handbook* for educated prisoners who have been selected to lead tutorial classes under the training and direction of highly paid professional penal instructors. The instructors get $60,000 a year and up. The tutors get maybe 29 cents an hour. Page 10 out of 34 in the *Handbook* lists and explains eight very helpful qualities that should be brought to any classroom: "patience, understanding, adaptability, kindness, enthusiasm and encouragement, sense of humor, perseverance, and preparedness."[16] A good list, but the truest meaning of these words for teachers gets lost in this handbook.

What are we to make of earlier commands in the handbook to a would-be tutor? "Do not change the teacher's lesson plans." "You do not ever have permission to use a staff computer." Notably, there *are* no formal plans actually offered by penal personnel in the prison in question, and teaching without computer instruction leaves everyone thirty-five years behind the times. Or take another directive: "When a teacher is working a compressed schedule or is absent, you may be left to lead the class." This one is a more direct lie. Official penal instructors often skip classes if prison tutors are available. Informants report that the instructors sit in their offices using staff computers for personal purposes, one of many reasons why no tutor ever gets to use one.[17]

On the record you have a fine handbook, groups of professional teachers, and a score of carefully trained prison tutors working through coordinated and carefully integrated course planning with as many eligible prisoners as possible. Why, then, do these programs fail to show more success? Why are there not more GED graduations in programs? As so often in prison administration, the paper record masks a different reality.

Official education in prison proceeds with the same lack of attention that exists up and down the penal chain of command. Every imagined security breach trumps the possibility of better collective use of prison tutors and educational settings. Ideas for reform break against an institutional wall fascinated by its own struggles. In the words of one leading prison study, "The hierarchy and paramilitary organization of the prison give rise to intense power struggles that affect the administration, the line staff, and the prisoners."[18]

So attenuated are the lines of communication on education up and down the penal administrative hierarchy that some prisoners actively refuse to complete their high school equivalency through GED programs for the incarcerated. The objectors believe that their participation only sanitizes officialdom's numbers through public relations gambits, and they want to do nothing that helps the authority that they hate for not paying real attention to them.[19]

A Philosophy for Prison Education

The first steps with the learned helpless have to be elemental: one must re-invoke the worthiness in wanting to learn. Effective philosophies in education are necessarily a mix of aspiration and pragmatism. The aspiration that must apply in prison education is simple enough. The desire to develop, to make oneself better than one has been, is never completely lost even if only a twisted vestige remains. Anyone who attends a graduation ceremony in a prison knows that the desire remains. There is something to work with.

Pragmatism, the other side of a philosophy of education, has more mundane virtues. It believes in many possibilities, directions, and thoughts over any single one. It is pluralistic. It welcomes totalities over unities. Its views are instrumental. Adaptation to reality is important. Practical consequences count. Verifiability is its truth.[20] The strongest claim that pragmatism can make for itself comes out of these practical strengths. Prison education *can* work, and it is *not* working *now*. Politically, it has a broader claim to make. Education is the answer that will work. It is the practical solution to criminal behavior.

Aspiration and pragmatism come together in possibilities that should apply to education in prison. A young child's education need not be option oriented. On the other hand, an adult's education requires an element of choice and some deference to personal agency. An adult must find meaning faster to go with an already formed personal identity. The ultimate goal is to free students to pursue further education on their own and as rapidly as possible. Sooner or later classroom prescription wearies the soul, and in prison it will happen sooner. That is why college programs like the Bard Prison Initiative let their students make the decisions about what direction they wish their education to take.

Almost nothing replaces the importance of some choice in prison education. Freedom as agency has two dimensions: power and control.[21] Power is beyond a prisoner. Control over one's thoughts, assumptions, temperament, and intellectual development provides the freedom that is available. Modern philosophers speak of this element of control in learning as a form of dignity very much in the way Francis Bacon did four centuries ago.

Think of it as the dignity to be instilled in the learned helpless. In modern parlance, dignity turns into a responsibility as well as a right. You are obligated to protect those rights in yourself and others.[22] Put another way, "the notion of dignity is closely related to the idea of active striving."[23] Vagaries in talk of dignity drop off through these insights. One can see whether a person tries to meet a responsibility. You can observe a process of active striving or the lack of it.

Call it pragmatism with an aspirational tinge. It opens thought to education, not as a lockstep development from one skill to another but as a mutual discovery. The legal philosopher Martha Nussbaum summarizes the difficulty when she suggests that education must first find the thresholds to apparent capabilities.[24] For a prisoner of very limited education, the process will necessarily be a slow and painful one at the outset.

The adjustment that a person without education must make asks a great deal and should be approached with that struggle in mind. It requires nothing less than a new landscape of meaning. Challenging oneself to think anew works only if a person has realized that only more learning will clarify matters of importance. At stake is a radical shift in a person's hierarchy of values, a shift that often requires painful acknowledgment of an unacceptable past.[25]

Prison Education Policy

Another good rule about teaching applies. No matter what the level, never assume interest. Find it and nurture it. Prison thought and activity are full of ingenuity for getting by in a tough world. Teachers have to be interested in what the people they teach already know. Penal institutions have to comprehend that shared knowledge and believe in the education of their charges. There is no such consideration now. "You'll be back, shitbird!" Prisoners released regularly hear this jeer from correction officers who know the recidivism rates and depend on them for their livelihood.[26]

Those recidivism rates prove by themselves that the educational system in prison is broken.[27] Illiteracy, to take the most obvious problem, exists at many levels in prison. Some inmates cannot read. Some can read without absorbing what they have read. Still others give up at the first sign of difficulty. Each of these problems requires a different approach and a nuanced sensitivity currently lacking in corrections instruction. Solutions must cope with a population that lacks basic skills, self-confidence, background in employment, external support, and the kind of work ethic that goes with daily endeavor.

Uneducated prisoners, the majority, live through denial. They trust no one, hide their vulnerabilities, show no feeling, don't engage, see kindness as weakness, resist the system, and ignore authority when they can. "I didn't realize I could be smart," a number have written to me.[28] Reinforcing each of these handicaps is a consuming bitterness. Most prisoners, even if they feel guilt over the crime they committed, blame the length of their sentence and the manner of its imposition on the adversarial process.[29]

Psychologically, the incarcerated see themselves as acted on more than acting, and this passiveness encourages a larger evasion of responsibility. Prisoners who do not accept personal blame for their incarceration are unlikely to want to change who they are. Their loyalty and identity hold to the familiar social environment of their crime, the world they know. It is therefore a major adjustment under trying circumstances to accept responsibility for what one has become and to want to change it.

This can happen in several ways. Religion in all of its forms is so important in prison because it answers the ultimate anguish in confinement: loneliness. The believer has the assurance that someone, the most important someone in the universe, listens and cares. A dialogue with the self under the imputed gaze of providence becomes more than possible even in the smallest prison cell; it becomes mandatory.

The most famous and influential conversion experience in Western literature, Augustine's *Confessions,* explains in detail how this works. God, brought into the psyche from outside, forces the sinner into a different level of self-scrutiny, often through a question. "Why are you relying on yourself, only to find yourself unreliable?" Interrogation of the self through the impetus of external agency turns identity on itself with new awareness, and it demands new answers. "I will reveal not who I was but what I have now become." The shift comes out of the despair of what one has been and done, a hopelessness felt by all prisoners. In conversion, desolation is the path to redemption. Augustine explains it in an image of pain that marries the external to the inward. "Wretch that I am. See [Lord], I do not hide my wounds. You are the physician, and I am the patient."[30]

Prisons supply a full variety of internal religious mentors capable of helping a searcher find and wield the language of conversion. The prospect of forgiveness from on high is also important, and in most creeds it leads to the avoidance of violence and other forms of criminal behavior. One developing Christian completed his own conversion when a more seasoned believer, a cellmate, questioned his continuing bitterness and his dislike of others around him. "How can you remain so angry," he was asked, "and call yourself a Christian?"[31] There is a foundation of communal belief to call upon in such cases.

Dramatic transformations of this kind are generally absent in a secular conversion. The person in this situation feels no one moment or epiphany but takes stock of himself or herself much more slowly. The secular convert begins to recognize that anger over confinement is self-damaging and corrosive. That step produces fatalism with few satisfactions. The now suffering individual asks, "How can I take back control of myself?" Examples of others all around tend to give both positive and negative reinforcement to the idea.

Mentors, often in informal prison focus groups, are a significant aspect of the solution. In one state prison in New York, prisoners who are working toward an education have formed motivational speaking groups called "Voices of Transformation" (VOT). Auditors who come to these sessions first express wariness and some disdain, but some of them slowly move from snide indifference and mild curiosity to real attentiveness, and by the end, the sessions, called "Critically Changing Lives," end with expressions of gratitude and handshakes. Everyone in prison wants some kind of change.[32]

The third form of conversion, all on one's own, is harder to explain. There is a mystery and a special power in it that others around the person recognize and either respect or shun. Crucial to it is a manufactured distance. "Only part of me, the physical part, is actually here. My sanctuary is in the mind and not in the actions required of me." At its best, this behavior pattern attracts others who cannot follow it. At its worst, it relegates the withdrawn owner to a form of craziness. To succeed, it requires extreme forms of asceticism and self-discipline that are rare. It can be found but not copied.

Each type of conversion has its educational possibilities. The religious person can be led to higher forms of literacy and educational involvement through a ready desire to know the words of the Lord. The Bible, Koran, Torah, Book of Mormon, or Bhagavad Gita can be handy tools in this process. The secular convert needs the leadership of prison elders and group support that authorities often discourage or at least frown on. The solitary autodidact should not be held to the ridiculous rule that applies in most prisons—namely, you must have only three or at most four books in a cell at a time.

Despite official claims to the contrary, frontline personnel reject learning as a security risk. Prisoners, the logic goes, belong in a stationary not a developmental state. Initiatives should be squelched. Education beyond the norm kindles envy. Helping a prisoner who wants to learn can also be seen as a sign of weakness in authority. Not all of this is a correction officer's fault.

Prisons are dangerous places for COs. Two related frames of reference identified by anthropologists and psychologists thrive in the negative thought patterns about prison education. The evil twins are "risk and blame," and they reinforce each other to the point of eliminating positive impulses. If you feel threatened enough in a community to feel that you are taking risks, you find someone to blame for it. The unavoidable allocation of mental energy to a risk undergone reinforces the desire to blame those who are making you take that risk.[33]

Risk also depends on acceptance of a time span, and it features a discrepancy in the mind of a correction officer entering a work shift. For the prison guard, the eight-hour tour of duty starts a race against time with potential harm coming from an angry prisoner who, already serving twenty-five years to life, may feel he has nothing further to lose. The magnitude of the risk on any given day may be small, but that is not the issue. Everything in risk depends "on the magnitude of the outcome." COs entering a facility have every right to place a high priority on their own health.

Blame, though intrinsically related to risk, has more corrupting qualities in thought and behavior. "Blaming is a way of manning the gates through which all information has to pass." It restricts thought to censure of the other. Blame enables an automatic response. It says arm yourself against the enemy, in this case every prisoner in sight. In terms of educational programs, the right to blame means that you do not have to care about the well-being of the other side.

Breaking through these quietly vicious mental circles will depend on new dimensions. It will require reciprocal advances in education for correction officers to reduce the hostilities and suspicions at the core of prison culture. The next chapter addresses those needs. For the moment, the questions are more directly about prisoner education. How do we translate philosophies and policies of education into a pragmatic plan with transformative implications? What kind of arrangements in education might actually work, and how do we get them to work?

A Plan for Prison Education

If lack of education has landed you in prison, logic dictates that compulsory education should apply during incarceration to make up for what was not accomplished earlier. "People who participate in correctional education programs are forty-three percent less likely to recidivate than people who do not." Prisoners who even manage to participate "in high school/GED programs are thirty percent less likely to recidivate than those who do not," and the odds of regular employment on release also go up.[34]

Sticks as well as carrots will be necessary for real progress to be made, and that will require more of an incentive system than is now available in prison. A reward system—more choice in leisure, more freedom of movement, better opportunities to meet with other prisoners, formal sport activities, better video arrangements, broader vocational choices, music opportunities, time reduced—any or all of these incentives should encourage the disenchanted to take education more seriously.

An ignored resource comes through those who arrive in prison in possession of a decent education. They can be used to assist basic learning with the same reward system through successful teaching results. It can be their way of paying back. And in return, prison teachers should be given independent agency as an incentive. All should work meaningfully while in prison, and they should be paid for their productivity. Vocation is a key to self-respect, identity, and personal dignity. It should be encouraged and applied to everyone there.

Many educated people in prison are happy to help with educational initiatives, but they lack the support system or the interest from authority. In breaking down everyone, correction officers dismiss the expertise right in front of them. Two incidents show what such leveling does to education in prison. A college teacher serving in prison has had letters held up by personnel because they came addressed with the prefix "Dr." attached to the name and address. The letters were held because the angry guard with a high school education who was sorting the mail insisted "you ain't no doctor in here!"[35] Another prisoner with a decade of teaching ready for use is assigned to the loading docks when he offers to be a classroom instructor. In penal humor, the closest he ever gets to a classroom comes when he is commanded to sweep the floors of one.[36]

The letters I receive from educated prisoners who actually get to act as scheduled tutors show that many of their students, along with the presiding personnel in education, do not take the learning process seriously. No one is made to care. Any system of compulsory requirements will be subject to abuse if not carefully watched. Accountability for everyone must take us beyond the extraordinary amount of waste in the system we have now. Getting out of prison should be a job, one worthy of having.

Coordinated teaching agendas should allow a group of educators to identify more exactly the level of instruction needed for a learner. At the most basic stages, one-on-one tutorials are probably necessary to give an uneducated person the amount of privacy and the confidence to proceed. There is an elemental incentive to be addressed and used. Writing a letter is a basic form of freedom, but it cannot be done without mastery of your ABCs. Just as a learner satisfies a work requirement in this way, so the educated tutor engages in the vocational requirement that should be put on everyone. Everyone can benefit. The in-house personnel is available. Missing is the institutional will and understanding of what education can mean for all concerned.

After basic skills in reading, writing, calculation, and computer knowledge have been mastered, education should be geared to vocational directions that make sense to the individual. Most prisoners correctly assume that the few programs available to them will prove useless on the outside. Development loves choice. Students willingly meet a challenge they accept for themselves.

Colleges are lending their assistance. Wesleyan College in Connecticut, Grinnell College in Iowa, Goucher College in Maryland, Notre Dame and Holy Cross College in Indiana, Washington University in Missouri, Cornell University in New York, and the Freedom Education Project in Washington state all have initiated programs. Boston University hosts Consortium on Prison Teaching. California recently created a Prison Education Program. Even so, the numbers actually helped have remained small against the millions incarcerated. As recently as 2003, "only fourteen states and the BOP (federal Bureau of Prisons) had more than 1,000 prisoners enrolled, and those systems had eighty-nine percent of the students involved."[37]

Colleges and universities were previously instrumental in reducing recidivism through the federal Pell Grant program that previously provided funds for prisoners seeking postsecondary correctional education. The elimination of prisoner eligibility for those funds through the congressional Omnibus Crime Bill of 1994 has had a stunning negative impact on the size and number of educational programs and recidivism. Existing studies offer every reason to believe that reinstating Pell Grant eligibility would again have many more institutions of higher learning contributing to "education as crime prevention."[38]

Right now the General Educational Development program leading to a high school diploma, the GED, is slavishly geared to tests to be given. The credential may be necessary, but that is no way to educate anyone. If you are searching for the answer to a question that someone else has set up, you are not thinking for yourself. So along with the rote GED classes, instructors in these classes should be encouraged to teach small thematic group classes on their own for those with the background to appreciate and work in them. Education should be a pleasure, not just a duty.

It should also contain meaningful incentives. Right now a person in prison receives $25 or $30 for completing the GED requirement. Make it $300, but on a sliding scale. If you do not work effectively toward the degree, the amount you receive drops by $50 on an annual basis. Rapid completion should also reward a learner. After earning a high school diploma, a beginner should have at least the possibility of being moved to a prison as close as possible to his or her family.[39]

Of course, the more elementary skill deficiencies must come first, and that is where so many people in prison need to begin. Left permanently behind, prisoners in this category forge a transgressive identity available through the adverse attitudes and pursuits all around them. "Compensation by violent behavior for low feelings of self-worth is an all-too-common aspect of criminal behavior." The numbers prone to such behavior are staggering. Among the incarcerated, statistics show, "19% of adult inmates are illiterate, and up to 60% are functionally illiterate."[40]

We have already said that individual tutorials must come first. Intensive one-on-one sessions have a chance to convince a prisoner that someone cares, and these sessions can quietly identify capacities without embarrassing a student or increasing low esteem through exposure in a public setting. In a two-pronged approach, small group classroom experiences should follow. To keep these small, more than educated prisoners will be needed to teach. Where should such instructors come from?

Variations on the Teach for America program are worth considering. Teach for America encourages young college graduates to work in impoverished school districts with full pay and benefits. Adult prisoners probably need more experienced and probably more worldly wise instructors. Successful retired individuals are an untapped resource in this regard. Already a number of older citizens enjoy the work they do in prisons. Individuals with college degrees who have a serious vocational background and who have worked closely with other people will probably do best. Pay them, too, but just enough to confirm it is a working relationship in a way that they have already experienced.

This second prong should rely on "a collective learning approach." Small groups of no more than five like-minded and similarly proficient prisoners working together. Some teachers can also be drawn from those who have been successful in the individual tutorial ranks. Lifelong prisoners who have developed a practical canniness about institutional norms and former prisoners who have made their way in the world can also supply a pool of potential instructors.

For the two-pronged approach to work, the teachers need more independence and flexibility than currently granted in American prisons. Alienation takes many forms. Getting past it requires patience, flexibility, ingenuity, and initiative rather than a set method. A good teacher looking at a writing assignment must figure out what to correct and what to let go for a later time or session. This will be hard work, and we should pay prison teachers well beyond the 29 cents an hour currently allotted in federal prisons. A living wage will not be necessary for either prison teachers or retirees from outside, but the sums allotted should be meaningful.

Everything proposed also depends on trust in educational programs that penal authority has been unwilling to grant thus far. Building that trust will require another kind of instruction: that of correction officers and their supervisors. COs work in a very stressful environment that breeds hostility. They should, in consequence, receive regular three-month paid sabbaticals to take classes in management training, criminology, and group dynamics. These classes should be mandatory. If there is resistance, it will probably be slight from frontline officers. Most of them will prefer the opportunity to learn in a classroom to walking the corridors of a prison floor. Instructors of the highest order will be necessary to instruct correction officers who will otherwise be cynical about further education. The goal in education here is to create an elite professional corps of correction officers that will make the term "prison guard" a misnomer.

Classes for correction officers, with stringent rules behind them, can focus, as well, on rooting out the astonishing levels of corruption in prison work forces. Smuggling—knives, drugs, and other weapons—is a cottage industry in most prisons. Officials will occasionally admit that it is at the heart of much prison violence. Most contraband comes in through correction officers, who can arrange to bring in many items at once by counting on the collaboration of fellow officers who will then take their own turn in a thriving racket. Special surveillance teams *separate* from the rest of the penal staff will be necessary to check *everyone* entering a facility.

The size of this problem cannot be ignored. At Rikers Island correction facility in New York City, a place of rampant violence, smuggling has continued despite tight municipal scrutiny and elaborate new screening mechanisms. The problem lies not in the scoping machines but in the personnel who run them. "In the last year and a half, 11 guards and civilian staff members have been arrested for contraband smuggling" at Rikers, and this figure includes just the smugglers who get caught. The amounts smuggled—sixteen packages concealed in one officer's pants recently—indicate acceptance of an illicit general practice. How could anyone believe he would not be caught by an honest search with that much contraband on his person?[41]

The painful truth is that correction officers lack the professional grounding that only a better education can give them. Correction officer unions will resist requirements for instilling a higher professionalism, one in which specialized knowledge leads to disciplined acceptance of a strict code of conduct enforced by common acceptance of absolute standards in performance. All professions enforce a set of standards beyond selfish regard, and correction officers claim to be professionals. Let them prove it. The benefit in heightened reputation and communal acceptance could be significant.

Education at this level must distinguish between professional behavior and everyday practice. It must address the important skills in a constituted field. Explicit values give stability to the definition of a field. It is not a field if anyone can walk into it in two months, as is virtually true today. The education of a correction officer should be a two-year course paid for by the state with possible advance in other forms of civil service after, say, ten years of service. As early as Aristotle, Western thought realized that no one should be a permanent punisher. To check "the odium" in it, he wrote, "different magistrates acting in turn should take charge of it."[42] One way to rethink the control of punishment is to rotate the performance of it.

Although such reforms will appear to be expensive, complaints about cost miss an essential point. The real problems in reform are ideological. The average expense for holding a person in prison for a year comes to over $30,000, and the price goes up dramatically in major cities and when aging prisoners need more health care, increasingly the case with long sentences. A Rand Corporation comprehensive cost analysis made in 2013 indicates that "providing correctional education is cost-effective compared with the cost of reincarceration." These education programs need not add to the overall cost of incarceration.[43]

Entrenched thought, not expense, stands in the way. External programs in a thriving educational atmosphere can also defer costs. As discussed above, a growing number of leading universities and colleges offer postsecondary educational programs in local prisons. Civic minded faculty and advanced students interested in teaching find it a natural outlet for pedagogical involvement, and their programs avoid the problem of institutional rote learning. The PEN Prison Writing Program out of PEN/America and the Minnesota Prison Writing Workshop are ongoing operations that might be expanded with more public support, and they are good models for other initiatives in this area.[44]

Intellectually and economically, the financial ledger in educating a life that will not return to prison has to be balanced against the spiraling costs of each year of renewed incarceration for an uneducated returnee. Those inside the system may not care about costs, but the average tax-paying citizen should.

The financial advantages of an education through individual tutorials and collective learning do not end there. The surveillance required to manage the hostile environment in current prison culture is expensive to maintain. What if one could reduce that hostility? The leading study in "cooperation theory" suggests how that can happen. Results "show that cooperation can get started by even a small cluster of individuals who are prepared to reciprocate cooperation, even in a world where no one else will cooperate." Great things often have modest origins. "Cooperation can emerge from small clusters of discriminating individuals as long as these individuals have even a small proportion of their interactions with each other."[45]

The ultimate advantages in reform through education come here. The ingrained warfare and misery of prison life might not be necessary with better understanding from all sides. Much would have to change in both thought and practice, but that is what education can hope to accomplish. The rewards in reduced risk, blame, and danger could be substantial for everyone. "Voluntary compliance" has purchase through cooperation. It offers a conceivable glimpse of community among governor and the governed.

The Reach for Community

The opposite tendency dominates prison culture. Two rules in ethnographic investigation apply. First, "science has not produced a run of people who do not wish to dominate one another." Second, "in an individualist culture, the weak are going to carry the blame for what happens to them."[46] In prison culture these rules generate a world of perpetual enmity and violence. The result is not a community but a habitat of each against all.

Prisoners are well aware of the destructive side of prison policies. Friendships, they write, "lead, in the eyes of authority, to the forming of power blocs and conspiracies." Accordingly, "a prisoner with too many friends or too much power may simply be transferred to another penitentiary." These notions—that friends are power and that personal relations should therefore be truncated—are devastating for any semblance of community. "Forgotten by the larger world, looked down on by prison authorities, and having to fight for survival with other inmates, each person stands alone."[47]

Discouragement has an aesthetic dimension, too. Prisons are made uniformly ugly places, and any attempt by a prisoner to change that receives a reprimand. The incarcerated in large medium-security prisons used to be able to wear variations in clothing and could personalize cell décor. These initiatives, once encouraged, are no longer tolerated. Writes a lifer in prison long enough to remember former privileges:

> Guards often came by my cell to compliment me on the latest improvement. Today, I live in a cell with a bare, scarred concrete floor. The walls are poorly painted off-white with peeling industrial blue on the metal, exactly the same as every other cell. . . . I'm not allowed any form of decoration in my cell. . . . I wear blue pants with a cheap elastic waistband and large, yellow letters, spelling out "PRISONER" down the right leg. The guards now comment on how my cell is "in compliance."[48]

The unrelieved sameness of drab space and clothing does more than indicate that you are like everyone else; it prohibits anything special about you and says: don't try to improve anything around you, least of all yourself. In the prison world of today, "good behavior" signifies a double negative. You have not done anything that you were not supposed to do. You lack demerits. Personal accomplishments count for little and earn suspicion rather than a modicum of appreciation.[49]

Education is the main answer to all of these problems. Learning is the spark in new communication. It stimulates an individual to reach toward others. Knowledge shared is not conspiratorial if it helps others to learn. As such, education should receive the highest priority for everyone, including those existing without hope when given life without parole. Human existence under any circumstances wants to improve at something. You develop or you regress, and it is to everyone's benefit that those who are filled with despair should have the opportunity to develop. Time weighs on everyone's hands in prison. Learning puts time back in those hands. Knowledge gained resists stasis. Improvement is an answer to stagnation.

It is the benign answer to confinement. An educated person can be at peace in a small space, particularly if surrounded by other educated people. Prison can force education on people, but it also requires a communal set of norms that are sympathetic to the process.

You may think that these aspirations ask too much of current prison facilities, but there is no reason why they cannot recover the possibility for at least the nonviolent and cooperative who are forced to reside there. Education is the main way to turn a prison toward community. Calculated deprivation is what we have instead: ignorance, despair, aggression, hostility, casual violence, and continuation of the crime that sent everyone to prison in the first place.

Objections to the possibility of change will come fast. They will also be thin. No one who objects to serious educational reform should be allowed to hide behind the costs, and they must accept that incarceration today is unfair, racist, unjust, unsuccessful, unproductive, unavailing, and dangerous for all there, including workers. No other leading enterprise could survive such accusations, and incarceration, as we have already noted, is the third largest business in the country.

How did the penal-industrial complex get so big and so inert? From 1978 to 2014 the United States prison population rose 408 percent. Its punishment regimes have grown without overall direction. They have increased brick by brick, and then cement cell by cement cell, with millions of spools of barbed wire on top for everyone to see and regret. Is it possible that this monstrosity has all happened through faulty premises? Nothing this enormous and broken can be working off of a constructive basis. What, then, is its basis? Theories of punishment have the answers.

9
What Is Punishment For?

The Language Used

MORE THAN HALF A CENTURY AGO A pioneer in criminology recognized most of what was wrong with the language of punishment—a language that we still use. Gresham Sykes, in *The Society of Captives* (1958), did not write as a prophet without honor. Many applauded his insights, and his book became a classic on prison culture. Yet little of that applause has influenced the major actors in the criminal justice system or the leaders in correction facilities, or even law professors teaching criminal law.[1]

Sykes exposed a language of punishment that did not reach the punished. The vocabulary used did not explain the act. Three glib theoretical terms—"retribution," "deterrence," and "rehabilitation"—gave "a beguiling neatness and simplicity" to theories of incarceration. But "this three-pronged aim" existed in such conflict with itself that it could not answer the crucial question. Were the convicted placed in prison *for* punishment or *as* punishment? Instead of answering that question, the three prongs held the distinction permanently aloft. Worse, they controlled debate, which devolved into "a set of clichés that closed off inquiry."

The small prepositional distinction means everything in punishment. Imprisoned *for* punishment indicates that punishment beyond mere imprisonment remains a logical possibility. Imprisoned *as* punishment suggests that loss of freedom becomes sufficient unto itself. Without recognition of the difference, punishment regimes of the United States have stumbled into contradictions that have made punishment too severe.

Decades of internecine squabbles among experts have helped to create these problems by failing to provide a coherent theory of punishment for communal understanding. Criminal theorists in favor of retribution have found no way of discouraging painful conditions in prison that reach beyond confinement, and this is where a transformation in understanding of punishment must occur. Those geared to deterrence favor extreme penalties to keep criminals in a state of fear without any reason to believe that longer sentences deter.[2] Those inclined toward rehabilitation insist on the possibility but have no plan for it. Sykes, in his drollest sally, makes these reformers surgeons holding scalpels with no idea about where to cut.[3]

So heated and extensive have been debates over the established terms of punishment that experts have turned on themselves. Embattled theorists belittle each other in academic forays that feed communal uncertainties instead of resolving them. Some have even thrown up their hands and said the scope of punishment should be left to the common sense of the people, but if so, when does common sense turn into popular whim in the hands and rhetoric of political leaders?[4]

One of the canniest American politicians of the late twentieth century predicted where lack of expert direction and precise definition would lead a culture of fear. In 1983, New York governor Mario Cuomo warned: "If we follow the logic that says getting tough on crime means incarcerating all felons, you will see this system grow to around fifty thousand inmates. . . . Do we as a society really believe that non-violent felons—the petty check forgers, the small time embezzlers—belong behind forty feet walls? Do we really believe that it is a better alternative than a lengthy sentence of community service? Because if we do, you had better get out your checkbooks. Because you are going to have to write me a check to build ten thousand more cells."[5]

Two popular phrases made punishment in the modern United States much worse than it had been, and they deserve our attention because of how far they strayed from realistic calculations about punishment as a legal act. In 1965, President Lyndon Johnson introduced the "War on Crime" to the American people. In 1971, President Richard Nixon followed with his decision to wage the "War on Drugs." Both leaders wanted to corral serious criminals at work, but their words cast a much wider net in a country that has been at war since 1941 and that has always been ready to accept ruthless negations when the subject is declared combat.

The presidents forgot that declaring "war" has murderous implications. It isolates a common enemy for destruction. Mere transgressors become foes to be eliminated. In war, galvanized hatred replaces concern, and desire for a solution insists on total victory. The patriotism invoked confuses more than it clarifies when it comes to crime. A search for "the enemy within" replaces normal communal sensibilities. Attacking that enemy calls for putting erring citizens behind bars permanently, and it asks that thoughts of citizenship be ignored for those who are caught and incarcerated. Mass incarceration has been one of many negative results.[6]

Wars rarely accomplish what they set out to prove, and the announced wars on crime and on drugs were no exception. Both had the unexpected consequence, or the added advantage, depending on whom you ask, of targeting impoverished minorities who had been given their long-delayed rights and who might now be encouraged to use their rights to join and thereby threaten established social hierarchies and privileges.[7]

Look at the results. During the "War on Crime," the risk of incarceration rose from 11 percent for African American men born between 1945 and 1949 to over 20 percent for those born between 1965 and 1969. The "War on Drugs" brought an explosion in the long-term imprisonment of women in prison, mostly for nonviolent crimes, especially on drug charges. "In 1980 there were just over 15,000 women in state prisons. By 2010 there were nearly 113,000. When the incarcerated in jail are added to the total, there are about 206,000 women serving time—nearly one-third of all female prisoners in the world."[8] And once again, the great majority of these women come from minority backgrounds stuck in a drug culture. It has not been farfetched for criminologists who study the problem to claim " 'the war on drugs' is really a war on women."[9]

The Emotions Used

Punishment is made unpleasant not just by the pain inflicted but through the emotions displayed in a punisher. To list them all at once is to see the problem. Infliction, to justify itself, encourages feelings of anger, hatred, contempt, dismissal, fear, and condemnation, all arranged to bolster the punisher's satisfaction, righteousness, and assumed superiority. The demeanor of the punished has an effect, but these emotions dominate many situations of punishment regardless of the receiver's stance. Are these reflexive reactions misplaced? Let's just say they are unhelpful for addressing the real purpose in punishment.

Anger is the most logical response from a punisher. A transgressor has broken a code of conduct known to all with disruption of social harmonies and harm to individuals directly affected. The philosopher Francis Bacon early saw the problem with anger; it feeds the other negative emotions of a punisher. To underline the point, he placed his essay on anger right after the one written on judgment.[10] A responsible punisher should focus anger more on the act in question than on the individual who performed it.

Hope for reform should be conveyed to one who has lost all moral standing, and the easiest way to do that is to acknowledge the individual worth that is still possible. What might that accomplish? The legal philosopher Richard Lazarus explains that "to hope is to believe that something positive, which does not presently apply to one's life, could still materialize." "The capacity to hope," he observes, "is a vital coping resource." Hope in what might be done can overcome despair in what has been done.[11]

A measure of hate, particularly through victim impact statements, may be inevitable in legal censure, but it promotes the usual punishment attitudes of contempt, dismissal, fear, and condemnation. The more subtle, inner feelings left in a punisher—satisfaction, righteousness, and assumed superiority—are harder to gauge but still pernicious. Although a punisher in forcing atonement for a crime will feel professional satisfaction in a job well done, the further step to self-satisfaction is a short one, and the same can be said of the difference between righteousness and self-righteousness. Assigning the criminal to another order is rarely helpful even if it appeals to the crowd to call the perpetrator of crime a monster.

Failure to maintain these delicate balances has three dangers. First, excess of any kind in the punisher supports worse excesses in public reactions and in the subordinate officers who will carry out punishment in prison. Second, the negative emotions forget the underlying purpose in punishment to correct, and third, those same emotions foster "the desire to punish" in a way that collapses the distance between "the responsible agent and the irresponsible offender." Hostility is left on the table instead of balanced judgment.[12]

When done too often, punishment also deadens the punisher to other sensibilities and increases the right, and even the need, to punish more heavily. The number of criminals judged can and has heightened levels of judgment. A judicial decider can reach the level of thinking "this is just what I do." The desire to punish flourishes on estrangement from the recipient of it.[13]

The Enigma in Confinement

Everyone urges confinement for conviction of a serious crime, but no one knows what legal confinement actually means unless she or he has experienced it. Some say you should lock yourself in a bathroom for a day to get a taste of the possibility, but that is not the half of it. Your bathroom should have an open door with other people constantly passing by and making threatening or deriding remarks. It should be either very hot or very cold and full of so much noise that you must shout to be heard, even though no one is ready to listen. We should, as well, add another person to your bathroom, someone you have no choice about and who has habits and a temperament you don't like, with maybe some of those habits being illegal ones.

With all of these elements added to your situation, you should extend the time involved from a day to years and then ask yourself how these conditions are supposed to make you a better person than the one whose criminal behavior led to confinement in the first place. People are appalled to learn that we confine so many people this way. The number is too large to grasp, and the plight remains abstract. Think instead of *one person* under the conditions just described as a solution to criminal behavior, and the problem becomes a visceral one.

"Individual compassion" moves some people; "statistical compassion" moves others, but the need to address a serious social problem requires both orientations.[14] This distinction was a major source of debate in *Brown v. Plata,* the Supreme Court's 5-to-4 decision in 2011, which addressed overcrowding in California's prison system as cruel and unusual punishment under the Eighth Amendment. The narrow majority made its decisions on the numbers; the angry minority thought that only individual cases were within the jurisdiction of the Court.[15] The ferocity of this debate kept both sides from reaching a basic issue. Dividing the justices, without the will to ask it, was a question. What *degree* of confinement can be called acceptable punishment?

All degrees of confinement are now used, including many thousands of prisoners held in single concrete bunkers for weeks, months, and sometimes years on end. As many as 80,000 prisoners live in solitary confinement on any given day in American prisons and jails, with 25,000 or more living that way on a long-term basis.[16] These figures, against common practice elsewhere, hold despite the fact that all serious studies of solitary confinement, starting with Jeremy Bentham's in the eighteenth century, have found that long-term solitary produces severe psychological damage in most people. In his concurring opinion in *Davis v. Ayala* in 2015, Justice Anthony Kennedy gave detailed attention to this long history, concluding, "years on end of near total isolation exact a terrible price." We need contact with others, a back and forth, for basic health.[17]

What can be behind penal disregard of so many *known* proofs of human wreckage from solitary confinement? Defects in current theories of punishment again lie at the root of the problem, particularly since answers are readily available. What are those answers? Criminologists like Margo Schlanger agree that long-term solitary should require the strictest justification and review; it should be for the least time possible; it should not be used on prisoners with serious medical and mental health issues except in the briefest of emergencies; it should not involve sensory deprivation; it should include regular out-of-cell time; it should be closely monitored by health as well as correctional staff; there should be realistic incentives for someone to get out of it; and it must have some independent oversight.[18]

The unresolved distinction between prison *as* punishment and prison *for* punishment stands in the way of these principles, and as long as the distinction remains unresolved, treatment in prison will depend on *unexamined* variations in the intensity and circumstances of confinement for prisoners up and down the penal system. Acceptance of overcrowding, haphazard cell assignments, poor physical conditions, harsh surveillance, rude supervisory techniques, and the willful disregard of reasonable requests all depend on the assumption that the incarcerated should suffer while in prison.

If confinement by itself is punishment, one can begin to ask very different questions. Are minimal exercises in partial freedom part of the learning process in confinement? Where and how soon should strict confinement be eased in the light of good behavior? Should levels of privacy be offered with advancement? Given that confinement itself is infliction, should prisoners be allowed to adjust the spaces in which they are held, with some individuality and personal comfort in mind? What should be the proportion of time spent in common rooms, and what measures should be taken to help prisoners keep cells as safe and hygienic as possible? What should be cell interactions in any given area of prison? What other kinds of deprivation should not be used? Breaking the cycles of hostility can be a first step to something better for everyone. So far so good, but what about the uncooperative and the permanently alienated?

The Worst of the Worst

In chapter 3, I analyzed the incorrigible criminal as the "Sisyphean Perplex," the person who cannot or will not refrain from transgressive behavior. Dictating current penal assumptions about the problem is a phrase with several meanings. It describes a percentage of prisoners with psychopathic criminal tendencies based on their inability to place any value on the feelings and worth of others and another percentage who define themselves through violence or other forms of compulsive criminal behavior. Together these recalcitrant groupings form a psychologically expansive category even though the actual percentages are small, and often enough, they define the parameters in penal thought. They receive a semi-official description used everywhere in prison jargon. They are "the worst of the worst."

Reflect on the phrase itself for what it actually says about punishment. Fascination over "the worst of the worst" may dominate thought in corrections precisely because it is so unhelpful. Obsession with "the worst" assumes that all in prison should be thought of as "worse," and it follows that those who are worse are very likely at any moment to become "much worse." Belief in this continuum gives correction officers a comfort zone for justifying policies of universal repression.

Keramet Reiter, in her study of one of the severest institutions in the country, Pelican Bay in California, has the best succinct description of an embroiled dynamic. "An institution premised on the existence of dangerous and bad prisoners has every incentive to make and remake, label and relabel, prisoners to fit this category." No one wants to admit a classification error. To let someone out of long-term solitary confinement is to admit that a mistake might have been made.[19]

The fallacy in assuming the broadest possibilities in "the worst of the worst" is that it defeats all thought of change. It welcomes harsh punishment for all. It forgets that even the violent tend to alter their behavior as they age. It supplies a category very hard for anyone to escape from. Instead of limiting that category to the truly dangerous and psychopathic, penal authorities target ever-growing numbers of prisoners who have become worse through the treatment of them.

Prison arrangements should not be based on the assumption that "the worst of the worst" includes very large numbers of prisoners. Nor should the nature of the crime dictate the kind of humane treatment that remains possible and therefore deserved. The logical recourse administratively has been to isolate prisoners assigned to this category in separate units, where they make everyone, including staff, worse. Far from being the answer, supermax prisons increase the problems involved.

We have already seen that total subjugation produces deeper levels of alienation and lack of cooperation. In the words of one highly self-educated and completely changed lifer in a maximum-security state prison who writes in search of more opportunities, "if [warehousing people] is the perspective society holds, then when prisoners behave 'animalistic' it should surprise no one."[20]

Most people behave a little better when treated well. A truism? Perhaps, but there is enough truth in the proposition to trust its possibilities until proven wrong. It is, regrettably, a truth that penal practices refuse to test and that current theories of punishment ignore. What is wrong with those theories? They ignore the real purposes in punishment.

The True Purposes of Punishment

There are only two real social purposes in punishment, and they unfortunately exist in subtle conflict with each other. The first purpose is *to reduce* levels of crime. The second purpose, dignified by the "War on Crime," is *to eliminate* crime. Seemingly the same, these two purposes are confirmed in their difference when mapped onto the previous distinction in punishment already noted: namely, imprisonment *as* punishment and imprisonment *for* punishment. Only the second possibilities in these binaries—the desire *to eliminate* crime and imprisonment *for* punishment—justify extreme punishment without limits.

This is where the real debate over punishment should take place, and it never does. If you try *to reduce* punishment and seek to imprison *as* punishment, you naturally express a degree of hope in correction. If instead you want *to eliminate* crime and imprison *for* punishment, retribution and incapacitation remain the keys to your understanding. Our criminal justice system leans toward the second option.

A stance that wants to eliminate crime falls into the impossibility of full achievement, and it answers that impossibility by depending on a theory of retribution disguised in the idea of ever more communal safety. It succeeds as a rhetorical stance, despite the impossibility of its claim, by ignoring the impossibility and playing on the public perception that there can never be enough safety. That is why we have most politicians appearing "tough on crime" even though crime levels have dropped in the opening decades of the twenty-first century. It is easier to be simple on this issue than complicated, and punishment is always a complicated proposition.[21]

In the desire to eliminate crime, all other currently fashionable terms on punishment—deterrence, rehabilitation, parole possibilities, proportionality—drop away. At the same time, no penologist or criminologist or punisher wants to be tarred with the lone brush of retribution, even while wielding it. To avoid the unseemly notion of appearing eager to punish just for the sake of punishment, retributivists like to create some room for the other concepts in punishment without really believing in them or operating with them in mind. An inchoate imbalance in theories of punishment forms the real rhetorical battleground.

Arguments that try to balance theories of punishment while holding to retribution naturally gravitate to the most extreme form of punishment: the death penalty. Here is where scrambled understandings of punishment become most obvious and are most easily observable. We need to return to a famous example of hidden levels of retribution on exactly this point. Punishment really gets tested only when the presumed "best of the best" wonder whether or not to treat "the worst" a little better.

The Supreme Court's divisions in *Furman v. Georgia* show us the rhetorical battleground at work in all of its imbalances. Put aside, for the moment, the reason why the case receives so much attention: the de facto moratorium on capital punishment that it created in 1972, a moratorium that lasted until 1976, when *Gregg v. Georgia* reinstituted the possibility under the more detailed procedural standards that thirty-seven states had enacted in the interim.[22]

The impact of these two court cases, taken together, has given us the most disastrous outcome possible in the punishment side of criminal justice. *Gregg* added questionable procedures to compromised theories of punishment with separate sentencing phases and led, logically enough, to *Payne v. Tennessee,* in 1991, with the introduction of mandatory victim impact statements.[23] Both innovations have brought angry emotional registers to the infliction to be imposed. The presumed objectivity of legal punishment has been pushed out the window at the critical final stage of consideration. Communal hatred, targeting not the crime but the individual who committed it, has allowed an orgy of personal display that should have nothing to do with the rendering of justice.

Gregg notwithstanding, the real opportunity to change the meaning of punishment came earlier, in *Furman v. Georgia,* and that opportunity was lost. When we concentrate on the case, we find, in the words of two experts on Supreme Court history, how "deterrence came to be quite beside the point," how rehabilitation became "an archaic artifact," and how "retribution provided all of the justification needed."[24]

Why is an emphasis on this case so important? Capital punishment, which might have been stopped in *Furman,* promotes the ratchet effect in all other levels of retributive punishment. Death, even as a rare penalty, makes the equally draconian sentence of life without parole a certainty in many court decisions and raises the legislative designation of sentences for crime proportionately all of the way down the line. There may be a larger intellectual problem. Is getting rid of capital punishment a necessary step toward a more enlightened theory of punishment?

Many incrementalists in punishment theory assume that capital punishment will gradually become an anachronism and go away. Against that way of thinking is the probability that at least the form and partial infliction of capital punishment is here to stay in America. The current configuration of the Supreme Court and the decision of the California electorate to retain capital punishment in a November 2016 referendum are signs and symptoms of our times.

One has to blame the nine men in *Furman v. Georgia* for this result and more. With a growing number of cultures rejecting the death penalty, *Furman* has left the United States in fifth place among the world's executioners. The four countries in front of it—China, Saudi Arabia, Iran, and Iraq—are all brutal totalitarian regimes.[25] Admittedly, the Supreme Court has picked away at the death penalty, eliminating execution in several categories: minors, the intellectually disabled, and those convicted of crimes other than murder. But 1,442 people have still died this way since 1976, and almost 3,000 more prisoners live under the threat on death row. This problem is not going away. A more courageous decision in 1972 would have prevented it.[26]

Confused on punishment in *Furman,* the nine justices could agree on nothing across 233 pages of contentious prose. At 50,000 words, it was the longest set of opinions in Court history at the time. Nine separate opinions were lodged in all, the most possible, and the Court's decision, rendered *per curiam,* because it disagreed on everything, consisted of a single paragraph of cryptic prose. On the sticking point, over arbitrary enforcement of the death penalty, the Court held only that "the imposition and carrying out of the death penalty *in these cases* constituted cruel and unusual punishment in violation of the Eighth and Fourteenth Amendments."[27] Never was so much written on so little decided. The tenuous majority of five could not even agree on how much arbitrariness had been necessary in the original court decisions to arrive at their decisions.

The Supreme Court in 1972 had an extraordinary opportunity to end capital punishment in the United States, but it did not have the courage or corporate wherewithal to seize it. For unmistakably, whoever is for capital punishment and whoever is against it, no one can deny that *everywhere* this penalty falls arbitrarily on the poor, the different, and, as often as not, on the mentally challenged. Arbitrariness *always* rules in these occasions given the very small numbers who are actually executed. Anyone rich enough to have a good lawyer at the trial stage is unlikely to be executed, and only a very small number of counties ever imposes the death penalty on anyone. A few counties in just three states—Texas, Georgia, and Missouri—were responsible for almost all executions in 2015.

Furman v. Georgia stands for two other things in the long term: first, the Supreme Court is at its most divided and most contentious over issues of punishment; second, theories of punishment become overt when "the worst of the worst" stand to receive *less* punishment than some think they deserve.[28] The two issues are related, but the second observation, fumbling differences over the language of punishment, is most relevant here. The Court's hopeless fight with itself reveals just how clumsy our understanding of punishment has become for even those most responsible for its enforcement.

How close did the Court come to abolishing capital punishment in *Furman v. Georgia*? No one can really say amid so much acrimony, but two justices, William J. Brennan and Thurgood Marshall, were absolutely against the death penalty, and a third on the fence, William O. Douglas, opposed it as arbitrary in many cases. Two others voting for death, Lewis F. Powell and Harry A. Blackmun, would later conclude that capital punishment was an unacceptable penalty.[29] One thing is clear. No other opportunity to repudiate legal executions has come as close in forty-seven years and counting.

William Henry Furman, a black man guilty of other crimes, killed a white father of five while committing a burglary at night in the victim's house. He was convicted and sentenced to death in a one-day trial.[30] The case before the Supreme Court was consolidated with two rape cases in which black men in Georgia and Texas entered the houses of white women at night and raped them.[31]

In other words, and although no one on the Court mentioned it explicitly in page after page of tortured prose, three southern juries were all dealing with the regional nightmare of home invasion by a black criminal who violated their white victims in the worst possible ways. The death penalty decisions in the lower courts were easily made—too easily for the barest but still sharply divided majority in the Supreme Court's 5-to-4 decision.

The closest to a deciding opinion in *Furman* is the shortest, that of Justice Potter Stewart, and there is little to admire in it. Stewart gains his authority by praising "my brothers" on all sides of the question and by concentrating on the unavoidable fact that the petitioners in these particular cases "are among a capriciously selective random handful upon whom the sentence of death has in fact been imposed." The truth of these words notwithstanding, they do not lead to the obvious conclusion that all defendants in successful death penalty decisions are arbitrarily chosen. The Court backs off from its own logic by limiting its decision to the *apparent* requirement that the penalty be imposed with greater consistency, a virtual impossibility given how our multifaceted criminal justice system works.[32]

Justice Stewart gets to his decision by qualification. He argues that "despite the inconclusive empirical evidence, only the automatic penalty of death will provide maximum deterrence." This is a shaky argument at best. To bolster it, Stewart immediately adds, "I cannot agree that retribution is a constitutionally impermissible ingredient in the imposition of punishment." Once again, retribution has taken over, and out come the heavy guns aimed at communal insecurities. "When people begin to believe that organized society is unwilling or unable to impose upon criminal offenders the punishment they 'deserve,'" Stewart thunders, "then there are sown the seeds of anarchy."

Notice how these rhetorical strategies work. Deterrence is a possibility especially when the death penalty is "automatic," a claim heavily contested elsewhere in the decision. Retribution reappears only as "an ingredient" when it is the whole thing. To cement his argument, Stewart raises the absurd prospect of chaos. If we do not kill a respectable and hopefully more consistent "handful" of criminals, "the people" will object, and in objecting we start down the slippery slope to anarchy.

By deflecting the argument on to the people instead of owning it, Stewart's strategy has a squeamish tone that appears somewhere in the language of the other justices in *Furman,* often with an agonizing overlay. No one wants to be tied directly to capital punishment, but seven of the nine don't want to deny it absolutely either. They all duck the main issue, and Stewart has given them that leverage. He insists that "the constitutionality of capital punishment in the abstract is not, however, before us in these cases," when it most certainly is.[33]

The sharpest debate over the alternative of deterrence in *Furman*—roughly comparable to how many angels can dance on the head of a pin—takes place between Justice Thurgood Marshall, who wants to abolish the death penalty, and Justice Lewis Powell, who writes to sustain it. Justice Marshall, for his part, proves that the arguments for deterrence in capital punishment are based on "logical hypotheses devoid of evidence." Empirically, the presence of the death penalty in law does not make police officers safer, and it has no effect on homicide rates (there is no difference in per capita murders between states that have the penalty and those that do not). In sum, deterrence supplies no statistical basis in the many studies on the subject.[34]

Justice Powell in dissent saves his own discussion of deterrence, one of many Court run-throughs of the same standard arguments about theories of punishing, until last because he knows it is his weakest argument. He admits that statistical studies "tend to support the view that the death penalty has not proved a successful deterrent," and he has to agree that "deterrence is a more appealing justification [than retribution]." Powell handles his problem by falling back on the notion that "opinions again differ widely," and those opinions take the place of logic. "Many are inclined to test the efficacy of punishment solely by its value as a deterrent, but this is too narrow a view." How many? Too narrow for what? Lurking, without being said, as in Potter Stewart's opinion, is retribution, the real source of Powell's argument.[35]

The conclusion reached by Justice Powell has already been assured at the outset. He holds to beliefs rather than the facts he has to admit. "*Prima facie* the penalty of death is likely to have a stronger effect as a deterrent to normal human beings than any other form of punishment, and there is some evidence (though no convincing statistical evidence) that this is in fact so."[36] "Prima facie" means at first sight. Powell, by his own definition, returns to what he first thought, ignoring the statistics that go the other way.

Nor does he bother to identify that strange caravan of "normal human beings" who will be deterred from committing crimes only by the threat of capital punishment.

Powell gestures to the presumed lack of absolute clarity on deterrence without recognizing that there can never be any degree of certainty beyond what has already been found. Hiding behind the words of others, he calls on "the *long-standing* and *still raging* debate over the validity of the deterrence justification for penal sanctions" to find more of a debate than exists. Debate, he claims "has not reached *any sufficiently clear* conclusions to permit it to be said that such sanctions are ineffective in *any particular* context or for *any particular group* of people who are able to appreciate the consequences of their acts."[37]

The hedging words in italics reveal Powell's problem. If the debate is "long-standing" and "still raging," on deterrence, he is safe in taking a position on it. But how "sufficiently clear" would most propositions have to be in order to apply for "any particular context" as well as members of "any particular group" who are also rational enough in committing crime "to appreciate the consequence of their acts"? The test is an impossible one.

Justice after justice in *Furman v. Georgia* supplies a long history lesson with hundreds of footnotes that reach all the way back to early English common law and through the history of precedents in both cultures on capital punishment. They show you can prove anything through history by cherry-picking your examples. Heavy in many of these arguments is reliance on a past that may have never been.

Still, there is the sincere effort involved. The exception, and the truly craven opinion in *Furman v. Georgia,* comes from Justice William Rehnquist, "well known for his support of capital punishment."[38] All of the other justices wrestle with their problem, and all of them indicate somewhere that if they were not officially sitting judges, they might personally think differently on the subject of capital punishment, but Rehnquist hides behind his office with "rigorous attention to the limits of this Court's authority," along with plenty of added boilerplate on the "Founding Fathers" and their writings.[39]

The shining light in this mess is the opinion of Justice William Brennan, and not because he is the second justice, along with Thurgood Marshall, to call for the abolition of capital punishment. I have already noted, in chapter 2, how Brennan in *Furman* parses the Eighth Amendment clause on "cruel and unusual punishments." Here he also slaps away the gratuitous arguments of others. He begins by noting the irrelevance of quoting the Founding Fathers on this issue, and, in another counter, reminds his colleagues "ours would indeed be a simple task were we required merely to measure a challenged punishment against those that history has long condemned."[40]

Justice Brennan sees what his colleagues do not. He understands that institutionally no one except the Court is in a position to decide the growing legal dilemma over capital punishment, and he realizes that the whole issue will continue to vex both the criminal justice system and the nation. Brennan adds another worry. He thinks time will only make it a more difficult problem to handle—an intuition the passing years have confirmed.

Referring to the unavoidable vagueness of the Eighth Amendment provision on "cruel and unusual punishments" and quoting from an earlier case, *Trop v. Dulles,* Justice Brennan decides "the Clause imposes upon this Court the duty, when the issue is properly presented, to determine the constitutional validity of a challenged punishment, whatever that punishment may be." Then this: "in these cases, '[t]hat issue confronts us, and the task of resolving it is inescapably ours.' "[41] The Court avoids a clear responsibility in *Furman.* "We must not, in the guise of 'judicial restraint,' " Brennan warns, "abdicate our fundamental responsibility to enforce the Bill of Rights."[42] That, of course, is exactly what the Court ends up doing in *Furman,* with a more muddled understanding of the Eighth Amendment than when it took up the case.

Like the others, Brennan's opinion gives its own detailed account of the history at issue, but Brennan's real decision comes early on in his opinion and on different grounds. He is that sure of his direction and his claims. The death penalty "is a denial of human dignity for the State arbitrarily to subject a person to an unusually severe punishment that society has indicated it does not regard as acceptable, and that cannot be shown to serve any penal purpose more effectively than a significantly less drastic punishment. Under these principles and this test, death is today a 'cruel and unusual' punishment."

The principles involved are fourfold, and any one of them is sufficient to decide the case in *Furman*. Capital punishment violates human dignity, it is arbitrarily imposed, many in society disapprove of it, and it is unusually severe where a lesser penalty will serve. In denying death, Brennan ends, "hope is given for the reformation of the criminal."[43] Much turns on a theory of punishment in this final statement.

Even the most intelligent and concerned figures have trapped themselves in a shopworn vocabulary without enough purchase to reach common understanding. In *Furman,* the justices were *unable* to agree on a theory of punishment on the most important criminal law issue of their time, and nothing has changed since then. Collectively understood, when punishment is up for discussion and decision, we still do not know what we are doing when we talk about it.

How, then, *should* we talk about it? The answers may be better if we accept the basic and simpler division between *incapacitation* and *correction,* but only if both of those terms are properly understood. Incapacitation welcomes at least the possibility of the death penalty, and it accepts long and perhaps permanent sentences. It also speaks to institutional and communal depression over high recidivism rates and lends itself to a tinge of fatalism over all other possibilities.

Against incapacitation is the fundamentally recognized right of people to a measure of freedom if they have learned how to use it responsibly. Incapacitation can be almost an instinct, but it works against important elements in human nature: it ignores the basic need to be able to move and plan some things on one's own. It cannot help but twist the people it affects into something troubling for everyone.

Correction presents an even more nuanced subject and problem. It is a term without real meaning in American punishment regimes today, and it is without meaning because so many in penal authority feel that it fails to change criminals into responsible citizens who can be returned to society. We have seen that the conditions for meaningful correction do not exist in current facilities. What would it take to make correction a viable alternative for a majority of those incarcerated? Logically, a majority of prisoners corrected is necessary if the goal of punishment through correction is to reduce the level of crime.

Real correction, in this sense, has not been tested. Under improved institutional conditions, it should be the opportunity for all in prison, whether or not the plan is ever to release them. As Justice Brennan saw, "hope is given for the reformation of the criminal." Hope should never be utterly denied, and it should offer welcome choices. But if so, how are choices to be managed? The biggest problem is one not talked about, and it reaches back to incapacitation.

Beyond adjustment into society, if not beyond some form of restoration, are the hundreds of thousands that we have held in prison who can no longer make it on the outside. Without prospects, skills, education, financial resources, or familial support, these are people who still deserve the measure of happiness that it might be possible to have while behind bars. More freedom for those who have proven themselves to be not dangerous should be a priority. Skill sets and detailed provision for potential release is the real hope against recidivism, but everyone should have the prospect to lead a useful life whether in or out of prison.

A prison with a more humane environment makes sense regardless of whether the orientation is toward correction or incapacitation. People who are treated inhumanely are not going to correct themselves, and they will make incapacitation three and four times as expensive as it should be. One answer to this predicament has been offered by a leading interdisciplinary criminologist, Austin Sarat, in an edited collection entitled "The Beautiful Prison."[44]

All of the participants in this collection of essays recognize that the term is an oxymoron. "The most beautiful prison," writes one contributor who is himself behind bars, "is the one not built." There is, in this regard, a movement to abolish prisons but with no real remedy in its place. Confinement of some kind for limited periods of time remains the safest form of punishment for violent crime, and as Aristotle saw first, "just punishments and chastisements do indeed spring from a good principle, but they are good only because we cannot do without them."[45]

The qualifiers in Aristotle's statement signify much. Punishment should be "just," and it has to spring from "a good principle." Somehow we have lost our way in maintaining those values and the moderation they entail. Too many people are harmed unnecessarily and permanently by our criminal justice system, and there is not enough motivation to improve the methods of incarceration that we now use. We intuitively know that current practices are wrong without being able to see what might be right. To engage in a meaningful spirit of correction with the prospect of incapacitation only when necessary, we need a different understanding of punishment than we currently find in legal doctrine.

10
The Architectonics of Reform

The Right to Be Heard

PUNISHMENT IS ABOUT DEPRIVATION, AND the intellectual puzzle in it. How do you turn deprivation into a positive transformation? Ovid gave us an inkling in *Metamorphosis* by making his ugliest views of punishment a loss of voice, a metamorphosis into the inability to speak. Prisoners today speak. They are not turned into spiders or other animals or olive trees, but when they speak they are not listened to. An idea lies buried here, and it has to do with the quality, eloquence, and range of voices in meaningful exchange. The right to be heard is one test of humanity and justice in a civilization.

Replacing a theory of punishment that shuns the transgressor with one that connects with that transgressor may sound plain enough in principle, but many things forestall the prospect of reciprocity between punisher and punished. Incarceration that shuns comes close to an instinct in American society, and it has created beliefs, applications, and institutional structures in its wake. Blame is its controlling reflex, and it does not like answers. To hold to blame is to tolerate harshness that is otherwise known to be wrong.

Even in the face of wrong, most people do not alter their ideas when troubled by them. Two reasons, one normative and the other pragmatic, indicate why people today should be concerned about our punishment regimes enough to want to do something about them. On normative grounds, we have moved well beyond George Bernard Shaw's classic warning about punishment from more than half a century ago. "If you are to punish a man retributively you must injure him," Shaw wrote in 1946. "If you are to reform him you must improve him. And men are not improved by being injured."[1]

In more pragmatic terms, the spreading net of enforcement and surveillance in American culture should be a general concern. We are approaching extraordinary levels of prosecution for anyone hauled in for a relatively minor offense who does not cooperate quickly with authority. The right to "a speedy and public trial" guaranteed by the Sixth Amendment is fast becoming a fiction except for a wealthy defendant who is willing to trust good counsel.

Stop and consider. Today, you, an ordinary citizen, could land in federal prison for five years and a $250,000 fine for a seemingly trivial offense if the legal system felt inclined to make it happen. Anyone who has borrowed a film knows the warning given right before every viewing. You are vulnerable to punishment if caught pirating a movie whether or not profit is involved, and "piracy," a former act of terrorism, is the identifying term for your crime.[2] The system is stoked to convict, and we now know that a number of people in prison were innocent of the charges leveled against them.

Prosecution depends on whether or not authority wants to target you or someone else through you. It turns on how badly the government wants to nail someone. The ratchet effects in our sentencing structures are frightening, and the carryover to severity in prisons should horrify anyone who knows anything about them. Punishment has reached beyond reasonable scales of correction.

There is much that can be done about these punitive impulses, which have increased in recent years.[3] Earlier chapters have outlined possibilities. Judges and legal counsel on both sides in criminal justice should take more active roles in improving prison conditions.[4] The people on all sides of incarceration need to be better educated and monitored. Correction facilities should not be sealed-away entities. A level of general communal surveillance is important. Technological means exist for preparing the incarcerated for a better return to civil life. Incarceration should include meaningful training toward a law-abiding life. No one should enter a facility with mere incapacitation as their lot. Correction demands improvement. That should be the byword for everyone in prison culture. But how do we get there?

The Words That Control Us and Free Us

Education at the levels required means a professionalism that can guide others. Highly trained people, the only ones who should be working in a prison, must know what they are willing to do or not do before a problem or threat arrives. The rules for being able to do that will vary, but beyond the skills taught they have the same significance. Intellectual restraint supplies the first rule in every profession, and solidarity through correct group behavior comes second. Both qualities are lacking in punishment regimes today.

Proper training resists the inclination to mistreat others. A professional person always knows whether individual behavior or that of the group is incorrect, and that person has been trained to speak out against it. To profess is to believe in what you are doing without giving up, even against heavy odds. How duty instills well-being originates in much earlier writings.

The Greeks first referred to the idea through the term *eudaimonia.* The word signifies happiness (as in the pursuit of it) or the good life, but it is understood more completely as "proper human flourishing." In Athens one could not flourish on one's own. It had to come through acceptance and meaningful participation in the community around one. Correct behavior gave understanding and peace against the heavy burdens of life and the cruelty of others.[5]

In the rampant consumer culture of today, professional identity is one of the few separating sources for the self-possession required in difficult circumstances, and it is what we must rely on for a better penal system. The ability to deal with violence without becoming overly violent oneself is a first step toward correction. Preceding that step, by making it easier, are the conduct, character traits, and demeanor that prevent violence in the first place.

Existing terminology does not help us here. "Prisoner" is the term we use for someone who has been confined. The word, from the French *prisoun,* originally meant "the condition of being kept in captivity," from *prisois,* "the action of taking prisoner" and *prensio,* "the power of making an arrest." These words, reaching further back, derived from the old French *prise* or "prize": "The sense of 'prisoner' (which occurs in Italian and Spanish as well as French English and Latin) appears to have arisen from a person taken [in war] and held as a captive."[6]

Think how much more useful it might have been in a theory of connection in punishment if incarceration could have been known through stoic philosophy as *prokopē* (meaning "a place of progress"), with a person held in one designated *ho prokopton* ("one who is in a state of progress"). "The distinctive character of the man who is in a state of progress is that he is on the right road." The term also covers "one who is beginning moral progress." "As soon as a man's feet are on the right path he may be called 'in a state of progress.' "[7]

A fanciful exercise? We are controlled by the words we use, and we need new words for a better theory of punishment. Someone punished makes progress out of a transgressive state only if aided by another's understanding. Making the transgressor better is the only true goal in an idea that claims to "correct."

Answers begin in mutuality of voice. In a postmodern world full of relative claims about truth, theorists of human nature concentrate more and more on the "talking animal," a conception whereby dialogue becomes a primary source of meaning.[8]

Punishment in the adversarial process involves exchange in this sense, and the nature, if not the shape, of those exchanges should continue in prison. They should not end, as they now do, at the stage of analysis in court. A continuing conversation between punisher and punished goes to the root of positive transformation. It should be the very definition of punishment if based on the goal of progress, which is to say if based on correction.

There is a precondition in these claims. Real exchange can take place only if all sides in a situation receive respect. A punisher must enlist reciprocity in order to make progress for the punished along a "right path." The call for mutual exchange and direction may sound outlandish, but it is no more outlandish than the wall of silence that now exists between correction officers and the incarcerated in prison life, a wall designed to be unhelpful (as described in chapter 7). As we saw earlier, correction officers who engage intellectually with prisoners are called "mud lovers" by their colleagues, and it is a powerful deterrent.

Training people to engage with each other is an art form based on education. A worried mother writing to her son in prison as he struggles with his education summarizes that art form in a sentence: "How you think is how you act."[9] The abilities to foster reflection, to mediate conflict, and to assist an individual beyond inconsistencies and unawareness, a major basis of crime and violence, are skills that every correction officer and educator in prison should possess and try to instill. There must be a common dimension in developing these skills. Mutuality as a virtue is more than just another individual recognized.

The Collective Voice

The history of civil rights tells us that no one is given them. Rights are taken. Their development has been marked from the inception of the republic by rebellion, civil war, civil disobedience, and public demonstration. No one who automatically has rights offers a piece of the body politic to those who lack them. Group consciousness with attending speech galvanizes the recognition demanded.

In yet another example of the hollowness we have documented in legal protections, that level of speaking consciousness has been taken away from the incarcerated by courtroom fiat. *Jones v. North Carolina Prisoners' Labor Union,* a 6-to-3 Supreme Court opinion in 1977, denied prisoners the right to unionize, but it went much further than it had to in reaching that outcome. *Jones* argued that "deference to the decisions of prison administrators and appropriate recognition to the peculiar and restrictive circumstances of penal confinement" took away from prisoners the fundamental rights to free speech, solicitation among themselves, and mutual association.[10]

Without access to those rights, the incarcerated lack standing to engage in a real conversation over their needs. They do not have the means to approach authority on the merits of the problems that all should want to recognize and fix. They have no effective means of answering malice and cruelty in behavior against them. In sum, they cannot be heard.

The legal imbalances created by *Jones v. North Carolina Prisoners' Labor Union* are as great as anyone can imagine. Without the prospect of a communal voice, each individual prisoner faces correction officers who belong to unions that protect their memberships despite every conceivable offense made by them. These same unions have sufficient power to intimidate penal management from promoting meaningful reform and from enforcing any real accountability in their ranks. "Qualified immunity" protects even rogue guards who go beyond all decency in the treatment of prisoners.

Jones will not be overruled, but a better understanding of punishment could distinguish its worst effects. Certainly the opinion is worth a closer look on these grounds. What, for example, might a theory of punishment based on interactive communication between prison authorities and the incarcerated do to the reasoning in *Jones*? Justice William Rehnquist, in writing the majority opinion, had to overrule two lower court opinions that found "there is not one scintilla of evidence to suggest that the Union [of prisoners] has been utilized to disrupt the operation of the penal institutions."[11]

Rehnquist overrides these findings with a blanket claim. He says "the fact of confinement and the needs of the penal institution" can impose across-the-board limitations "on constitutional rights, including those derived from the First Amendment." Eliminated are "those associational rights that the First Amendment protects outside of prison walls."[12] None of the common rights of association apply anywhere inside prison walls! In effect, the logic of *Jones* depends on whatever administrative discretion imposes when filtered through a peculiarly narrow definition of place.

Abdication to administrative penal discretion, as we have seen before, comes first. Prisoners' rights "may be curtailed *whenever* the institution's officials, in the exercise of their informed discretion, *reasonably conclude* that such associations, *whether through group meetings or otherwise,* possess *the likelihood* of disruption to prison order or stability, *or otherwise interfere* with the legitimate penological objectives of the prison environment." The impossibility of a meaningful challenge can be seen in the highlighted phrases.[13]

Authorities only have to *think* some activity might "*naturally* result in increasing the existing friction between inmates and prison personnel." "It is enough to say that they have not been *conclusively shown to be wrong* in this view."[14] To make this abdication to prison authorities even stronger, Chief Justice Warren Burger weighs in with a concurrence of his own. The Court's opinion " 'reflects no more than a healthy sense of realism' on our part to understand that needed reforms in the area of prison administration must come, not from the federal courts, but from those with the most expertise in this field—prison administrators themselves."[15]

When has an ascendant institution ever reformed itself without outside pressure? Justice Thurgood Marshall, with Justice William Brennan concurring in dissent, deplores the sweeping nature of *Jones* as a return to servitude. "The Court . . . takes a giant step backwards toward that discredited conception of prisoners' rights and the role of the courts [that prevailed in the nineteenth century]." Marshall and Brennan also see the handwriting on the wall. "If the mode of analysis adopted in today's decision were to be generally followed," they warn, "prisoners eventually would be stripped of all constitutional rights, and would retain only those privileges that prison officials, in their 'informed discretion,' deigned to recognize."[16] That, in fact, is what occurs in decisions that follow *Jones.*

What could possibly justify such a broad assertion of powers? The crux in *Jones v. North Carolina Prisoners' Labor Union* comes down to the second argument, and it is about location. Prisons, it turns out, are not public places. Nor, for that matter, are they private places. When it comes to incarceration, the majority in *Jones* throws out the basic organizational rubric of Anglo-American legal understanding and protection offered since Sir William Blackstone's *Commentaries on the Laws of England* (1765–1769). Gone is Blackstone's insistence on a comprehensive working definition of the distinction to be kept between public and private spheres.[17]

Prisoners, by occupying neither zone of legal entitlements and protections, have no rights that might apply in either sphere. Civilization in itself has lost one of its definitions. Prisoners are left on their own. "A prison may be no more easily converted into a public forum than a military base," Justice Rehnquist argues. "Thus appellants [prison authorities] need *only* demonstrate a rational basis for their distinctions."[18] Only? The Court says it will not subject the abstract reasons given by authorities to serious scrutiny.

The logic of *Jones* specifies that the views of prison authority will conquer the rights of everyone under penal sway and that these views will win out against verified facts in the record of cases. "Since a prison is most emphatically not a 'public forum,'" Rehnquist asserts, "reasonable beliefs of appellants [the penal administration] are sufficient." It follows that "the District Court's further requirement of a demonstrable showing that the Union was in fact harmful is inconsistent with the deference federal courts should pay to the informed discretion of prison officials."[19]

Prisons are "most emphatically" not a public forum? Does saying it repeatedly and more firmly make it true? Shouldn't prisons be public places? They are the people's institutions. Openness to view and discussion could end abusive practices. As it is, penal authority can block any behavior in the incarcerated without a show of anything beyond potential harm, and in that process, they also block public perception of what is not a public place.

Against the Court's claims, realize that discussion, dialogue, mediation, and debate in any legitimate conflict always depend on *some* friction. It is the way institutions and groups of people work together and improve. Arbitration begins with strategies worked out and adopted in an acceptable private sphere. Only then does discussion move into the public sphere, where conflict might arrive at a solution. Negotiation of any kind is invariably a two-step process.

Jones v. North Carolina Prisoners' Labor Union stands in the way of a theory of punishment based on more transparency between punisher and punished, but its logic is fragile through the contextual basis it claims. Prisons *are* public spaces. Rules and regulations apply with public consequences, and the lack of accountability of officialdom in them does not keep them from being small cities with movement in and out. The interstice created between public and private spheres leaves a legal void, a hole in which law degenerates into nothing more than the imposition of authority.

"Tyranny" is not too strong a term to apply to the consequences. Collectivities exist in penal institutions, but they have no voice. In chapter 3 we saw that people robbed of voice drop out of humanity. Lost is "the talking animal," and the implications should be clear. The only way prisoners can protest terrible treatment from those in authority over them today is by putting their physical bodies on the line, as many prisoners in California prisons did together in 2013 by going on a dangerous sixty-day hunger strike.[20]

What were the prisoners' requests in the hunger strike? Reasonableness presided. They wanted the elimination of group punishments for individual violations, a more realistic policy on gangs, compliance with the U.S. Commission on Safety and Abuse over conditions in long-term solitary confinement, adequate food, and more constructive programs and minimal privileges for those held in solitary. At the time, hundreds had been held in extreme solitary for a decade or more. Should people in prison have had to risk their lives to get a decent hearing for their requests?[21] Unions may be barred to prisoners by legal declaration; the joint right to speak to authority should not be.

What would it require to overcome professional and communal fear of a collective voice from the incarcerated when they have serious grievances that anyone should recognize? In *Jones,* Justice Rehnquist alludes to that fear. He accepts without question the "apprehensive" stance of prison authorities. All evidence put to one side, authorities can legitimately fear "a power bloc within the inmate population which could be utilized to cause work slowdowns or stoppages or other undesirable concerted activity."[22] The vocabulary used here is telling. "A bloc," relying on cold war terminology, can also be a communal resource instead of a power grab. What if those prison work conditions are truly intolerable? That has happened in prison after prison.

Rehnquist recognizes only "undesirable concerted activity." Prisons, he declares, "are populated, involuntarily, by people who have been found to have violated one or more of the criminal laws established by society for its orderly governance."[23] The remark is technically accurate. People in prison "have been found" to have broken the law. But the rhetorical stance and placement of the statement imply much more. We are to see an entire population ready to commit more crime and eager to challenge orderly governance if allowed to speak.

Nothing could be more inaccurate. Most prisoners want everything in a facility to run smoothly. Life is much safer for them that way. Rehnquist's countering projection should be seen for what it is: a gratuitous play on communal apprehensions. *Jones v. North Carolina Prisoners' Labor Union* lets speculation run wild in order to keep thought away from the real problem at hand. When, if ever, should a prison population be able to question the unfair treatment it receives?

An Act of Imagination

Just about everyone takes for granted that violent criminals should be locked away to keep them from harming more people. So far so good. Still, much of what we take for granted contains uncertainties when pursued beyond the surfaces in opinion. Just how much and under what conditions should criminals be locked up, and for how long? These questions spawn more problematic answers, and it is here that an act of imagination, as opposed to the prevailing kernel of self-evidence, deserves consideration.

Self-evidence has the problem of relying on what the self already knows. Imagination reaches beyond the information already processed.[24] To engage in "a thought experiment" beyond accepted views about crime and punishment requires a mental leap, and that leap must entertain an unseen but possibly better future.[25] Somewhere in generations to come our progeny may look back on the hostility and cruelty we not only tolerated but encouraged in today's prisons with amazement, shame, and even contempt. Far-fetched? Not if you realize that nineteenth-century slavery has had that effect on current generations.

It helps that practical contingencies are ripe for a different kind of thinking. In 2015, Governor Dannel Malloy launched a series of initiatives that are turning prisons in Connecticut into "reintegration centers," with new education programs to fight recidivism. Also on the table are less harsh laws for juvenile offenders and minor drug charges. Reform of the unfair state bail and parole systems with more emphasis on community supervision instead of incarceration is another part of his plan. Malloy's goal is to turn Connecticut into a "Second Chance Society," and there is a payoff in sight. "Overall, crime in Connecticut is at a 48-year low and falling faster than almost anywhere in the country."[26]

Such reforms would have been unthinkable a decade ago. In 2014, when the governor of New York proposed a plan for college courses for prisoners, the project floundered under an avalanche of political mockery about "kids before cons." By 2016, after sustained coverage of prison abuse, this same governor, Andrew Cuomo, has been able to earmark millions of dollars for college programs, with matching funds coming from private sources. Other elected officials have quickly agreed with him. Proposed programs for the education of prisoners have suddenly become "just really common sense."[27] Again in reaction, in July 2015, the U.S. Department of Education announced a return to grants for prisoners' education with the Second Chance Pell Pilot program.[28]

In the search for another way, everything depends on the questions that you are willing to ask against the unpleasant manifestations in all of punishment. Orpheus, you will recall, asks Hades to choose between a return of life for his wife against an untimely death right there for himself, and it makes everyone present reconsider what they are doing. A moment of imagination transforms Roman ruthlessness about fate into mercy.

Forget for a moment the wrangling over prisoners' rights and ask yourself a deeper set of questions with imagination at the ready. Just how much equality should a person sacrifice when entering prison? Most rights are routinely stripped away during incarceration, and that is generally understood and accepted. Equality, in contrast, is a residual category that we are never presumed to lose and are supposed to remember in dealing with each other. Everyone, it is said, is equal before the law, and it is a claim beyond aspiration. The integrity of law depends on it. Why else would the Supreme Court insist that anyone put to death feel the least possible amount of pain?[29]

Now compare the question about equality to a reality at work against the presumption. Faced today with constant contempt and abuse by his handlers, a long-time prisoner can come to a starkly different conclusion. "Most people," he says, "take it for granted that they are human." In prison, "you realize that being human isn't a birthright." If not a birthright? That means it can be taken away from you and has been.[30]

Add a related question. How must we regard others when they are under our control?[31] Prisoners are routinely denied minimal consideration and ownership over themselves in the battle zone that prison culture establishes. They belong to a special category of conflict and vulnerability associated with the denial of identity. The best naming of that category comes in a description of fascist tyranny: "complaints do not exist where they cannot be made."[32]

Consider the plight of an elderly, sick prisoner in a federal prison who had fallen asleep and "failed to stand count" immediately in a sloppily run afternoon roll call. He quickly identifies himself and does everything possible with the officer still present to verify his presence. His assigned punishment in 2015—this for a man incarcerated for a number of years without a single infraction—came to ninety days of lost telephone and commissary privileges and loss of a valued two-man rooming arrangement. His appeals fell on deaf ears.[33]

Or absorb the following, an exercise to force testimony against another prisoner. In February 2013 in the open courtyard of the far northern New York state Bare Hill Correctional Facility, ten men were made to take off their coats, hats, and gloves in 5 to 10 degree weather and forced to clasp their bare hands on the chain-link fence behind them for between fifteen minutes (according to authorities) and thirty to forty-five minutes (in reports from the men). Either way, it was long enough for all of the men to suffer serious frostbite; some were hospitalized.

How were formal grievances dismissed and quickly forgotten at Bare Hill? The men had suffered. That could not be denied, but officially they were said to have suffered through "failure to properly dress for the weather." One angry thwarted complainer would confirm the reality by sending an envelope full of dead skin from his injured fingers to his lawyer, who published photographs of it.[34]

Only colossal levels of mean-spiritedness can explain these two incidents. Think again about the deeper questions just asked. "How much equality does one sacrifice in prison?" "How must we regard others under our control?" Both questions should get the same response if taken seriously. They turn on a belief in inviolability. Philosophers from Immanuel Kant to John Rawls have insisted that a moral sense requires that you put yourself in the other person's shoes in acceptance of the mutual opportunity for integrity that life gives to each of us.

What is at stake in failing to answer these questions? We have given birth to a system where the elements of human status and recognition of elemental need can be removed. Penal behavior, as currently understood, lacks basic consideration. If we respond by summoning worthiness and empathy, what must they entail? They insist on a reciprocity in feeling and understanding, and there can be no positive contact without them. Nor can anyone insist on his or her own worth without a voice to respond when that worth is challenged. There must be the capacity to assert, "I am standing here, and you who hold power over me can ease the unnecessary part in my predicament."

Better exchange, really very different exchange, is therefore the key to a new theory of punishment. To be well understood is the gift in human intelligence. Martin Buber's theory of "I and Thou" insists that "all real living is meeting." "Existence cannot be possessed, but only shared in." "Where there is no sharing there is no reality." Only through meaningful dialogue, "the sphere of 'between,'" can existence reach "an 'essential We.'"[35] Marianne Constable makes the same point in a legal context.[36]

Obviously exchange can complicate matters instead of easing them. Ability to share understanding defines us and makes for elementary social cohesion. Just as often its mechanics separate us, and for painful reasons. For truly the most difficult art in conversation has less to do with speaking than with listening well, the much harder talent to develop. One must, in theories of dialogue, be willing "to listen to the voice of the other and to suspend all pre-determined categories and concepts that one may have of the other." Even trickier, you have to be receptive to change by what you have heard.[37]

Three serious handicaps prevent us from listening well, and they are worth remembering because no one overcomes them completely. First, observing without evaluating is a very difficult thing to do, but it is the means to overcoming the other two difficulties. Second, it is very hard to know what another person is feeling. Many people are not in touch with their feelings, and have difficulty in articulating them. The vulnerabilities involved stop them and us. Third, it is that much harder to feel empathy for someone in an adversarial relationship despite the fact that empathy is the essential tool for understanding another person.[38]

In a prison setting, these three handicaps must be very consciously met. In the censorious atmosphere, full of negative evaluation and hostility, that permeates incarceration, prisoners and correction officers prove equally reluctant to show their feelings. Everyone hides behind a mask that tries to say, "I feel nothing." Everywhere in the oven of incarceration, strident smaller demands disguise colossal needs or hopes that the possessor cannot bear to face.

Given a more ideal prison setting, these negative behavior patterns would still be hard to adjust. Hard but not impossible. One of the stronger traits in human nature is adaptability, and when everyone is knowingly miserable over where they are and what they are doing, the opportunity for change is real. It is where penology must go if it is to clean up the waste and cruelty in current punishment regimes.

To communicate is "to make something common." Dialogue as communication involves "something new, which may not have been in the starting point at all. It's something creative. And this shared meaning is the 'glue' or 'cement' that holds people and societies together."[39] The word "dialogue" has two roots: *dia,* which means "through," and *logos,* or "the word"; hence, "discovery through use of the word." Dialogue with a purpose adds the notion of inquiry, and in the alienation of prison culture, inquiry has no choice but to focus on "the basic tenet . . . that if people are not engaged, there must be a reason."[40]

Penal dialogue tries to find voices previously unheard in combination with those that are heard. Typical groupings in prison dialogues involve between fifteen and twenty people. The necessity for such a method depends on the further assumption "that cultural change can be brought about only when everyone is involved." Full participation is not just about "voice" either. "There is something essentially human about face-to-face communication between people, and only a small part of the meaning of what is communicated is carried by the bare words."[41]

The simplest demonstrations of respect succeed because of the sincerity they instill—a sincerity that most people in prison instinctively yearn for once they get past a suspicion that is justified. Sincerity is what is missing from their environment. In the words of one expert in "prison dialogue," "my practice in the prison was based on respect. Because I offered respect, it opened the door for people to be genuine, and as they were genuine they got listened to."[42]

Those who work with dialogue in prisons also argue that being listened to can spark personal involvement in the many who have not been listened to. "The future of imprisonment," if it is to change, must take place through the development of such exchanges. Those who work in this area agree that "American corrections must transform itself from the inside out." *This* is what is meant by metamorphosis.[43]

Is it still difficult to accept that imagination is a tool to correct corrections? Stop for a moment and realize where we are. Our extant policies are not without a journey into their own fantasy land. We are warehousing people in prison for years without attention to their development, and we then expect them to emerge as law-abiding citizens. The arrangement, if it can be called that, couples a ludicrous agenda to no plan at all. Don't let the status quo define practicality when it comes to prison culture. Current policies hide the fairy tale in law enforcement.

Corrections as Communication

Believing in the role of imagination is one thing. A realistic worry has to be our other guide. For if language is the source of all accommodation, it provides every rationale for violence and then justifies violence after the fact. That is what now happens in prison culture. Time and again, accommodation and justification come limping after.

A pithy comment can direct us. "Symbolic power," writes the sociologist Pierre Bourdieu, "is a power to create things with words." Bourdieu couches this thought within the larger capacity of "making a new group." That group then has "the power granted to those who have obtained sufficient recognition to be in a position to impose recognition." Bourdieu wants to know "on what conditions a symbolic power can become a power of constitution," which means "keeping" while also "transforming." These comments go to the very definition of metamorphosis.[44]

Better language and a full understanding of its purposes can start to transform penology in reform-minded groups if those groups can present a cohesive agenda for larger recognition. Success, if it is to come, will depend on detailed study of penal tactics and reactions to them rather than high theory. The answers do not lie in hollowed-out legal mechanics so much as in the dynamics of articulation that control group behavior.

The human race is the only animal with a comprehensive vocabulary, and the only one that will physically and mentally torment its own species for prolonged periods of time. Speech allows an extraordinary range of human relations. Moving from the negative to the positive will take a lot of effort. Currently, prison discourse is entirely negative, characterizing the incarcerated as unacceptable in civilized society.

We can begin to reach for an architectonics of reform by proceeding from manners. André Comte-Sponville's impressive treatise on Western ethical tradition gives an account that surprises most readers. The first virtue he lists, before all others, is "politeness," and his explanation resonates. "Politeness comes before the other virtues in the sense that it serves as a foundation for the moral development of the individual."[45]

Civility builds the accomplished adult. "Morality is like a politeness of the soul, an essential etiquette of the inner life, a code of duties, a ceremonial of the essential." It comes first, before all other virtues, because it exists in a temporal rather than a cardinal frame of reference, but that does not deride its importance. Politeness is the "small thing that paves the way for great things." Psychologically, politeness makes someone externally what they really should be. It holds us to a higher standard of ourselves. Emphasis on "a code of duties"—reaching back to doing one's duty no matter what—is especially noteworthy here. Courtesy invokes restraint, and restraint is what is currently lacking in prison culture.

Translating these high-sounding terms into a prison context is not as difficult as may appear. For starters, no person in authority in corrections should ever swear or use vulgar expletives. Profanity, except in the rare circumstance of mutual humor, is aggressive, hurtful, full of anger, and demeaning for the recipient of it. Professional people never use it in their assigned obligations, and eliminating it should be part of the professionalization of correction officer units. A curse welcomes a similar return. It is one of the most powerful catalysts in hostility, a form of microaggression that no professional wants to encourage.

Laughter greeted this suggestion against potty-mouthed talk when I presented it to a large academic audience, but when I asked who used profanity in the classroom, no one in a crowded room raised a hand. The proverb holds on this score: "A soft answer turneth away wrath" and "grievous words stir up anger."[46] Prisoners are already reflexively angry. Why on earth should anyone want to make them angrier? The whole idea in corrections is to get people to rise above their former modes of behavior, and the point can include formality in speech.

A careful, accurate application in language enhances self-discipline and the ability to show respect. Used well, it is a sign of strength, not weakness. Profanity, in contrast, projects a loss of emotional control. Eliminating it can improve any organization, including a professional football team where streams of invective and vituperation are as frequent as breathing.[47] Curse words never describe the situation at hand; they are boilerplate for emphasis. In a correction officer, the right use of language is proof of professional standing and a good way to avoid being drawn into prison demeanor.

Three admonitions from a study of nonviolent language can carry us further. First, "the key ingredient of empathy is presence." Second, "there is considerably less violence in cultures where people think in terms of human needs than in cultures where people label one another as 'good' or 'bad.'" Third, "at the core of all anger is a need that is not being fulfilled."[48] Each point applies with special intensity in prison culture.

We have seen that stark separations in communication between punisher and punished breed a lack of understanding and empathy. All prisoners should have a more-or-less private conversation with someone in authority twice a week. If this requires upper echelons in prison authority to engage in frontline operations, all the better. Think of the benefits. Prisoners become persons who know someone cares, or at least listens. The wall against communication built by "a snitch mentality" falters if it doesn't fall. The possibilities for adjustment in unnecessary and irritating policies triple. Real conversation eliminates trivializing tendencies. It is a way to be heard.

There are other benefits in opening the lines of communication. Authorities will be able to distinguish idiosyncratic crotchets ("I don't like the soap") from serious complaints ("Shining a strobe light in our faces at 3 a.m. is not necessary").[49] The idea of a responsible collective voice can begin to take hold through these conversations. Authorities might not fear a collective voice if the practice of regular communication enables group conversations.

One exchange does not a conversation make. Barriers come down only through gradual and earned recognition. Sooner or later, however, even deeply alienated prisoners will realize they are missing an opportunity. To get one's view across is to assert one's human status. Patience in this process will be a difficult virtue, and it must begin with those in power. Sincerity in the moment of exchange is a necessity for the longer-range goal of authenticity, the truth with time behind it. One can be sincere by believing what one says even if it is not true. Authenticity is that long-range check on truth. Only the test of many conversations reaches that higher goal.[50]

For similar reasons, one can expect less violence if the assumption of "badness" gets assigned to specific action instead of becoming a lumped category in which all present are assumed to be bad all of the time. When a correction officer tells a prisoner that something is wrong, the accusation should be in concrete terms and not as a wholesale condemnation or a withering put-down. If we add that anger grows out of needs not met, the reason why those needs cannot be met should be explicit. Deliberately ignoring a simple request, a frequent prison guard ploy, should not be acceptable practice in a correction officer.

A reasonable need that can be met should be met. Prison mattresses are notoriously thin and ill-fitting on very hard bunks. When a well-behaved sixty-seven-year-old prisoner with back problems takes an extra pillow to ease his pain, the decision to send the designated culprit to the SHU (special housing unit for delinquents) is gratuitous and counterproductive. The better response to a reasonable need lets a person safely request and receive a second pillow or hear the reason why not.[51] Better yet, general recognition might lead to more comfortable mattresses.[52]

Translated into psychological terms, current policies rely on aversive stimuli and do little to provide fulfilling stimuli. The imbalance can best be understood through a familiar domestic lesson. When children learn not to put a hand on a hot radiator or stove, the experience teaches them to stay away from both but not how to get heat when necessary or how to cook; that requires a different kind of fulfilling stimulus. A lesson with a radiator valve or a decision to bake bread together under supervision will be more effective.[53]

Consigning a prisoner to a tougher unit for taking an extra pillow represents an aversive stimulus without the possibility of fulfillment. It blocks the right to make a reasonable request for fear of punishment, and it takes away a vestige of the right to appear human.[54] If you multiply that mentality a thousandfold, you have the make-up that controls prison behavior on all sides.

There is a better answer for the truly professional correction officer. "To be beneficent where one can is a duty"—literally, "the highest of all." A stickler for retributive punishment like Immanuel Kant could still insist with such words that this duty extend to those in prison. Prisoners could not be shunned. They deserved full connection through "the dignity of humanity in another person."[55] "Good will" through reason is Kant's available engine for reaching universally toward the recognition and care of others. He calls it the one "good without qualification." There is no other. "Good will" alone "has its full value in itself." It is absolute because it thrives on its desire for the reciprocities and affinities available.[56]

One does not have to be a philosopher to see this much. Thirty men in the maximum-security wing of the Jessup Correctional Institution in Maryland recently came up with pretty much the same thing by stressing the goal of meaningful growth over stasis during corrections. The mechanism to that transformation would again be good will. "It mattered greatly, several said, to have someone who cares." With good will anything was possible. "The enlightened prison, we concluded, would embody the following five core attitudes: *hope, growth, recognition of merit, individuality,* and *community.*"[57]

Good will can even claim to be the route to right language. How much can be accomplished by common courtesy, sincere exchange, and attention to minimal needs in a context of such general discomfort? It is time to find out, particularly since transformations in the language used can be done and monitored immediately. Sincerity cannot be measured. Improper and inconsiderate address can be. Identifying vile language requires no judgment call; it is a simple matter of overhearing the words, and if that language is corrected, it will promote the look and, in time, the presence of sincerity.

Value over Ruin

Of course, good language and consideration are never going to be enough. Think of them as first planks in a general platform. The thought and hence the behavior behind language are our real goals. Listen to the renowned psychologist Steven Pinker on how we think. "Human characterizations of reality are built out of a recognizable inventory of thoughts." We can adjust that inventory to the obligations that duty places on behavior. Obligations work through the frequent exercise of common norms: "acting, going, changing, being, having."[58] The common norm in an architectonics of reform is within reach: call it *value over ruin*—the well-being, personal and common, that communal engagement seeks.

Adjustments of this kind, value over ruin, can lead to an incorporated sense of responsibility. However hidden, prisons exist as one of the foundational institutions in modern society, and their sheltered nature and rapid expansion away from public scrutiny have become serious problems for the body politic. In the common philosophical understanding of a democratic republic, writes the philosopher of equality Thomas Nagel, "we are responsible through the institutions which require our support, for the things they could have prevented as well as for the things they actively cause."[59]

Accept a new structure in attitudes that begins with correct language and courteous treatment. They can help guide in the heightened professionalism that will be required for broader reform. Many other recommendations have been made in the course of these pages. The task here is to pull them together in a framework, a sequence of viable changes that allow correctional facilities to adjust themselves to what is needed. Incremental change will encourage larger transformations.

There will be plenty of resistance. Habit and established interests control institutions, and the low standards for becoming a correction officer and the political nature of higher-level appointments reinforce the status quo in prison culture. Metamorphosis does not occur without some discomfort and bewilderment. Change will also require outside investment with internal cooperation from authorities in corrections, a change in habitat, as it were. Appointments at the highest echelons of correctional facilities will have to demand this spirit of cooperation and general well-being instead of business as usual.

What might be the best sequence for transformation? Who will set the new standard? First and foremost, with new thoughts about actual punishment in mind, those involved in prosecution and sentencing must involve themselves more in corrections. Presentencing report officers, prosecutors, defense counsel, and judges all need to follow the people they imprison into the shadows of incarceration. The judicial branch, from the lowest to the highest, must know more about prison culture and its impact on those who are held in the state's name.

Involving these legal actors could aid in later prison reviews of the sentenced. Presentencing officers will learn more about the range in sentencing, their trade. Prosecutors who become involved should feel less pressure to keep conviction levels up and to never admit an error.[60] Defense counsel have their own special obligation to follow a client further; they supply the part of the legal process that objected to the sentencing arrangement in the first place and would still have corroborating evidence to offer. Washing one's official hands at the moment of sentencing leaves the person convicted without representation in a system where individual voices are silenced and a collective voice is forbidden.

Judges should follow the person they have sentenced for additional reasons. They are in a position to protest in a way that will be listened to both in and out of the system. They can claim, as no other can, "this is not what I meant to happen through the sentence I handed down." A federal district court judge recently urged the possibility of "a second look" at those in prison. So many people are in prison much longer than common sense dictates that a sentencing judge may indeed want to see what has transpired in a sentence that has proven to be much longer than necessary.

How is a judge on the spot supposed to gauge whether an expression of remorse during sentencing—standard practice in a defendant—accurately reflects the person's decision to overcome a criminal past? It cannot be done, and it is telling that the judge in question had to visit a prisoner after prolonged incarceration to find out. Federal district court judge Stefan R. Underhill, on the bench since 1999, used his visit to recommend "a mechanism for judges to re-evaluate the sentences they've imposed." Only the sentencer can know whether a defendant got a break or fell under mandatory minimums and tough sentencing guidelines.[61]

Controls will be essential against manipulation and possible intimidation, and Judge Underhill suggests some. "Second-look review" for early release would allow a single opportunity based on a warden's recommendation, a clean disciplinary record, completion of relevant training, vocational readiness, health circumstances, and outside support. Judge Underhill wants "second-look review" for another reason. After sitting on the bench for more than seventeen years, he has no faith in programs of "compassionate release" or in parole systems to accomplish the purposes he has outlined. They haven't worked. Think, as well, of the incentives this attention might give to a reform-minded prisoner. An architectonics of reform depends on a viable instillation of prisoner cooperation.

For any of these professional involvements to succeed in assisting a metamorphosis to a better system, judges will need independent monitors in correction facilities to help them collect evidence when it is relevant. In response to the classic question asked earlier "Who will watch the watchers?" prison hierarchies have exhibited a marked inability to control the behavior of frontline officers under their command. Nor have they handled legitimate grievances fairly. Outside monitors trained in penology will be necessary.

Until safeguarding watchers or monitors can be arranged, judges and other officials in the sentencing process will have to use their clerks and interns to monitor prisoner grievances directly. Depending on volume, special courts to deal with penal obfuscation or procedural avoidance might be necessary. The implementation of more comprehensive video and sonar surveillance systems should aid this process. In the meantime, no correction officer should be allowed to discipline a prisoner in an area beyond the reach of current surveillance mechanisms.

I have previously argued, in keeping with surveillance mechanisms, for more beneficial, careful, and moderate uses of technology. Technology alienates when it does not help and when it is not understood well. It should never be used as a substitute for personal contact.

The greatest stumbling block will take time and care to remove. The professionalization of prison guards into correction officers is long overdue and an absolute necessity. Nobody can be expected to handle the pressures of such a multifaceted and vexed position based on the current stipulation of six weeks or two months of instruction. Correction officer academies prepare their students through tough boot camps and mostly for combat readiness. Prison administrations then reinforce these negative lessons by placing their newest recruits, people without union seniority, in the worst possible environments.

"Correction officer" has been an honored position in the facilities of other nations, where officers "fill both rehabilitative and security roles" and each prisoner has an experienced "contact officer."[62] That is not the case in the United States. Proper training, care, and professionalization are the answers to this problem, and there are no others. What would such an education look like? Once again Steven Pinker's observations are useful. "The goal of education is to make up for the shortcomings in our instinctive ways of thinking about the physical and social world."[63] Acting through instinct presents a proven danger in the negative impulses of punishment, and it works at cross purposes where nuanced social understanding is required.

It follows that education succeeds, again from Pinker, "not by trying to implant abstract statements in empty minds but by taking the mental models that are our standard equipment, applying them to new subjects in selective analogies, and assembling them into new and more sophisticated combinations." Concreteness from out of the familiar is again important, but it needs new applications. The sophisticated combinations called for in corrections should center on the ability to develop a lawful life in others.

If, as claimed earlier, a person should never be a permanent punisher, correction officers must be trained for several things at the same time. After more careful applicant screening, a program should involve a two-year plan covered by the state. You get what you pay for. The importance of training in professional language, restraint, patience, accurate reporting, personal relations, and willing exchange have already been covered. All of these skills have the added advantage of preparing a successful recruit for other positions in government after a required term of service. There are parallels in the military academies of the country.

Physical control procedures must still be taught to penal staff, but violent responses from an officer have to be made a last rather than a first resort and must be as limited as possible without incurring personal injury. Further punishment in prison should also be a last resort, and again limited in time and scope. Correction officers should be schooled to think of themselves as civil servants on a trajectory toward other governmental work. The limit in frontline corrections should be ten years at most. Punishment, by its very nature, is an odious function. No one should be allowed to grow fond of it or even comfortable in applying it.

Correction officer unions will fight these changes, but not continuously if they are properly urged and rewarded. These are dangerous positions to fill and, as in the armed services, there should be regular periods of rest and recuperation with pay for people who work in corrections. Recovery periods can be a valuable source of additional training. Scheduled time away from prison management should go to further education in the art of generating a law-abiding life in others.

Correction officer unions should want to help. They have elected leaders with public functions. Political enablers must expose those union leaders who stand in the way of eliminating proven violence in jails and prisons.[64] Union contracts currently allow officers to refuse to answer questions from investigators. Those contracts also give final say on dismissal to arbitrators rather than to a corrections commissioner. All too often an abusive officer is reinstated after an investigation finds fault.[65]

Many incidents of brutality illustrate that there is a serious challenge to be met here. One such incident can suffice on the question of professionalism. When a New York City correction officer repeatedly hit a prisoner over the head with his radio, causing fractures to an eye socket and nose as well as serious cuts to the face, the head of the New York City Officers' Benevolent Association, Norman Seabrook, wanted to know "why *an otherwise exemplary officer and military veteran* would respond in that way."[66]

Is being a military veteran relevant other than to praise the correction officer? And how could one possibly see such an officer as exemplary? The attacker used his radio out of convenience. It allowed him to protect his hands while doing as much damage as possible in the knowledge that penal authorities would come up with another radio and that the event itself would be routinely denied. This one could not be. The attacking officer's mistake? A video camera recorded the attack this time, and it showed two other correction officers trying to restrain their companion.

Unions should be given the chance to clean up the corrupt product they now turn out in the recognition that corruption and ignorance go together. If they remain uninterested in better educational arrangements and penal reform, they must be made to ensure improvement and compliance. Union obstructionism over proven cases of mistreatment is a frequent problem.

Disciplinary systems are "so stacked in the union's favor that a guard could be found guilty of brutalizing an inmate and not be fired."[67]

Since 2010 New York state efforts to dismiss thirty prison guards accused through clear evidence of abusing prisoners prevailed only eight times because of "a convoluted arbitration process that is required under the union contract."[68] Everywhere in the country the political clout of unions and provisions of qualified immunity blunt most charges of abuse against prison guards.[69]

The negative consequences of failure are in front of us on a weekly basis. How bad does corruption get in the rank and file when union leaders do everything they can to protect their memberships from accountability? In the Rikers Island jail complex in New York City, twenty-six department employees were arrested on contraband charges between 2014 and early 2016, despite guard knowledge of "a highly publicized campaign to tighten security."[70] Prosecutors subsequently found that kickbacks, bribes, and contraband involving rogue guards created a "climate of danger and fear" throughout the penal system.[71]

Corruption rarely confines itself to one level in an organization completely oriented to its own self-interest and to defense of its illegal behavior. In June 2016, after a rare open-and-shut conviction of five correction officers for abuse of a prisoner by a jury in front of a packed audience of other correction officers, union leader Norman Seabrook called the verdict "an absolute travesty." All correction officers had been "disrespected." A day later, Seabrook was himself indicted on fraud charges related to a kickback scheme using union funds for his own enrichment.[72]

Take one last example, on February 6, 2016, when the second officer in less than a week was arrested for bringing drugs into the Rikers Island complex. The officer admitted to having sexual relations in a jailhouse closet with, as she claimed, the only inmate to whom she gave drugs. When questioned, her explanations for these offenses revealed fathoms of unprofessional understanding. "I thought I was falling in love" vied, on the one hand, with her excuse about the time spent in the closet, on the other. "It only lasted five minutes," she said, during which everyone else was held in lockdown.[73]

Records across the country show that most contraband—including drugs and weapons as well as most initial instigations of violence and intimidation—flow into jails and prisons through corrupt prison guards. These offenders need to be identified, fired, and replaced with honest, better-trained employees. Until that happens, independent monitors should inspect every officer who enters a prison or jail facility, with dismissal the immediate consequence for smuggling. Drugs are a primary source of conflict among prisoners, and a medical source of frustration in dealing with addiction.

Structure with a path is the key to an architectonics of reform. Right now stagnation and fatalism reign in an atmosphere of futility. Prisoners criticize correction officers most consistently for not caring about what they are doing, and there is plenty of corroborating evidence.[74] Introducing a spirit of development and engagement can supply the vitality and approachability currently missing. All institutions require initiative to engineer a better product, and here the product is more successful human lives.

I have argued that education is the best answer against so many returns to prison. With everyone in a penal authority geared toward success in some way, correctional facilities can transform lives and begin to live up to their name. Better tiered systems in training based on attainment levels are required. More people will want to work in prison education if there are better achievement rates coupled to technological innovations that encourage responsiveness. An educated person looks for ways to improve a situation.

If the tragedy of mass incarceration can be reduced, there is no reason why prison facilities should not be more comfortable places. Well-being must again be the gauge. A spirit of development includes the duty to improve. Extra comforts and opportunities—better rooming conditions, freer access to certain facilities, better work options, more group meetings, more contact electronically—can be significant incentives for prisoners to progress through educational and other improvement programs.

Grave problem areas are not going to go away. What is to be done with the unreachable, the violent, the gang affiliated, and the mentally ill, all of whom bring their own measure of chaos to prison culture? Part of structure is more knowing compartmentalization. Identifying distinct areas, screening them, and separating them as much as possible for expert counseling and treatment would be a start instead of lumping everyone together as part of a common problem. The idea of care depends on the acceptance of individuality.[75]

Some will see these last recommendations as an evasion, but over time most prisoners are not unreachable, or violent, or committed to further gang activity if positive reinforcements are offered. The reasonable people in prison—the ones who can be reasoned with—want to get out, and everything should be done to help them develop responsibly with that possibility in mind.

Mental illness falls into a separate category. It should be understood as an *illness for treatment in getting better* rather than as a project in tactical control through medication. Physicians and their interns, not correction officers, should diagnose these problems in separate facilities that have instilled an appropriate professional atmosphere.

It goes without saying that the negative categories just mentioned should never be assigned permanent status. An effective theory of corrections applies to everyone within a facility. Prisoners should not be permanently assigned a label such as incorrigible, and this applies just as firmly to people who will never be able to leave a facility. Some people cannot be helped; most can be. People grow in some way whatever is done to them. The plan must be to keep that growth from twisting against itself or others.

Will there be added expense? That depends on how much cooperation can accomplish in facilities where there is now none and where so much manpower must be given to constant negative surveillance. Mass incarceration is expensive. "The law of diminishing marginal benefits applies to incarcerating additional people or adding years to sentences."[76] The cost in change depends on whether we can turn static warehouses into working communities where cooperation rather than resistance guides behavior.

The idealism at the heart of these suggestions is real, but no one can claim that either the ideals or the specific suggestions behind them would be out of place in a prison environment oriented to lawful behavior and respect for human nature. Remember our two controlling questions, and let them be abiding ones. First, "how much equality should a person sacrifice when entering prison?" The answer has to be none. Second, "how must we regard the interests of others in our control over them?" The answer this time says, with care. Honestly asked, both questions steer us toward different understandings in punishment. An architectonics of reform can succeed with these kinds of understanding.

Why It Is So Important to Get There

Prisons are at best a primitive answer to the ailments that beset society. Logic demands that they be used sparingly. But our incarceration practices have gone far beyond logic in two ways: First, the size of penal restriction is unmanageable; the United States now has the largest number of people in prison in the world. Second, the excessive cruelty found everywhere in American punishment regimes is unsustainable. These manifestations have created a powder keg that will explode if not answered. Patterns in prison riots are already an indicator.[77]

Critics can argue this is not a problem but a condition. Prisons are one of the first necessary institutions in any civilization, and by design they have never been appealing to those forced to inhabit them. True enough, but current conditions have become an acknowledged problem, and that problem has evolved into a crisis waiting to be solved. Movement along that continuum—from condition to problem to crisis—occurs when interventions begin to define a new reality.[78]

Four such interventions have changed the picture in the first decades of the twenty-first century. Facts have revealed that minority populations have been targeted and now form an incongruous majority in prison populations. This is a social scandal that will not go away. At the same time, overcrowding in correctional facilities has created intolerable conditions and eliminated the semblance of meaningful programs for the imprisoned. That is one reason why recidivism rates continue to hover above 60 percent. Third, the explosion in the number of women in prison is so far out of line with the rest of the world as to be a cultural aberration. Finally, the cruelty in incarceration, often with racial accents, has received dramatic verification through the publicized deaths of prisoners under official control. Cameras are part of that verification. Through electronic surveillance that cannot be dismissed, everyone now knows that prisoners are subjected to the unchecked rage of frustrated prison guards who are not held accountable for their actions.

Is this how we want to be thought of and remembered as a people? The shame in recognition can be pushed away only so far, and only if you are quite certain that you and all of those you care about will never find themselves in prison. That certainty should be shaken by the continuing spread of drug addiction, with related crime factors in middle-class and all youth segments of the culture. Geographically, there is a corresponding spread of crime into rural and suburban communities as well as the poor sections of cities. If not before, we are now in this problem together.

Punishment will always be called for against criminal behavior, but how much punishment for what kind of crime? Almost any felony under existing laws—with more laws on the way in every session of a legislature—will ruin a good life just beginning or one near the edge of uncertainties or dependent on limited means.[79] Prisons must be understood for what they have become and what they produce: more serious felons.

Other dangers are harder to see, but they are there. The size and behavior patterns in control of incarceration are a submerged cancer metastasizing into the rest of American society. Any tattooed youngster on the streets in poorly fitting pants and unlaced shoes reproduces the style of prison culture. For generations of young teens in ghetto neighborhoods, a recent study proves "the penal system has largely replaced the educational system as the key setting of young adulthood." Prison, not an unavailable job, becomes the measure of who is a man.[80] Maybe so, but countless families are wrecked by current incarceration rates.

Really at stake is how we want to think of ourselves with others. Innovations in thoughtfulness depend on adjustments in the boundaries of value networks that define comfort zones. Institutions, by the very success of their presence, the status quo, block us from seeing as far as we should and allow us to live with limitations and commonplaces that lead toward failure without our realizing it until it is upon us.[81]

Putting people in prison is a failure if it does not lead to correction, and there is plenty of evidence to prove the point. One prisoner facing that dead end writes about it in an acutely moving way. Paralyzed by utter despair, her declared worthlessness, and a long sentence, she decided out of desperation that "with all this 'me time' on my hands it was time to do some work. Time to take a long and painful look at myself," and she adds, from hindsight, that it was not "an endeavor for the faint of heart." In pride over her lonely attempt, she would also conclude "real help is not readily available." No, it isn't, but it should be.[82]

Without that help, most people in prison are going to fail, and that awareness should yield a "painful look" of our own. Improvement as well as retribution is a human reflex. Which one are we ready to emphasize? The problems reach well beyond mass incarceration. How long will we tolerate an intrinsic malice and endemic cruelty at all levels in our penal institutions—levels that we would not tolerate anywhere else?

Law can show us in ways that it hasn't. One of the best comments on turning legal aspiration into reality comes from the law-educated poet Archibald MacLeish. "The business of law," he wrote in the *Harvard Law Review,* "is to make sense of the confusion of what we call human life—to reduce it to order but at the same time to give it possibility, scope, even dignity."[83] Possibility, scope, and dignity are the virtues—really the necessities—currently missing in our carceral understandings. We can do something about it if we want to.

Coda: Being in Prison

IN NOVEMBER 2014, I was asked to speak at the projected January graduation ceremony of prisoners who would receive their college degrees at the Fishkill Correctional Institution in conjunction with programs run by Nyack College in upstate New York. Graduation oratory is all about telling people to apply what they have learned in the world. What do you say to people who are not going out in the world and who must remain right where they are? My wife and I—she accompanied me—discussed this problem at some length.

Anyone who visits even the best parts of the inside of a prison feels some claustrophobia. The only unlocked or permanently opened doors are on toilet or inspection stalls. You must be "let in" everywhere you go. You have been stripped of all of your possessions—wallets, money, keys, travel tickets, identification cards, prescriptions, and everything else of value—and you already have been told what not to wear, including certain colors, high-heeled shoes, underwire bras, and jewelry of any kind. You are completely in the hands of somewhat reluctant officials who must guarantee your identity when it is questioned, and that occurs frequently.

The families of those to receive diplomas were already gathered around tables in a long, narrow reception room without windows. The warden and other luminaries sat behind a podium. The graduating class was to file in at the last minute in their caps and gowns. While waiting, I learned from the families that many had come from a great distance, and most had not seen these sons, grandsons, husbands, fathers, and nephews in many years. I was also told that they would only have a short meal with their graduate after the ceremony. Some had come from as far as Florida. I therefore cut my remarks in half to make sure there would be as much time as possible for them. Relatives are always proud of a graduate, but the pride and joy shown here came to another level. Graduation meant that someone who had been disgraced and whom they loved had turned himself around.

After the ceremony, my wife and I mixed with the families. It was a pleasant time under the clear pressure of another kind of time, with correction officers waiting by the locked doors. The valedictorian of the class came up to me and said sadly, "I am the black sheep of my family." He had done well at the podium and I told him so. I then added, "There are no black sheep; only sheep. You owe no one an apology after what you have accomplished here."

As we ate with the graduates and their families, one of them said, "I haven't had a piece of lemon meringue pie in ten years." Making small talk, I suggested it was nice of the facility to provide such a meal. Still wearing his gown over shirt and tie, this man fixed me with a look and said, "Administrative tangles were too much for that. We paid for the meal ourselves!" So there you have it. The hope and the hopelessness of prison life all bound together.

I've never had a more attentive audience. My address, if it can be called that, is printed below. I spoke from notes but have it in this final form because the graduates asked for a copy and later printed and distributed it as a pamphlet. I've not changed a word as I remember it. Like my intention for this book, I want these words to help the people in prison, some of whom will never leave it.

Fishkill Correctional Institution, January 22, 2015
Six Ways in Which Education Can Be Immediately Useful

It is a pleasure to be with you here today, and I know time right now is short even though time weighs daily on your hands. Your families wait to be with you, so my remarks will be brief but heartfelt. I have organized them around six ways in which the education you have just completed can be immediately useful to you in ways that you might not have thought about or recognized. My goal is to get you to think about that.

I. The More You Know, the More You Realize You Don't Know. Your education should teach you to keep learning, to thirst for further understanding of the things you know. Instead of being intimidated by feelings of not understanding, you are now part of an engagement with thought. With your degree, you should be able to build a meaningful reading program along intellectual interests that you have established. That will keep you mentally involved and curious about the world and its ways. One famous definition of an educated person is one who can spend time alone in a room well.

II. Recognizing What You Don't Know Is a Social Tool. In the law, we call this *docta ignorantia*, or learned ignorance. It realizes that everyone makes mistakes through the limitations that bind all of us in, and that, in consequence, no one should be quite so certain in judging another or in accepting definition through a mistake made. *Docta ignorantia* contains, in other words, mercy and toleration. Law does not recognize mercy as a formal concept, but that is no reason why those involved in it cannot show mercy to one another. If you grasp how fallible we all are, you are better equipped to understand why someone is showing you intolerance, anger, despair, or hostility. Education, in this sense, should make you humble without defeating you. It teaches you about the world all around you.

III. Education Is Self-Knowledge. Most of you have been grappling with the reasons why you are here and undoubtedly have regrets on that score. It takes a lot for anyone to really take serious stock of the self, and it is much harder if you have to recognize some vital and very public failures. Many of you will have come from difficult backgrounds with perhaps little or not enough early help. You begin to realize why you did what you did, but it is also very easy to feel victimized by this. Self-knowledge reminds you that "I did this to myself and must find a way to change that." One knowledge that education brings is self-comprehension. You learn to examine yourself through the examples that literature, history, philosophy, sociology, science, and psychology give you. You develop the tools that explain behavior in anyone but most certainly in yourself. Reading becomes a way to live many lives at once and to make your own more interesting.

IV. Education Is Also About Learning to Write Well. I cannot emphasize this enough from the many letters I have received from people in prison. I believe that it isn't really an idea until you have written it down. Writing is the realization of thought. Writing well opens avenues to others. We are social animals, a difficulty when you are too close to others but also far away from a listening audience. Writing to your family or even to a stranger on the outside is one of the greatest satisfactions that my correspondents from prison always mention. It is a skill like any other, and you get better with practice. Mastering it is a lifelong challenge but also an adventure. Leaving a record of who you are is one of the things that defines a human being, particularly in relation to others who know you or who need to know you in a different way. Be a letter writer. Find an ideal correspondent.

V. Education Is Self-Improvement. We either develop or we decline. There is no middle ground in human life. Prison has a stasis, a lack of momentum that must be fought against. The satisfaction in living comes in getting better at doing something. We are made to achieve. When that is taken away from us, we lose ourselves. You have time on your hands and must find a way to lift that burden. Engagement with knowledge, the development of a skill, the advance of the mind are what education brings to you no matter where you are.

VI. Education Is a Place of Its Own. All of you would prefer to be somewhere else, and one of my hopes is that it will be possible for all of you, but it will not happen for some, and it can take far too long for many others. Education is your guard against this despair. The mind, often a torment, is also a sanctuary. Your education is your own place. It is a room that can become a house. The knowledge you build into the room can become a house that reaches the many other houses that have gone before you. It is knowledge that holds us all together as a community across time. As you think, so others before you have thought, and people who come after will recognize you through that commonality. This kind of house has no race, no inequality, no class distinctions, no time limits, no restrictions. It is what you make of it. It is the resting place that will never let you down.

You have just been officially credentialed with a degree that says you can be the master of all six of these forms of mental endeavor. Your job now is to make them continuously valid by expanding on the implications of each of them. Your education is one of the few things in life where the harder you work at it, the easier it will get.

Don't let yourself down. Others who are here are very proud of what you have accomplished, and I have been honored to be able to represent you today. The really hard part comes now. What's next? What is next is your continuing adventure in making yourself better than you were. You are, in my view, ideally equipped for this even in circumstances that are not the best. Why? You have the best of educations because it has been the hardest to obtain, and you therefore know the value of it, not in the world, but to yourself and your families.

NOTES

Introduction

1. The United States has the largest prison population in the world. At the end of 2013, 6,899,000 adults in the country lived under the formal supervision of the criminal justice system through probation, parole, prison, and jail. Of those, 1,574,700 were in state or federal prisons with 215,000 in federal prisons and roughly another 730,000 in jails where circulation is hard to tabulate. Twelve million people cycled through jails in the United States in 2013. See David Brown, Chris Cunneen, Melanie Schwartz, Julie Stubbs, and Courtney Yount, *Justice Reinvestment: Winding Back Imprisonment* (New York: Palgrave Macmillan, 2016), 19–21.
2. *Oxford English Dictionary*, s.v. "metamorphosis": "The action or process of changing in form, shape, or substance."
3. William James, "Pragmatism" (1907), in *Pragmatism and Four Essays from The Meaning of Truth* (New York: Meridian, 1955), 51–52.
4. George Orwell, "Politics and the English Language" (1945), in *George Orwell: Essays*, ed. John Carey (New York: Knopf, 2002), 964.
5. Albert O. Hirschman, "Two Hundred Years of Reactionary Rhetoric," in *The Rhetoric of Reaction: Perversity, Futility, Jeopardy* (Cambridge: Harvard University Press, 1991), 2–8.
6. David J. Rothman, *The Discovery of the Asylum: Social Order and Disorder in the New Republic* (1971), rev. ed. (New Brunswick, N.J.: Aldine Transaction, 2008), 78–79, 83, 294–295.
7. I paraphrase from John W. Kingdon, *Agendas, Alternatives, and Public Policies,* updated 2nd ed. (Boston: Longman, 2011), 3–19, 109.
8. Alan Feuer, "Judge Calls for End to 'Madness of Mass Incarceration,' " *New York Times* (June 24, 2016), A22.

9. Barack Obama, "Remarks by the President After Visit at El Reno Federal Correctional Institution" (White House, Office of the Press Secretary, July 16, 2015).
10. Martin Luther King Jr., "Letter from Birmingham Jail," in *Why We Can't Wait* (New York: New American Library, 1964), 94–95. Prison Letters, 2014–2017, in author's possession.
11. Alice Goffman, *On the Run: Fugitive Life in an American City* (New York: Farrar, Straus and Giroux, 2014), xiii, 3.
12. See Francis X. Clines, "Tough Matriarch, Easy Touch, and Good Listener; Women Doing Hard Time Find a Warden with Her Own Way of Keeping the Lid On," *New York Times* (April 24, 1993), www.nytimes.com/1993/04/24/nyregion/tough-matriarch-easy-touch-good-listener-women-doing-hard-time-find-warden-with.html?mcubz=3. Additional information comes from someone who spent a lot of time in Bedford Hills.
13. Dr. Robert Jay Lifton, quoted in "Letters to the Editor," *New York Times* (December 17, 2014), A30.
14. Orwell, "Politics and the English Language," 954.
15. The *Oxford English Dictionary* defines "cruelty" in these ways.
16. I paraphrase from Michael Anteby, *Manufacturing Morals: The Values of Silence in Business School Education* (Chicago: University of Chicago Press, 2013), 7–9.
17. Matthew 7:12, and Robert Axelrod, *The Evolution of Cooperation*, rev. ed. (New York: Basic, 1984), viii, 20, 202–205.
18. Winnie Hu and Kate Pastor, "Trial of 5 Rikers Guards Brings out Culture of Violence at Jail," *New York Times* (June 19, 2016), A17.
19. Edmund Burke, "The First Letter on a Regicide Peace" (1796), in *Edmund Burke: Revolutionary Writings: Reflections on the Revolution in France and the First Letter on a Regicide Peace*, ed. Ian Hampsher-Monk (Cambridge: Cambridge University Press, 2014), 310.
20. I paraphrase from Stuart Firestein, *Ignorance: How It Drives Science* (New York: Oxford University Press, 2012), 11.

Chapter 1. The Linguistic Tangle in Treatment of the Incarcerated

1. For negative treatment in court, see Nicole Gonzalez Van Cleve, *Crook County: Racism and Injustice in America's Largest Criminal Court* (Stanford: Stanford University Press, 2016).
2. Prison Letters, 2014–2017, in author's possession. I change enough of the circumstances to protect the identity of the source.
3. Prison Letters, 2014–2017. When a correction officer behaves correctly that term or C.O. is used to describe the person. Where there is unprofessional behavior, I use the term "guard."
4. Prison Letters, 2014–2017.
5. Timothy Williams, "Panel to Set Terms to End Abusive Reign to Los Angeles County Jail System," *New York Times* (December 17, 2014), A18.
6. Williams, "Panel to Set Terms," A18.

7. *Webster's Third New International Dictionary of the English Language Unabridged* and *Oxford English Dictionary*, s.v. "inmate."
8. Williams, "Panel to Set Terms," A18.
9. On prison grievances, see Kitty Calavita and Valerie Jenness, *Appealing to Justice: Prisoner Grievances, Rights, and Carceral Logic* (Berkeley: University of California Press, 2015).
10. Aldous Huxley, "Speech Delivered at the Albert Hall, London, 1936," quoted in *In a Dark Time*, ed. Robert Jay Lifton and Nicholas Humphrey (Cambridge: Harvard University Press, 1984), 10.
11. Winnie Hu and Kate Pastor, "5 Rikers Officers Convicted in Beating of Inmate," *New York Times* (June 8, 2016), A16.
12. Michelle Alexander, *The New Jim Crow: Mass Incarceration in the Age of Colorblindness*, rev. ed. (New York: New Press, 2012).
13. Michael B. Beverley, "A Perspective on Prison," in *Fourth City: Essays from the Prison in America*, ed. Doran Larson (East Lansing: Michigan State University Press, 2013), 27.
14. "You are not to expect any thing, either in this or any other case, further than the practice have established them into habit." Locke, *Some Thoughts on Education* in *The Works of John Locke in Nine Volumes*, 12th ed. (London: C. and J. Rivington, 1824), 8:13.
15. For the legal definitions, see *Black's Law Dictionary*, 6th ed. (St. Paul, Minn.: West, 1990), 958, and Jack N. Rakove, ed., *The Annotated U.S. Constitution and Declaration of Independence* (Cambridge: Harvard University Press, 2009), 238–240.
16. *Black's Law Dictionary*, 1234. See as well, In re Kemmler, 136 U.S. 436 (1889); Coker v. Georgia, 433 U.S. 584 (1977); Holt v. Sarver, D.C. Ark., 309 F. Supp. 362 (1970); Jackson v. Bishop, 404 F. 2d. 571 (1968); and Furman v. Georgia, 408 U.S. 238 (1972).
17. Harmelin v. Michigan, 501 U.S. 957 (1991) at 957, 994.
18. Furman v. Georgia, 408 U.S. at 281. Emphasis added.
19. Montaigne, "Of Cruelty," in *The Complete Essays of Montaigne*, trans. Donald M. Frame (Stanford: Stanford University Press, 1958), 313, 316, 311.
20. William Blake, "A Divine Image," in *English Romantic Writers*, ed. David Perkins (New York: Harcourt, Brace & World, 1967), 65.
21. Furman v. Georgia, 408 U.S. at 376.
22. *Oxford English Dictionary*, s.v. "malice."
23. Matheny v. United States, 469 F.3d 1093 (7th Cir. 2006), at 1097.
24. Jendusa-Nicolai v. Larsen, 677 F.3d 320 (7th Cir. 2012), at 322–324.
25. United States v. Delaney, No. 12–2849 (7th Cir. 2013), 5, 9; Rollin M. Perkins, "A Re-examination of Malice Aforethought," *Yale Law Journal* 43 (February 1934): 537–570 at 570.
26. Farmer v. Brennan, 114 S.Ct. 1970 (1994) at 1972–1973, 1977–1979. Emphasis added. See, as well, Robert A. Ferguson, *Inferno: An Anatomy of American Punishment* (Cambridge: Harvard University Press, 2014), 153–155.

27. Farmer v. Brennan, 114 S.Ct. at 1978–1979.
28. Estelle v. Gamble, 429 U.S. 97 (1976) at 105.
29. Helling v. McKinney, 509 U.S. 25 (1993).
30. Huxley, "Speech Delivered at the Albert Hall," 10.
31. Michael Schwirtz and Michael Winerip, "Head of Jails Is Criticized on Violence at Rikers," *New York Times* (October 9, 2014), A27, A32.
32. Aristotle, *The Politics and the Constitution of Athens,* ed. Stephen Everson, trans. Jonathan Barnes (Cambridge: Cambridge University Press, 1996), 163–164, 184 (6.8.1-11:1322a; 7.13.10:1332a); Aristotle, *Nicomachean Ethics,* 2nd ed., trans. Terence Irwin (Indianapolis: Hackett, 1999), 73 (5.4.6:1132a). See, as well, W. D. Ross, "Politics," in *Aristotle: A Complete Exposition of His Works and Thoughts* (New York: Meridian, 1959), 242.
33. Charles-Louis de Secondat, Baron de Montesquieu, *The Spirit of the Laws,* trans. Thomas Nugent, 2 vols. (New York: Hafner, 1949), 81–82 (1.6.9).

Chapter 2. Do Americans Like to Punish?

1. "A Living Death: Life Without Parole for Nonviolent Offenses" (New York: American Civil Liberties Foundation, 2013), 4–5.
2. James Q. Whitman, *Harsh Justice: Criminal Punishment and the Widening Divide Between America and Europe* (Oxford: Oxford University Press, 2003), 12–13, 55, 92–95, 196, 207. See also Charles-Louis de Secondat, Baron De Montesquieu, *The Spirit of the Laws,* trans. Thomas Nugent, 2 vols. (New York: Hafner, 1949), 1:223 (6.21).
3. See Robert A. Ferguson, "The Role of Mercy in Legal Discourse," in *Merciful Judgments and Contemporary Society,* ed. Austin Sarat (Cambridge: Cambridge University Press, 2012), 19–82.
4. See Austin Sarat, *Knowing the Suffering of Others: Legal Perspectives on Pain and Its Meaning* (Tuscaloosa: University of Alabama Press, 2014), 1–13.
5. Whitman, *Harsh Justice,* 38.
6. Whitman, *Harsh Justice,* 206–207.
7. Franklin E. Zimring, Gordon Hawkins, and Sam Kamin, *Punishment and Democracy: Three Strikes and You're Out in California* (New York: Oxford University Press, 2001), 202.
8. Andrew E. Taslitz, "The Criminal Republic: Democratic Breakdown as a Cause of Mass Incarceration," *Ohio State Journal of Criminal Law* 9 (Fall 2011): 133–193.
9. For the most extended debate over retribution, see Jeffrie C. Murphy and Jean Hampton, *Forgiveness and Mercy* (Cambridge: Cambridge University Press, 1988), 65, 119, 129.
10. Drew Leder and the Jessup Correctional Institution Scholars, "The Enlightened Prison," in *The Beautiful Prison,* ed. Austin Sarat, special issue of *Studies in Law, Politics, and Society* 64 (2014): 28.
11. Meghan J. Ryan, "Finality and Rehabilitation," *Wake Forest Journal of Law and Policy* 4 (2014): 121–149 at 122.

12. Katherine Beckett and Theodore Sasson, *The Politics of Injustice: Crime and Punishment in America* (Thousand Oaks, Calif.: Pine Forge Press, 2000), 186.
13. *Oxford English Dictionary*, s.v. "condemn."
14. Nigel Walker, *Why Punish?* (Oxford: Oxford University Press, 1991), 1–3.
15. Lon Fuller, *The Morality of Law*, rev. ed. (New Haven, Conn.: Yale University Press, 1969), 22–23.
16. Michael B. Beverley, "A Perspective on Prison," in *Fourth City: Essays from the Prison in America*, ed. Doran Larson (East Lansing: Michigan State University Press, 2014), 28.
17. Laron Ounce, *Correction Officer's Guide to Understanding Inmates* (Atlanta: Ga.: Ounce Publishing, 2012), 53.
18. Dean Faiello, "Impermanence," in Larson, *Fourth City: Essays from the Prison in America*, 81–84. Also Prison Letters, 2014–2017, in author's possession.
19. Prison Letters, 2014–2017.
20. Faiello, "Impermanence," 80.
21. Beverley, "Perspective on Prison," 26.
22. Beverley, "Perspective on Prison," 28.
23. Walton v. Tryon, 21 English Reports 262 (1753); repr., *English Reports*, vol. 21, *Chancery*, sec. 1 (London: Stevens & Sons, 1902), 262–263.
24. Arthur Schopenhauer, "Human Nature," in *Complete Essays of Schopenhauer*, trans. T. Bailey Saunders (New York: Wiley, 1942), 14–15.
25. Erving Goffman, *Stigma: Notes on the Management of Spoiled Identity* (New York: Simon & Schuster, 1986), 3, 5, 130.
26. Nigel Walker, *Punishment, Danger & Stigma: The Morality of Criminal Law* (New Jersey: Barnes & Noble Books, 1980), 155, 159.
27. Goffman, *Stigma*, 144, 70.
28. Goffman, *Stigma*, 101, 13.
29. Marla Pisciotta, "Former Potomac Center Workers Arrested," *State Journal* (December 16, 2014), www.statejournal.com/story/27639376/former-potomac-center-workers-arrested; Pisciotta, "More Arrests Related to Potomac Center Abuse and Neglect of Charges," *State Journal* (December 22, 2014), www.statejournal.com/story/27685655/more-arrests-made-related-to-potomac-center-abuse-and-neglect-charges. For the prisoner's words, see James Ridgeway, "The Overseer," *Mother Jones* (July/August 2011), 51.
30. United States Attorney, Southern District of New York, "CRIPA: Investigation of the New York City Department of Correction Jails on Rikers Island" (August 4, 2014), 21.
31. "CRIPA Investigation of Rikers Island," 22–23.
32. David Brown, Chris Cunneen, Melanie Schwartz, Julie Stubbs, and Courtney Young, *Justice Reinvestment: Winding Back Imprisonment* (New York: Palgrave Macmillan, 2016), 31–36.
33. Nicole Flatow, "Supreme Court Justices Blast the Corrections System," *Think Progress* 24 (March 24, 2015), http://thinkprogress.org/Justice/2015/02/24/3637885/supreme-court-justices-implore-congress-reform-criminal-justice-system-not-humane/.

34. Baz Dreisinger, *Incarceration Nations: A Journey to Justice in Prisons Around the World* (New York: Other Press, 2016), 284.
35. Jim Dwyer, "Guards' Union Flexes Muscles in Albany," *New York* (December 19, 2014), A27. See Joshua Page, *The Toughest Beat: Politics, Punishment, and the Prison Officers Union in California* (New York: Oxford University Press, 2011).
36. Ronald Dworkin, *Religion Without God* (Cambridge, Mass.: Harvard University Press, 2013), 20; see also 15.

Chapter 3. Accounting for Unaccountability

1. Daniel Baraz, *Medieval Cruelty: Changing Perceptions, Late Antiquity to the Early Modern Period* (Ithaca, N.Y.: Cornell University Press, 2003), 11, 32, 45, 175–180.
2. In exile Ovid continues to work on "the unfinished" *Metamorphosis,* but it remains unfinished. He has been punished for "two sins," a poem and an error; no crime. Ovid, *Tristia,* trans. L. R. Lind (Athens: University of Georgia Press, 1975), 33, 52, and 34, 39 (6.63–64, 55–56, and 92, 207).
3. John C. Thibault, *The Mystery of Ovid's Exile* (Berkeley: University of California Press, 1964). For Ovid's protests, see *Tristia,* 33, 38 (2:43–52, 187–194).
4. L. R. Lind, introduction to *Tristia,* xiii. Lind indicates "the semi-legal nature" of book 2 of *Tristia,* or "sad poems."
5. Ovid, *Metamorphosis: A New Verse Translation,* trans. David Raeburn (New York: Penguin Books, 2004), 5. (1.18). Subsequent references in text. In book 2 of *Metamorphoses,* the earth itself warns how near "we are back to confusion and primal chaos" (2.298).
6. Robert Cover, "Nomos and Narrative," *Harvard Law Review* 4 (1983); repr. in *Narrative, Violence, and the Law,* ed. Martha Minow, Michael Ryan, and Austin Sarat (Ann Arbor: University of Michigan Press, 1992), 105, 112.
7. Deborah Sontag, "Push to End Prison Rapes Loses Earlier Momentum," *New York Times* (May 13, 2015), A16.
8. Sharona Coutts and Zoe Greenberg, "Women Incarcerated: Investigative Series Shows Systemic Abuse of Women in Prisons and Jails," *Prison Legal News* 26 (June 2015): 1–16; Victoria Law, "Reproductive Health Care in Women's Prisons 'Painful' and 'Traumatic,'" *Prison Legal News* 27 (March 2016): 26–28; Michael Singer, *Prison Rape: An American Institution?* (Santa Barbara, Calif.: Praeger, 2013).
9. Singer, *Prison Rape.*
10. Benjamin Weiner, "Female Inmates' Suit Says Sex Abuse Is Persistent in State Prisons," *New York Times* (February 26, 2016), A24. See, as well, "Women Behind Bars" (editorial), *New York Times* (November 30, 2015), A22; Chandra Bozelko, "Why We Let Prison Rape Go On," *New York Times* (April 18, 2015), A19. Bozelko gives the Bureaus of Justice Statistics on rape.
11. K. Balsley, "Truthseeking and Truthmaking in Ovid's *Metamorphosis,* I: 63–245," *Law & Literature* 23 (2011): 48–70.
12. Balsey, "Truthseeking and Truthmaking," 49, 57–59.

13. The story of Arachne is a "*mise en abyme* of the *Metamorphoses*, a 'miniature model' mirroring much of the poem's content and illuminating ways by which the narrative operates." Barbara Pavlock, *The Image of the Poet in Ovid's Metamorphoses* (Madison: University of Wisconsin Press, 2009), 3–7, 138–139n. See, as well, Patricia J. Johnson, "The Weaving Contest," *Ovid Before Exile: Art and Punishment in the Metamorphoses* (Madison: University of Wisconsin Press, 2008), 74–95.
14. Horace, *Epistles*, ii, 62.
15. Pilar Opazo, *Appetite for Innovation: Change and Creativity at elBulli* (New York: Columbia University Press, 2016).
16. Albert Camus, *Le mythe de Sisyphe* (1942), trans. and repr. as *The Myth of Sisyphus and Other Essays*, trans. Justin O'Brien (New York: Knopf, 1955), 120.
17. Cover, "Nomos and Narrative," 103.

Chapter 4. Rights Talk and the Enabling of Wrongs

1. Marshall, dissenting opinion in Jones v. North Carolina Prisoners' Labor Union, Inc., 433 U.S. 119, 139 (1977), quoting Ruffin v. Commonwealth, 62 Va. (21 Gratt.) 790, 796 (1871).
2. Michelle Alexander, *The New Jim Crow: Mass Incarceration in the Age of Colorblindness* (New York: New Press, 2010).
3. Margaret R. Somers, *Genealogies of Citizenship: Markets, Statelessness, and the Right to Have Rights* (New York: Cambridge University Press, 2008), 1, 25.
4. Ronald Dworkin, *Taking Rights Seriously* (Cambridge, Mass.: Harvard University Press, 1997), p. 198.
5. Mary Ann Glendon, *Rights Talk: The Impoverishment of Political Discourse* (New York: Free Press, 1991), x, xii, 9; Richard Thompson Ford, *Rights Gone Wrong: How Law Ignores Common Sense and Undermines Social Justice* (New York: Farrar, Straus and Giroux, 2011), esp. "Why Do Rights Go Wrong?" (pp. 18–31).
6. Mark Tushnet, "An Essay on Rights," *Texas Law Review* 62 (May 1984): 1371.
7. Alan C. Hutchinson and Patrick J. Monahan, "The 'Rights' Stuff: Roberto Ungar and Beyond," *Texas Law Review*, 62 (1984), 1483.
8. Tushnet, "Essay on Rights," 1373.
9. Michael J. Perry, "Taking Neither Rights-Talk nor the 'Critique of Rights' Too Seriously," *Texas Law Review* 62 (1984): 1409. See also Sharon Dolovich, "Cruelty, Prison Conditions, and the Eighth Amendment," *New York University Law Review* 84 (October 2009): 881–979.
10. William J. Stuntz, *The Collapse of American Criminal Justice* (Cambridge, Mass.: Harvard University Press, 2011), 68, 80, and generally 67–80.
11. Mary Douglas, *How Institutions Think* (Syracuse, N.Y.: Syracuse University Press, 1986), 63.
12. Turner v. Safley, 107 S.Ct. 2254 (1987). Subsequent citations in text. Citations to the earlier district (1984) and appellate decisions (1985) in notes below.
13. Thomas L. Haskell, ed., *The Authority of Experts: Studies in History and Theory* (Bloomington: Indiana University Press, 1984).

14. For the balance against the success of prisoner grievances, see Kitty Calavita and Valerie Jenness, *Appealing to Justice: Prisoner Grievances, Rights, and Carceral Logic* (Berkeley: University of California Press, 2015), esp. 111–115, on "the operational realities."
15. For the factual information, see Leonard Safley, et al., v. William R. Turner, et al. 586 F.Supp. 589 (1984).
16. Safley v. Turner, 586 F.Supp. at 589–590, 596.
17. Safley v. Turner, 586 F.Supp. at 591–593.
18. Safley v. Turner, 586 F.Supp. at 593, 590.
19. Virtually every prison letter that I receive raises this point. Prison Letters, 2014–2017, in author's possession.
20. Safley v. Turner, 586 F.Supp. at 590, 592–593.
21. See Safley v. Turner, 586 F.Supp. at 593.
22. Safley v. Turner, 586 F.Supp. at 597.
23. Safley v. Turner, 586 F.Supp. at 596–597.
24. Safley v. Turner, 777 F.2d. 1307 (8th Cir. 1985), at 1309–1310, 1315.
25. Safley v. Turner, 777 F.2d. at 1310, 1313, 1315–1316.
26. Procunier v. Martinez, 416 U.S. 396 (1974).
27. Emphasis added for purposes of identification.
28. Whitley v. Albers, 475 U.S. 312 (1986) at 313 and 318–326. The case involves careless and unnecessary use of force during a prison uprising.
29. Procunier v. Martinez, 416 U.S. at 405–406. Emphasis added.
30. Jones v. North Carolina Prisoners' Labor Union, Inc., 433 U.S. 119, denied the right of people in prison to organize collectively in protecting their rights. Bell v. Wolfish, 441 U.S. 520 (1979), sharply restricted inmates' receipt of hardback books.
31. O'Lone v. Estate of Shabazz, 107 S.Ct. 2400 (1987) at 2405. A qualified exception on *individual* religious rights comes much later in Holt v. Hobbs, 574 U.S. __ (2015). Penal authority wins when prisoners engage in collective action, not necessarily over a passive decision by a single prisoner.
32. See O'Lone v. Estate of Shabazz, 107 S.Ct. 2400 at 2408.
33. Barbara Belbot and Craig Hemmens, *The Legal Rights of the Convicted* (El Paso, Tex.: LFB, 2010), 59.
34. Thornburgh v. Abbott, 490 U.S. 401 (1989).
35. Overton v. Bazetta, 539 U.S. 126 (2003).
36. Shaw v. Murphy, 532 U.S. 223 (2001) at 229.
37. James E. Robertson, "The Rehnquist Court and The 'Turnerization' of Prisoners' Rights," *New York Law Review* 10 (2006): 97. See, as well, Washington v. Harper, 494 U.S. 210 (1991) at 224–225. Here the *Turner* test justifies the involuntary use of psychotropic medications on prisoners as a reasonable need in prison security). Shaw v. Murphy, 532 U.S. 223, finds no First Amendment free speech right to advise another prisoner.
38. Hudson v. Palmer, 468 U.S. 517 (1984). Subsequent citations in text.
39. Palmer v. Hudson 468 U.S. 517 (1983), "Joint Appendix," at 6, 18, 20, 22, 23.

40. Douglas, *How Institutions Think,* 49–50.
41. John F. Pfaff, *Locked In: The True Causes of Mass Incarceration—and How to Achieve Real Reform* (New York: Basic, 2017).
42. Brown, Governor of California, et al. v. Plata et al., 131 S.Ct. 1919 (2011). For hopeful analyses, see Margo Schlanger, "Plata v. Brown and Realignment: Jails, Prisons, Courts, and Politics," *Harvard Civil Rights–Civil Liberties Law Review* 18 (2013): 165ff, and Jonathan Simon, *Mass Incarceration on Trial: A Remarkable Court Decision and the Future of Prisons in America* (New York: New Press, 2014).
43. Brown v. Plata, 131 S.Ct. at 1924–1925, 1933–1934.
44. Brown v. Plata, 131 S.Ct. at 1933–1934.
45. Brown v. Plata, 131 S.Ct. at 1928.
46. Brown v. Plata, 131 S.Ct. at 1953 (Scalia dissenting).
47. Adam Liptak, "Justices Order California to Shed 30,000 Prisoners, *New York Times* (May 23, 2011), A1. See also, Brown v. Plata, 131 S.Ct. at 1968 (Alito dissenting).
48. Albert Sabbaté, "Overall California Crime Drops amid Prison Realignment" (January 9, 2013), http://abcnews.go.com/ABC_Univision/News/crime-drops-california-economy-early-release-inmates/story?id=18167411.
49. Brown v. Plata, 131 S.Ct. at 1950–1951 (Scalia dissenting).
50. Douglas, *How Institutions Think,* 19, 79.
51. Montgomery v. Louisiana, 577 U.S. __ (2016), at 3, 14 (majority opinion).
52. Montgomery v. Louisiana, 577 U.S. __ at 21, 3, 15–16.
53. Montgomery v. Louisiana, 577 U.S. __ at 21.
54. Dworkin, *Taking Rights Seriously,* 181; Richard A. Primus, *The American Language of Rights* (Cambridge: Cambridge University Press, 1999), 232–233.
55. Jeremy Waldron, "Dignity, Rights, and Responsibilities," NYU School of Law, Public Law Research Paper no. 10–83 (November 17, 2010), https://ssrn.com/abstract=1710759.
56. Martha Nussbaum, *Creating Capabilities: The Human Development Approach* (Cambridge, Mass.: Harvard University Press, 2011), p. 18ff.
57. Amartya Sen, "Well-Being, Agency, and Freedom: The Dewey Lectures 1984," *Journal of Philosophy* 82 (April 1985): 169–221.
58. For how deviance works, see Michel de Certeau, *The Practice of Everyday Life,* trans. Steven Rendall (Berkeley: University of California Press, 1984).
59. See Brett Dignam, "Learning to Counter Mass Incarceration," *Connecticut Law Review* 48 (May 2016): 1224–1227 ("Investment in Higher Education Pays Dividends").

Chapter 5. Sentencing the Disappearing Convict

1. Michael Tonry, "The Fragmentation of Sentencing and Corrections in America," *Sentencing and Corrections: Issues for the 21st Century* 1 (September 1999): 1, and generally 1–7. Judge Gerard Lynch writes, "So far, the federal guidelines have influenced state sentencing regimes mostly as a negative model and a distraction,"

in "Introduction: Sentencing: Learning from, and Worrying About the States," *Columbia Law Review* 105 (May 2005): 933.

2. United States v. Booker, 543 U.S. 220 (2005), at 225–226. "Stevens, J., delivered the opinion of the Court in part, in which Scalia, Souter, Thomas, and Ginsburg, JJ., joined. Breyer, J., delivered the opinion of the Court in part, in which Rehnquist, C.J. and O'Connor, Kennedy and Ginsburg, JJ., joined, *post* p. 244. Stevens, J. filed an opinion dissenting in part, in which Souter, J. joined, and in which Scalia, J., joined except for Part III and footnote 17, post, p. 272. Scalia, J., *post*, p. 303, and Thomas, J., *post* p. 313, filed opinions dissenting in part. Breyer, J., filed an opinion dissenting in part, in which Rehnquist, C.J., and O'Connor and Kennedy, JJ., joined, *post*, p. 326."
3. For the problems in *Booker*, see Nancy Gertner, "What Yogi Berra Teaches About Post-Booker Sentencing," *Yale Law Journal* 115 (August 5, 2006), Pocket Part 137, at www.yalelawjournal.org/forum/what-yogi-berra-teaches-about-post-booker-sentencing; Gertner, "A Short History of American Sentencing: Too Little Law, Too Much Law, or Just Right?" *Journal of Criminal Law and Criminology* 100 (2010): 691–708; and William W. Berry III, "Discretion Without Guidance: The Need to Give Meaning to §3353 After Booker and Its Progeny," *Connecticut Law Review* 40 (2008): 631ff.
4. United States v. Booker, 543 U.S. at 38–39.
5. Paul J. Hofer and Mark H. Allenbaugh, "Guideline Departure" in "The Reason Behind the Rules: Finding and Using the Philosophy of the Federal Sentencing Guidelines," *American Criminal Law Review* 40, no. 19 (2003): 84.
6. *Oxford Latin Dictionary* (New York: Oxford University Press, 2003), s.v. "sententia"; Jill Harries, "The *Queastio*-Statutes," *Law and Crime in the Roman World* (New York: Cambridge University Press, 2007), 16–21.
7. William J. Stuntz, *The Collapse of American Criminal Justice* (Cambridge, Mass.: Harvard University Press, 2011).
8. The observations that follow are based on fifty judicial sentences by federal judges and leading state judges.
9. J. L. Austin, *How to Do Things with Words*, 2nd ed., ed. F. O. Urmson and Marina Sbisà (Cambridge, Mass.: Harvard University Press, 1975), 4–7, 99–109.
10. Federal District Judge Katherine B. Forrest, "Transcript of Sentencing Proceedings," United States v. Vicente Rodriquez, S.D.N.Y. 15 Cr. 16 (March 11, 2015) (KBF), 29.
11. See "Sentencing Procedure," *Benchbook for U.S. District Court Judges*, 6th ed. (Washington, D.C.: Federal Judicial Center, 2013), 125–137.
12. For elaborate justifications of variations in sentencing after *Booker*, see Kimbrough v. United States, 552 U.S. 85 (2007), and Spears v. United States, 555 U.S 261 (2009).
13. "Sentencing Memorandum and Order of Rajat K. Gupta," United States v. Rajat Gupta, S.D.N.Y. 11 Cr. 907 (JSR) Docket no. 127 (October 24, 2012), at 1–2, 9, 14, and generally, 1–7. See, as well, Hon. Jed S. Rakoff, "Why the Sentencing Guidelines Should Be Scrapped," *Federal Sentencing Reporter* 26 (October, 2013): 6–9,

and Rakoff, "Why Innocent People Plead Guilty," *New York Review of Books* (November 20, 2014), 16–18.

14. Rakoff, "Why Innocent People Plead Guilty," 17.
15. Alex Kazinsky, "Preface to the 44th Annual Review of Criminal Procedure," *Georgetown Law Journal* 103 (2015): i, xi, and, more generally, xxii–xxvi.
16. Judge Robert P. Patterson Jr., "Transcript of Sentencing Proceedings," United States v. Marino Cruz-Gonzalez, S.D.N.Y. 14 Cr. 414 (RPP) (October 9, 2014), at 11, 18, 24–27.
17. Judge Denise Cote, "Transcript of Sentencing Proceedings," in United States v. Pena Pichardo, S.D.N.Y. 13 Cr. 172 (DLC) (January 9, 2014), at 18.
18. "Sentence," United States v. Faisal Shahzad, S.D.N.Y. 10 Cr. 1184 (MGC), 7; Stephanie Clifford, "U.S. Judges Questioning Harsh Justice in a New Era," *New York Times* (August 28, 2015), A10, A15.
19. "Sentencing," United States v. Gupta, S.D.N.Y. 11 Cr. 907 at 11.
20. 18 U.S.C. § 3553(a) (1) and (2).
21. United States v. Gupta, S.D.N.Y. 11 Cr. 907 at 13.
22. "Transcript of Sentencing Proceedings," People v. DeLoatch, Sup. Ct. Westchester County, Ind., no. 203/2013 (October 1, 2013), at 5.
23. "Transcript of Sentencing Proceedings," United States v. Boyd, S.D.N.Y 13 Cr. 890 (RPP) (January 8, 2015), at 27.
24. "Transcript of Proceedings," United States v. Barrett, S.D.N.Y. 13 Cr. 600 (WHA) (February 26, 2014), at 10, 11, 24; "Transcript of Sentencing Proceedings," United States v. Marinto Cruz-Gonzalez, S.D.N.Y. 14 Cr. 414 (RPP) (October 9, 2014), at 8–11.
25. Michael L. Owens, "Making the Case for Suicide," and Dortell Williams, "Making Sense out of Life Without the Possibility of Parole," both in *Too Cruel, Not Unusual Enough: An Anthology Published by the Other Death Penalty Project*, ed. Kenneth E. Hartman (Lancaster, Calif.: The Other Death Penalty Project, 2013), 5, 48.
26. "Sentence," United States v. Bernard L. Madoff, 9 Cr. 213 (DC) (June 29, 2009), 49–51.
27. "Sentence," United States v. Theodore Levy Freedman, S.D.N.Y, 11 Cr 599 (DAB) (September 17, 2013), at 3–5, 10–11, 13–14, 27–29. "Anything else that we can do to confuse this record any further?" Judge Deborah A. Batts concludes in exasperation with both counsel (26).
28. See Richard Weisman, "Towards a Constructionist Approach to the Study of Remorse," *Showing Remorse: Law and the Social Control of Emotion* (Surrey, Eng.: Ashgate, 2014), 1–21, and M. Catherine Gruber, *"I'm Sorry for What I've Done": The Language of Courtroom Apologies* (New York: Oxford University Press, 2014), 159–160.
29. "Sentence," United States v. John Fazio Jr., 11 Cr. 873 (KBF) (September 13, 2012), 67, 72, 74, 80–81, 85.
30. Justice Anthony Kennedy in Harmelin v. Michigan, 501 U.S. 957 (1991) at 998, 1001. Kennedy's strictness is worth quoting because of his later words regarding "deference" in Brown v. Plata, 563 U.S. (2011).

31. Harmelin v. Michigan, 501 U.S. at 994–995.
32. Hartman, *Too Cruel, Not Unusual Enough,* xxi, 66, 43, 156, 40.
33. John Simon, *Mass Incarceration on Trial: A Remarkable Court Decision and The Future of Prisons in America* (New York: New Press, 2014), 140, 144.
34. *Oxford English Dictionary,* s.v. "defer."
35. *Black's Law Dictionary,* 10th ed. (St. Paul, Minn.: West Group, 2014), 513–514, 1515. There is no entry for "deference" in the 6th through the 9th editions.
36. *Oxford English Dictionary,* s.v. "defer."
37. For one of the best articles on deference, see Thomas W. Merrill, "Judicial Deference to Executive Precedent," *Yale Law Journal* 101 (1992): 969, esp. 1032.
38. The other landmark opinion, 5 to 4, on health insurance is National Federation of Independent Business v. Sebelius, 576 U.S. __ (2012), 132 S.Ct. 2566.
39. Chevron U.S.A., Inc. v. Natural Resources Defense Council, Inc., 467 U.S. 837 (1984). For the standard work on judicial deference to administrative authority, see Harry T. Edwards and Linda A. Elliott, *Federal Courts Standards of Review: Apellate Court Review of District Court Decisions and Agency Action* (St. Paul, Minn.: Thomson/West, 2007), 137–186, esp. 155ff.
40. King et al. v. Burwell, Secretary of Health and Human Services, et al., 576 U.S. (2015) No. 14–114 (June 25, 2015), at 7–9, 15.
41. King v. Burwell, 576 U.S. at 8.
42. 417 U.S. 817 (1974).
43. 433 U.S. 119 (1977).
44. 452 U.S. 337 (1981).
45. 459 U.S. 460 (1983).
46. 468 U.S. 576 (1984); 468 U.S. 517 (1984).
47. 511 U.S. 825 (1994).
48. 538 U.S. 63 (2003).
49. Overton v. Bazzetta, 539 U.S 126 (2003).
50. Hon. Harold Baer Jr., with Arminda Bepko, "A Necessary and Proper Role for Federal Courts in Prison Reform: The *Benjamin v. Malcolm* Consent Decrees," *New York Law School Law Review* 52 (2007/2008): 4, 7–8, 64.
51. Richard A. Posner, *Reflections on Judging* (Cambridge, Mass.: Harvard University Press, 2013), 123. See, as well, Philip Hamburger, "Chevron Bias," *George Washington Law Review* 84 (September 2016): 1188–1251.
52. 18 U.S.C. § 3553(a), under "Title 18: Crimes and Criminal Procedure," restores the normative dimension to sentencing away from guideline point totals.
53. Even Louisiana, sometimes called the punishment capital of the United States, calls for regular "comprehensive review" of "the extent to which education, job training, and reentry preparation programs can both facilitate the readiness of inmates to transition into the community and reduce recidivism." La. Rev. Stat. Ann. §15,321(E)(4). Texas, another state with high incarceration rates, seeks "to prevent arbitrary or oppressive treatment of persons suspected, accused, or convicted of offenses." Tex. Penal Code Ann. §1.02(1)(5). Illinois indicates that "the purposes of this Code of Corrections are to . . . prevent arbitrary or oppressive

treatment of persons adjudicated offenders or delinquents; and restore offenders to useful citizenship." 730 Ill. Comp. Stat. Ann. 5/1-1-2(d). Alabama, another state with a harsh penal system, has as one of its "general purposes . . . to prevent arbitrary or oppressive treatment of persons accused or convicted of offenses." Ala. Code §13A-1-3 (6). Against the many examples of prison abuse in New York, N.Y. Penal Law §105(6) calls for "the rehabilitation of those convicted, the promotion of their successful and productive reentry and reintegration into society."

54. Miranda v. Arizona, 384 U.S. 436 (1966). See, as well, "Admissibility of Confessions," U.S.C. §3501(a)(b). For the Miranda warning under challenge, see Dickerson v. United States, 530 U.S. 428 (2000), and Charles D. Weisselberg, "Mourning *Miranda*," *California Law Review* 96 (December 2008): 1521–1601.
55. Michael J. Graetz and Linda Greenhouse, "Minimizing *Miranda*," in *The Burger Court and the Rise of the Judicial Right* (New York: Simon & Schuster, 2016), 43–46.
56. 42 U.S.C. §1997e (a)(e); 28 U.S.C. §1915 (b)(g).
57. See Margo Schlanger, "Trends in Prisoner Litigation as the PLRA Enters Adulthood," *Prison Legal News* 26 (October 2015): 1–15.

Chapter 6. The Technology of Confinement

1. See Jacques Ellul, *Le bluff technologique* (Paris: Hatchette, 1988) and *The Technological Bluff*, trans. Geoffrey W. Bromiley (Grand Rapids, Mich.: Eerdmans, 1990); Neil Postman, *Technopoly: The Surrender of Culture to Technology* (New York: Vintage, 1993), 20; John Pratt, *Punishment and Civilization: Penal Tolerance and Intolerance in Modern Society* (London: Sage, 2002), 121; Erving Goffman, *Asylums: Essays on the Social Situation of Mental Patients and Other Inmates* (Garden City, N.Y.: Anchor, 1961), 4–7, 23, 28, 48, 61–64; and Bernard Harcourt, "The Mortification of the Self," in *Exposed: Desire and Disobedience in the Digital Age* (Cambridge, Mass.: Harvard University Press, 2015), 224–225, and, more generally, 217–233.
2. Langdon Winner, *The Whale and the Reactor: A Search for Limits in an Age of High Technology* (Chicago: University of Chicago Press, 1986), 36.
3. Jürgen Habermas, *The Lure of Technology*, trans. Ciaran Cronin (Cambridge: Polity, 2015), 11–12.
4. Stephen C. Richards, ed., *The Marion Experiment: Long-Term Solitary Confinement and the Supermax Movement* (Carbondale: Southern Illinois University Press, 2015), viii, 2.
5. Erick Markowitz, "Chain Gang 2.0: If You Can't Afford This GPS Ankle Bracelet, You Get Thrown in Jail," *International Business Times* (September 21, 2015), www.ibtimes.com/chain-gang-20-if-you-cant-afford-gps-ankle-bracelet-you-get-thrown-jail-2065283; James Kilgore, "The Spread of Electronic Monitoring: No Quick Fix for Mass Incarceration," *Prison Legal News* 26 (April 2015): 22–24; James C. McKinley Jr., "State's Chief Judge, Citing 'Injustice,' Lays Out Plans to Alter Bail System," *New York Times* (October 2, 2015), A23.

6. Eric Markowitz, "Inside the Shadowy Business of Prison Phone Calls," *Prison Legal News* 26 (August 2015): 16–21; Matt Stroud and Joshua Brustein, "Expensive 'Prison Skype' Is Squeezing Out In-Prison Visitation," *Bloomberg News* (April, 27, 2015), www.bloomberg.com/news/articles/2015-04-27/expensive-prison-skype-is-squeezing-out-in-person-visitation.
7. Michael Ollove, "State Prisons Turn to Telemedicine to Improve Health and Save Money," *Stateline: The Pew Charitable Trusts: Research and Analysis* (January 21, 2016), www.pewtrusts.org/en/research-and-analysis/blogs/stateline/2016/01/21/state-prisons-turn-to-telemedicine-to-improve.
8. Jeremy Bentham, *Panopticon* (1787; repr., Middletown, Del.: Perfect Library, 2015), 5–9, 14.
9. Bentham, *Panopticon,* 16.
10. "Rikers Guard in Shiv Bust," *New York Post* (October 12, 2015), 13; Michael Schwirtz, "Report to Criticize City on Pace of Rikers Reform," *New York Times* (October 16, 2015), A28.
11. Bentham, *Panopticon,* 16.
12. Bentham, *Panopticon,* 1–13, 17–18, 25, 29, 30, 39.
13. Bentham, *Panopticon,* 53–54.
14. Nicholas Carr, "World and Screen," in *The Glass Cage: Automation and Us* (New York: Norton, 2014), 125–152, at 149, 219.
15. David Reutter, "Federal Court Orders Cameras to Cover Blind Spots at North Carolina Prison," *Prison Legal News* 26 (September 2015): 35.
16. Richard Jones, "Digital Rule: Punishment, Control, and Technology," *Punishment and Society* 2, no. 1 (2000): 8.
17. Ted Conover, *New Jack: Guarding Sing Sing* (New York: Random House, 2000), 282.
18. Sarah Glowa-Kollisch et al., "Data-Driven Human Rights: Using the Electronic Health Record to Promote Human Rights in Jail," *Health and Human Rights Journal* 16 (June 2014): 159–160; Ariel Ludvig et al., "Injury Surveillance in New York City Jails," *American Journal of Public Health* 102 (June 2012): 1108–1111.
19. Michael Winerip and Michael Schwirtz, "Family Files Suit in Prison Homicide as an Ex-Inmate Speaks Out," *New York Times* (September 10, 2015), A27. The *New York Times* "reviewed sworn affidavits and letters from 19 inmates" who witnessed the encounter.
20. Conover, *New Jack,* 282. It is common practice to kick a prisoner down stairs with his hands tightly handcuffed behind him. Prison Letters, 2014–2017, in author's possession.
21. David M. Reutter, "Florida's Department of Corrections: A Culture of Corruption, Abuse, and Deaths," *Prison Legal News* 27 (February 2016): 1, 8, 9; David M. Reutter and Rod L. Bower, "Widespread Corruption in L.A. County Jails Leads to Federal Investigation, Indictments," *Prison Legal News* 27 (February 2016): 5.
22. Lewis Mumford, *The Myth of the Machine* (New York: Harcourt, Brace & Jovanovich, 1970), 2:185–186; J. David Bolter, *Turing's Man: Western Culture in the*

Computer Age (Chapel Hill: University of North Carolina Press, 1984), 232–238. For the "technological imperative," see Nicholas Carr, *The Big Switch* (New York: Norton, 2013), 22.

23. Jeremy Bentham, *La théorie des peines et des récompenses* (1775), trans. and repr. as *The Rationale of Punishment*, ed. James T. McHugh (Amherst, N.Y.: Prometheus, 2009), 49, 97, 120, 127–128; Bentham, *Panopticon*, 10, 13, 18, 23–25, 31.
24. Prison Letters, 2014–2017.
25. Edward T. Hall, *The Hidden Dimension* (1966; repr., New York: Anchor, 1990), 1, 14, 51, 53, 57, 63, 104, 116–124, 172.
26. Barack Obama, "Remarks by the President After Visit at El Reno Federal Correctional Institution" (White House Office of the Press Secretary, July 16, 2015).
27. Daniel W. E. Holt, "Heat in US Prisons and Jails: Corrections and the Challenge of Climate Change" (New York: Sabin Center for Climate Change Law, Columbia Law School, 2015), i–iii, 5–6, 32–35, 89–90.
28. Conover, *New Jack*, 41.
29. Allan Turner, "Biometrics: Applying an Emerging Technology to Jails," in *Corrections Today* (Lanham, Md.: American Correctional Association, 2000), 1–2; "New Device Unveiled to Stop or Lessen Inmate Assaults: Assault Intervention Device (AID)," *Los Angeles Daily News*, August 20, 2010, www.dailynews.com/article/zz/20100820/NEWS/100829895.
30. The Prison Litigation and Reform Act (PLRA), with its "physical injury requirement," 42 U.S.C. § 1997e (e). See also Lorna A. Rhodes, *Total Confinement: Madness and Reason in the Maximum Security Prison* (Berkeley: University of California Press, 2004), 91–92.
31. Conover, *New Jack*, 92.
32. Robert B. Reich, "Big Tech Has Become Way Too Powerful," *New York Times* (September 20, 2015), SR3; Naomi R. Lamoreaux, *The Great Merger Movement in American Business, 1895–1904* (Cambridge: Cambridge University Press, 1985); Carlota Perez, *Technological Revolutions and Financial Capital: The Dynamics of Bubbles and Golden Ages* (Cheltenham, U.K.: Edward Elgar, 2002).
33. Alan Blinder, "Alabama Grapples with Fixing Prisons as Uprisings Occur," *New York Times* (March 16, 2016), A11–12; Richard Pérez-Peña, "Rampaging Inmates Kill 2 at a Nebraska Prison Described as Understaffed," *New York Times* (May 12, 2015), A13; Pérez-Peña, "Investigations into Deadly Nebraska Prison Riot Yields Few Answers," *New York Times* (May 13, 2015), A12; Jon Hurdle and Richard Pérez-Peña, "Delaware Prison Standoff Ends with Correction Officer Dead," *New York Times* (February 3, 2017), A9. There were ninety vacant correction officer positions in Delaware.
34. Pratt, "Bureaucratization and Indifference," in *Punishment and Civilization*, 121–144.
35. Max Weber, *The Protestant Ethic and the Spirit of Capitalism*, trans. Talcott Parsons (New York: Charles Scribner's Sons, 1958), 181; Weber, "Bureaucracy," in *Economy and Society: An Outline of Interpretive Sociology*, ed. Guenther Roth and Claus Wittich (Berkeley: University of California Press, 1978), 2:960, 973, 975, and more

generally 956–1005; Caroline Levine, *Forms: Whole, Rhythm, Hierarchy, Network* (Princeton: Princeton University Press, 2015), 97–104.

36. Peter B. Kraska and John J. Brent, eds., *Theorizing Criminal Justice: Eight Essential Orientations*, 2nd ed. (Long Grove, Ill.: Waveland, 2004), 195–197.
37. Weber, "Bureaucracy," 992.
38. See Barbara A. Owen, *The Reproduction of Social Control: A Study of Prison Workers at San Quentin* (New York: Praeger, 1988), 20, 106. Owen writes "at the upper levels of the hierarchy, concerns with prisoners are secondary to concerns over maintaining the status quo" (20).
39. William K. Rashbaum, "Guards Provoked Attack on State Inmate, Inquiry Finds," *New York Times* (January 8, 2016), A18.
40. Conover, *New Jack*, 77, 103, 140, 144.
41. Prison Letters, 2014–2017.
42. Prison Letters, 2014–2017.
43. Christopher Zoukis and Rod L. Bower, "Aramark's Correctional Food Services: Meals, Maggots, and Misconduct," *Prison Legal News* 26 (December 2015): 1–18. It is easier to sell food that does not reach proper standards to prisons than elsewhere in the market.
44. Chris Walsh, *Cowardice: A Brief History* (Princeton: Princeton University Press, 2014), 6–7, 100–130.
45. Mumford, *Myth of the Machine*, 200–201.
46. See Turner, "Biometrics," 1–2, and "New Device Unveiled."
47. Robin I. M. Dunbar, "Neocortex Size as a Constraint on Group Size in Primates," *Journal of Human Evolution* 22 (1992): 469–493; Malcom Gladwell, *The Tipping Point: How Little Things Make a Big Difference* (Boston: Little, Brown, 2000), 177–181, 185–186.
48. Michael Schwirtz, "Prosecutors Overwhelmed by Violence Cases from Rikers," *New York Times* (September 26, 2015), A23; Tom Robbins, "Abused Inmates, Strong Unions and Hard-to-Fire Prison Guards," *New York Times* (September 28, 2015), A1, A22.
49. Mumford, *Myth of the Machine*, 188–189, 228.
50. Captain M. B. Stewart, U.S. Army, *Military Character, Habit, Deportment, Courtesy, and Discipline* (Menasha, Wis.: George Banta, 1913), 58, 18.
51. Michael Huckabee, quoted in "Transcript: Read the Full Text of the Primetime Republican Debate," *Time* (August 6, 2015), http://time.com/3988276/republican-debate-transcript-full-text. See, as well, John H. Faris, "The Impact of Basic Combat Training: The Role of the Drill Sergeant," in *The Social Psychology of Military Service*, ed. Nancy L. Goldman and David R. Segal (Beverly Hills, Calif.: Sage, 1976), 14–18; *Handbook: Drill Sergeant* (Center for Army Lessons Learned, no. 09–12, January 2009), 6–8, 13, 16, 19; and https://info.publicintelligencenet/USArmy-DrillSergeant.pdf.
52. I paraphrase from Roberto Mangabeira Unger, *Passion: An Essay on Personality* (New York: Free Press, 1984), 193–196.
53. Conover, *New Jack*, 18, 30, 33, 86.

54. Conover, *New Jack,* 30.
55. Conover, *New Jack,* 160.
56. Conover, *New Jack,* 21, 213, 246, 248, 281, 285, 315.
57. For the isolation and distrust in correction officer work, see Owen, *Reproduction of Social Control,* 23, 38, 68, 84–85.
58. Conover, *New Jack,* 41.
59. Clayton M. Christensen, introduction to *The Innovator's Dilemma: The Revolutionary Book That Will Change the Way You Do Business* (New York: HarperCollins Business, 2011), xvi.
60. Perez, *Technological Revolutions and Financial Capital,* 8, 108.
61. Kraska and Brent, *Theorizing Criminal Justice,* 206–214, 217–230, 7–159; Joshua Page, "Monopolizing the Beat: The Fight Against Prison Privatization," in *The Toughest Beat: Politics, Punishment, and the Prison Officers Union in California* (New York: Oxford University Press, 2011), 137–159.
62. Christensen, *Innovator's Dilemma,* 259.
63. Arbinger Institute, "People or Objects" and "How to Use Leadership and Self-Deception," in *Leadership and Self-Deception: Getting out of the Box* (San Francisco: Berrett-Koehler, 2010), 42–49, 180–186.
64. Postman, *Technopoly,* xii, 52–55.
65. Prison Letters, 2014–2017.
66. Carr, *Glass Cage,* 232.
67. "Common commodities become contraband. . . . Seemingly innocuous objects, such as a toothbrush, can be turned into a deadly weapon. A tube of shampoo can be transformed into a syringe for injecting drugs." Owen, *Reproduction of Social Control,* 19.
68. Christensen, *Innovator's Dilemma,* 34–36.
69. Sherry Turkle, *Alone Together: Why We Expect More from Technology and Less from Each Other* (New York: Basic, 2011).
70. Gresham M. Sykes was the first to analyze the complicated need for prisoner cooperation in depth. See Sykes, "The Defects of Total Power," in *The Society of Captives: A Study of a Maximum Security Prison* (1958; rev. ed., Princeton: Princeton University Press, 2007), 52–62.
71. Roberto Mangabeira Unger, *Knowledge and Politics* (New York: Free Press, 1984), 249–262.
72. Michael Oakeshott, *On Human Conduct* (Oxford: Clarendon Press, 1990), 323–324.
73. Americans for Effective Law Enforcement, "Prisoners, Parolees, Sex Offenders, Computers and the Internet," parts 1 and 2, *Americans for Effective Law Enforcement Monthly Law Journal* 5 (2015): 301–309, 6 (2015): 301–309; Ben Branstetter, "The Case for Internet Access in Prisons," *Washington Post* (February 9, 2015), www.washingtonpost.com/news/the-intersect/wp/2015/02.09/the-case-for-internet-access-in-prisons/; Kimberley Railey, "Some Prisons Let Inmates Connect with Tablets," *USA Today* (August, 18, 2013), www.usatoday.com/story/news/nation/2013/08/17/tabletsforinmates/2651727/.

74. Kim Severson and Robbie Brown, "Outlawed, Cellphones Are Thriving in Prisons," *New York Times* (January 3, 2011), A12.

Chapter 7. Prison Talk

1. Michel Anteby, *Manufacturing Morals: The Values of Silence in Business School Education* (Chicago: University of Chicago Press, 2013), 7–9, 130.
2. Lorna A. Rhodes, *Total Confinement: Madness and Reason in the Maximum Security Prison* (Berkeley: University of California Press, 2004), 172, 54–55.
3. Joshua Page, *The Toughest Beat: Politics, Punishment, and the Prison Officers Union in California* (Oxford: Oxford University Press, 2011), 165–166.
4. Larone Koonce, *Correction Officer's Guide to Understanding Inmates* (Atlanta, Ga.: Koonce, 2012), 105–110, 206–208.
5. Ted Conover, *New Jack: Guarding Sing Sing* (New York: Vintage, 2001), 167. "Blood in/Blood out" also mandates that you slash someone to get in the gang and will be slashed if you try to get out.
6. David Skarbek, "What Works?" in *The Social Order of the Underworld: How Prison Gangs Govern the American Penal System* (New York: Oxford University Press, 2014), 157–162.
7. Koonce, *Correction Officer's Guide,* 112, but see *Oxford English Dictionary,* s.v. "bing." In modern American parlance "bing" is "slang: a solitary-confinement prison cell," and an exclamation: "They've hit you with something." See also *Webster's Third New International Dictionary,* s.v. "bing."
8. I take prison slang from Doran Larsen, ed., "Glossary," in *Fourth City: Essays from the Prison in America* (East Lansing: Michigan State University Press, 2013), 299–309, from published prison narratives, and from Prison Letters, 2014–2017, in author's possession.
9. Jean Casella, James Ridgeway, and Sarah Shroud, eds., *Hell Is a Very Small Place: Voices from Solitary Confinement* (New York: New Press, 2016), 81, 32.
10. Anthony Giddens, *Central Problems in Social Theory: Action, Structure and Contradiction* (Berkeley: University of California Press, 1979).
11. Victor Hassine, *Life Without Parole: Living and Dying in Prison Today,* ed. Robert Johnson and Sonia Tabriz, 5th ed. (New York: Oxford University Press, 2011), 52.
12. Prison Letters, 2014–2017. See, as well, Pascal, "No. 80," *Pascal's Pensées,* trans. Martin Turnell (London: Harvill, 1962), 127.
13. Charles Taylor, *The Language Animal: The Full Shape of the Human Linguistic Capacity* (Cambridge, Mass.: Harvard University Press, 2016), 7, 25, 46, 264–265.
14. Conover, *New Jack,* 316.
15. "New York City Jail Guards Are Fighting to Keep Their Records Secret" *Marshall Project* (October 20, 2015), www.themarshallproject.org/2015/10/20/new-york-city-jail-guards-are-fighting-to-keep-their-records-secret.
16. T. C. Esselstyn, "The Social System of Correctional Workers," *Crime and Delinquency* 12 (April 1966): 117–124, at 119; Barbara A. Owen, *The Reproduction of*

Social Control: A Study of Prison Workers at San Quentin (New York: Praeger, 1988), 23, 38, 68, 80, 83–84.

17. Koonce, *Correction Officer's Guide*. Subsequent references in text.
18. Herman Melville, "Chapter XII: Biographical," in *Moby-Dick or, The Whale* (1851; repr., New York: Bobbs-Merrill, 1964), 89.
19. Owen, *Reproduction of Social Control*, 84.
20. Lorna A. Rhodes, *Total Confinement: Madness and Reason in the Maximum Security Prison* (Berkeley: University of California Press, 2004), 86–90.
21. Victor Hassine, "Gauntlet of Despair," in *Life Without Parole: Living and Dying in Prison Today*, ed. Robert Johnson and Sonia Tabriz (New York: Oxford University Press, 2011), 23.
22. Jeff Smith, *Mr. Smith Goes to Prison: What My Year Behind Bars Taught Me About America's Prison Crisis* (New York: St. Martin's Press, 2015), 140–141, 148, 64. From the other side, a correction officer was slashed with twenty-two stitches to his face in the Rikers Island Juvenile facility on Friday, November 6, 2015. Michael Schwirtz, "2 Teenage Inmates Charged in Attack on Rikers Island Officer," *New York Times* (November 7, 2015), A21.
23. Prison Letters, 2014–2017. Birds fascinate prisoners. A group in solitary confinement kept their sanity by watching a pair of owls nest on a security light. "We watched [the owlets] grow up and fly away" in a way the watchers could not. Casella, Ridgeway, and Ṣhourd, *Hell Is a Very Small Place*, 82.
24. Casella, Ridgeway, and Shourd, *Hell Is a Very Small Place*, 127.
25. Gresham M. Sykes, *The Society of Captives: A Study of a Maximum Security Prison* (Princeton: Princeton University Press, 2007), 91, 99; Doran Larson, ed., *Fourth City: Essays from the Prison in America* (East Lansing: Michigan State University Press, 2013), 206.
26. Robert Johnson and Sonia Tabriz, "Closing Reflections on Living and Dying in Prison Today," in *Life Without Parole: Living and Dying in Prison Today*, by Victor Hassine, ed. Robert Johnson and Sonia Tabriz, 5th ed. (New York: Oxford University Press, 2012), 149.
27. Pierre Bourdieu, "Social Space and Symbolic Power," in *In Other Words: Essays Towards a Reflexive Sociology*, trans. Matthew Adamson (Stanford: Stanford University Press, 1990), 134.
28. Keramet Reiter, *23/7: Pelican Bay Prison and the Rise of Long-Term Solitary Confinement* (New Haven: Yale University Press, 2016), 111.
29. Kenneth E. Hartman, ed., *Too Cruel, Not Unusual Enough: An Anthology Published by the Other Death Penalty Project* (Lancaster, Calif.: Other Death Penalty Project, 2013), 74–75.
30. Hartman, *Too Cruel, Not Unusual Enough*, xxii, 6, 17, 21, 26, 43, 59, 80, 176.
31. Hartman, *Too Cruel, Not Unusual Enough*, 177.
32. Christopher H. Mumola, *Suicide and Homicide in State Prisons and Local Jails* (Washington, D.C.: U.S. Department of Justice, 2005), 11; Morris L. Thigpen, Thomas J. Beauclair, Virginia A. Hutchinson, and Fran Zandi, *National Study of*

Jail Suicide 20 Years Later (Washington, D.C.: National Institute of Correction, 2011), 44.

33. Hartman, *Too Cruel, Not Unusual Enough,* p. 3.
34. Koonce, "Key 19: Know Your Inmates (The Aquarium)," in *Correction Officer's Guide,* 117–118.
35. Mark Binelli, "Inside America's Toughest Federal Prison," *Prison Legal News* 26 (November 2015): 6, 8, 5.
36. Larson, *Fourth City,* 78, 149, 164–165.
37. Larson, *Fourth City,* 27–28.
38. Conover, *New Jack,* 227–230.
39. Bureau of Justice Statistics show a sharp downward trend in discretionary parole releases. See "Reentry Trends in the U.S.," www.bjs.gov/content/reentry/releases.cfm, and Beth Schwartzapfel, "Life Without Parole: Inside the Secretive World of Parole Boards Where Your Freedom May Depend on Politics and Whim," *Prison Legal News* 26 (September 2015): 1–15.
40. William J. Genego, Peter D. Goldberger, and Vicki C. Jackson, "Parole Release Decision Making and the Sentencing Process," *Yale Law Journal* 84 (March 1975): 810–902. See pp. 899–900 for a list of suggested reforms never followed. See, as well, "Calif Lifers Search for Parole," in Larson, *Fourth City,* 210–211.
41. Governor Deval Patrick of Massachusetts asked for and received the resignations of the parole board that released Dominic Cinelli after Cinelli killed a police officer in an armed robbery in December 2010. In response, the new parole board had even lower levels of release. See Beth Schwartzapfel, "Life Without Parole," *Prison Legal News* 26 (September 2015): 7.
42. "A Chance to Fix Parole in New York" (editorial), *New York Times* (September 5, 2015), A18.
43. The Supreme Court has held in Greenholtz v. Inmates of Nebraska Penal and Correctional Complex, 442 U.S. 1 (1979) at 2, that "a reasonable entitlement to due process is not created merely because a State provides for the *possibility* of parole" and that "nothing in due process concepts requires the Board to specify the particular 'evidence' in the inmate's file or at his interview on which it rests its discretionary determination to deny release."
44. I paraphrase from the Model Penal Code § 305.10.
45. Joan Petersilia, "Parole and Prisoner Reentry in the United States," *Crime and Justice* 12 (1990): 479–529, at 490, 494–496. The shift away from the idea of parole as a desirable aspect of rehabilitation has been dramatic and constant from the 1970s until now.
46. Robert A. Ferguson, "The Ratchet Effect in Theory," in *Inferno: An Anatomy of American Punishment* (Cambridge, Mass.: Harvard University Press, 2014), 32–64.
47. Petersilia, "Parole and Prisoner Reentry," 487ff.
48. Prison Letters, 2014–2017.
49. I follow my usual policy in this paragraph and the ones to follow of not revealing prisoners' names. My information in this case comes from the petitioner's brief

appealing the rejection of parole but with access to the transcript of the actual parole hearing, and I have been able to confirm each of the assertions in the appellate brief. See Appellant's Brief: Appeal from Denial of Parole (October 1, 2013) in State of New York Division of Parole Appeals Unit DIN 89G1015, NYSID 06327128Q Appellant (submitted on December 30, 2013). Hereinafter "Appellant's Brief (December 30, 2013)."

50. Appellant's Brief (December 30, 2013), 15. Emphasis added.
51. Appellant's Brief (December 30, 2013), 15–16.
52. Michael Wilson, "Crime's Details Are Rehashed and Parole Is Denied, Again and Again," *New York Times* (July 4, 2015), A18. Samuel Hamilton, another model prisoner with "an exemplary record and unprecedented support," was denied in seven straight parole hearings. In response to an appeal, the New York Judicial Appellate Division said that as long as the parole determination did not evince "irrationality bordering on impropriety" the courts could not interfere with the discretion invested in a parole board. Hamilton v. New York State Division of Parole, 518301; see also John Caher, "Split Panel Uphold Parole Denial for Exemplary Inmate," *New York Law Journal* (July 25, 2014).
53. Andrew Cohen and Beth Schwartzapfel, "Life Without Parole: Opening Statement," *Marshall Project* (July 13, 2015), 2, and more generally 2–10, www.themarshallproject.org/2015/07/10/life-without-parole. Many articles detail the failure of parole boards. See Daniel Weiss, "California's Inequitable Parole System: A Proposal to Reestablish Fairness," *Southern California Law Review* 78 (2005): 1573–1605; Daniel S. Medwed, "The Innocent Prisoner's Dilemma: Consequences of Failing to Admit Guilt at Parole Hearings," *Iowa Law Review* 93 (2008): 491–557; and Paul J. Larkin Jr., "Parole: Corpse or Phoenix?" *American Criminal Law Review* 50 (2014): 303–340.
54. Beth Schwartzapfel, "Life Without Parole," *Prison Legal News* 26 (September 2015): 1.
55. Sara Mayeux, "The Origins of Back-End Sentencing in California: A Dispatch from the Archives," *Stanford Law and Policy Review* 22 (2011): 529–530.
56. Samson v. California, 547 U.S. 843 (2006) at 846.
57. Jonathan Lippman, "Remarks" (New York State Permanent Commission on Sentencing, John Jay College of Criminal Justice, May 27, 2015), 2, 5; Andrew Keshner, "Lippman Moves to Reform Sentencing for Most Felonies," *New York Law Journal* (May 28, 2015); Rebecca Davis O'Brien, "New York's Chief Judge Proposes Fixed Prison Terms," *Wall Street Journal* (May 28, 2015), A19.
58. Background records on these commissioners show one with three terms in a district attorney's office. Another was a senior investigator for the New York State Crime Victims Board.
59. John Dewey, *The Public and Its Problems* (New York: Henry Holt, 1927), 3.
60. New York State Permanent Commission on Sentencing, "The Argument for Full Determinacy," in *A Proposal for Fully Determinate Sentencing for New York State: A Recommendation to the Chief Judge of the State of New York* (New York: John Jay College of Criminal Justice, December 2014), 5; Cohen and Schwartzapfel, "Life Without Parole," 8.

61. Amartya Sen, "Well-Being, Agency, and Freedom: The Dewey Lectures 1984," *Journal of Philosophy* 82 (April 1985): 174, 180, 186–187.
62. Hannah Arendt, *The Human Condition*, 2nd ed. (Chicago: University of Chicago Press, 1958), 247, 9.
63. Prison Letters, 2014–2017. For the quotation, see Larson, *Fourth City*, 72.
64. Alan Rosenthal and Patricia Warth, "New York Still in Need of Parole Reform," *Atticus* 24 (Spring 2012): 1–4.

Chapter 8. Education in Prison Reform

1. Lois M. Davis, Robert Bozick, Jennifer L. Steele, Jessica Saunders, and Jeremy N. V. Miles, *Evaluating the Effectiveness of Correctional Education: A Meta-Analysis of Programs That Provide Education to Incarcerated Adults* (Washington, D.C.: Rand Corporation, 2013). The report, sponsored by the Bureau of Justice Assistance of the U.S. Department of Justice, finds "on average, inmates who participated in correctional education programs had *43 percent lower odds of recidivating* than inmates who did not." See "Results," xvi. Also see Laura E. Gorgol and Brian A. Sponsler, *Unlocking Potential: Results of a National Survey of Postsecondary Education in State Prisons* (Washington, D.C.: Institute for Higher Education Policy, 2011), 16, and Caroline Wolf Harlow, "Education and Correctional Populations," *Bureau of Justice Statistics: Special Report* (Washington, D.C.: U.S. Department of Justice, 2003), 10. For the details on recidivism reaching 67.8 percent after three years, see Matthew R. Durose, Alexia D. Cooper, and Howard N. Snyder, "Recidivism of Prisoners Released in 30 States in 2005: Patterns from 2005 to 2010," Bureau of Justice Statistics (Washington, D.C.: U.S. Department of Justice, 2014), 1–29.
2. Daniel Karpowitz, *College in Prison: Reading in an Age of Mass Incarceration* (New Brunswick, N.J.: Rutgers University Press, 2017); Ellen Condliffe Lagemann, *Liberating Minds: The Case for College in Prison* (New York: New Press, 2016).
3. Sarah Wynn, "Mean Women and Misplaced Priorities: Incarcerated Women in Oklahoma," *Journal of Law, Gender & Society* 27 (2012): 281–304.
4. Aleks Kaistura and Russ Immarigeon, "States of Women's Incarceration: The Global Context," Prison Policy Initiative, www.prisonpolicy.org/global/women/.
5. Carolyn L. Sandoval, Lisa M. Baumgartner, and M. Carolyn Clark, "Paving Paths Toward Transformation with Incarcerated Women," *Journal of Transformative Education* 14 (March 2016): 34–52.
6. Francis X. Clines, "Tough Matriarch, Easy Touch, and Good Listener: Women Doing Hard Time Find a Warden with Her Own Way of Keeping the Lid On," *New York Times* (April 24, 1993), at www.nytimes.com/1993/04/24/nyregion/tough-matriarch-easy-touch-good-listener-women-doing-hard-time-find-warden-with.html.
7. Harlow, "Education and Correctional Populations," 1.
8. John Stuart Batchelder and J. Marvin Pippert, "Hard Time or Idle Time: Factors Affecting Inmate Choices Between Participation in Prison Work and Education Programs," *Prison Journal* 82 (June 2002): 269–270.

9. Prison Letters, 2014–2017, in author's possession.
10. Motoko Rich, "Test Scores Under Common Core Show That 'Proficient' Varies by State," *New York Times* (October 7, 15), A1, A17.
11. Adrian Novotny, Roger G. Seifer, and David R. Werner, "Collective Learning: A Pro-Social Teaching Strategy for Prison Education: The Strategy and Methodology of Group Performance in the Prison Classroom," *Journal of Correctional Education* 42 (1991): 80.
12. Prison Letters, 2014–2017.
13. Michelle Alexander, "The Cruel Hand," in *The New Jim Crow: Mass Incarceration in the Age of Colorblindness* (New York: New Press, 2012), 140–177.
14. T. A. Ryan and Kimberly A. McCabe, "Mandatory Versus Voluntary Prison Education and Academic Achievement," *Prison Journal* 74 (December 1994): 450–461.
15. Francis Bacon, "The Advancement of Learning," in *Francis Bacon: The Major Works*, ed. Brian Vickers (Oxford: Oxford University Press, 1996), 148. "The Advancement of Learning" makes the point as early as 1605; *De dignitate et augmentis scientiarum* in 1623 gives it titular significance. See, as well, Michael Rosen, *Dignity: Its History and Meaning* (Cambridge, Mass.: Harvard University Press, 2012), 15.
16. *Inmate Tutor Handbook* (Marianna, Fla.: FCI Marianna Education Department, n.d.), 10.
17. *Inmate Tutor Handbook*, 7, 9.
18. Barbara A. Owen, *The Reproduction of Social Control: A Study of Prison Workers at San Quentin* (New York: Praeger, 1988), 14–15.
19. Prison Letters, 2014–2017.
20. William James, *Pragmatism and Four Essays from The Meaning of Truth* (New York: Meridian, 1955), 42, 90, 127, 133.
21. Amartya Sen, "Well-Being, Agency and Freedom: The Dewey Lectures 1984," *Journal of Philosophy* 82 (April 1985): 208.
22. Jeremy Waldron, "Dignity, Rights, and Responsibilities," NYU School of Law, Public Law Research Paper no. 10–83 (November 17, 2010), 10, 24–28, https://ssrn.com/abstract=1710759.
23. Martha Nussbaum, *Creating Capabilities: The Human Development Approach* (Cambridge, Mass.: Harvard University Press, 2011), 31.
24. Nussbaum, *Creating Capabilities*, 39–40.
25. Charles Taylor, *The Language Animal: The Full Shape of the Human Linguistic Capability* (Cambridge, Mass.: Harvard University Press, 2016), pp. 195–197.
26. Jeff Smith, *Mr. Smith Goes to Prison: What My Year Behind Bars Taught Me About America's Prison Crisis* (New York: St. Martin's, 2015), 209. On being called "a shitbird" on release: "if I heard it once, I heard it a dozen times. It's what CO's told inmates nearing their release date."
27. "Soaring recidivism rates indicate that efficient and effective functioning for release inmates is a secondary consideration among program administrators." John Stuart Batchelder and J. Marvin Pippert, "Hard Time or Idle Time: Factors Affecting Inmate Choices Between Participation in Prison Work and Education Programs," *Prison Journal* 82 (June 2002): 279.

28. Prison Letters, 2014–2017.
29. Gresham M. Sykes and David Matza, "Techniques of Neutralization: A Theory of Delinquency," *American Sociological Review* 22 (December 1957): 664–670.
30. Saint Augustine, *Confessions* (397–400), trans. Henry Chadwick (New York: Oxford University Press, 1991), 151, 282, 202.
31. Prison Letters, 2014–2017.
32. Prison Letters, 2014–2017.
33. Mary Douglas, *Risk and Blame: Essays in Cultural Theory* (New York: Routledge, 1996), 16–19, 31, 36.
34. I rely on Brett Dignam's collection of data, using Davis et al., *Evaluating the Effectiveness of Correctional Education:* Dignam, "Learning to Counter Mass Incarceration," *Connecticut Law Review* 48 (May 2016): 1217–1230, at 1227.
35. Prison Letters, 2014–2017.
36. Smith, *Mr. Smith Goes to Prison*, 84–87, 205.
37. Dignam, "Learning to Counter Mass Incarceration," 1228–1229, 1223.
38. Daniel Karpowitz and Max Kenner, *Education as Crime Prevention: The Case for Reinstating Pell Grant Eligibility for the Incarcerated* (Annandale-on-Hudson, N.Y.: Bard Prison Initiative, 1995), 1–8; Joshua Page, "Eliminating the Enemy: The Import of Denying Prisoners Access to Higher Education in Clinton's America," *Punishment & Society* 6 (2004): 357–378; Richard Tewksbury and Jon Marc Taylor, "The Consequences of Eliminating Pell Grant Eligibility for Students in Post-Secondary Education Programs," *Federal Probation* 60 (1996): 60–63; Jonathan E. Messemer, "College Programs for Inmates: The Post-Pell Grant Era," *Journal of Correctional Education* 54 (March 2003): 32–39.
39. These suggestions come from an active GED prison tutor. Prison Letters, 2014–2017.
40. Adrian S. Novotny, Roger G. Seifer, and David R. Werner, "Collective Learning: A Pro-Social Teaching Strategy for Prison Education: The Strategy and Methodology of Group Performance in the Prison Classroom," *Journal of Correctional Education* 42 (June 1991): 80. For statistics on illiteracy, see Karpowitz and Kenner, *Education as Crime Prevention*, 4.
41. Michael Schwirtz, "Rikers Guard Is Charged with Having Contraband," *New York Times* (November 26, 2015), A33.
42. Aristotle, *The Politics*, ed. Steven Everson (Cambridge: Cambridge University Press, 1988), 153–154 (6.1322a.1–25).
43. Davis et al., *Evaluating the Effectiveness of Correctional Education*, iii, 59.
44. See www.pen.org/prison-writing and www.mnprisonwriting.org/who-we-are.html.
45. Robert Axelrod, *The Evolution of Cooperation*, rev. ed. (New York: Basic, 1984), 173, 175.
46. Douglas, *Risk and Blame*, 9, 36.
47. Drew Leder and the Jessup Correctional Institution Scholars, "The Enlightened Prison," in *The Beautiful Prison*, ed. Austin Sarat, special issue of *Studies in Law, Politics, and Society* 64 (2014): 28–29.

48. Kenneth E. Hartman, "Searching for the Beautiful Prison," in *Beautiful Prison*, ed. Sarat, 13–14.
49. Leder and the Jessup Correctional Institution Scholars, "Enlightened Prison," 25.

Chapter 9. What Is Punishment For?

1. Gresham M. Sykes, *The Society of Captives: A Study of a Maximum Security Prison* (Princeton: Princeton University Press, 2007), 9–11, 31, 136.
2. Emily Bazelon, "The Soft Evidence Behind the Hard Rhetoric of 'Deterrence,'" *New York Times Magazine* (October, 25, 2015), 13.
3. Sykes, *Society of Captives*, 10–11; and Robert Martinson, "What Works?—Questions and Answers About Prison Reform," *Public Interest* 35 (Spring 1974).
4. James Q. Wilson, *Thinking About Crime: A Powerful Indictment of the American Criminal Justice System* (New York: Basic, 1975).
5. *Report of the Department of Correctional Services* (Albany, N.Y.: Department of Correctional Services, 1985–1986); John Pratt, *Punishment and Civilization: Penal Tolerance and Intolerance in Modern Society* (London: Sage, 2002), 18, 183–184. For the racial implications in a culture of fear, see Bruce Western, "Chapter 3: The Politics and Economics of Punitive Criminal Justice" and conclusion, in *Punishment and Inequality in America* (New York: Russell Sage Foundation, 2006), 52–81, 189–198. Western concludes, "Policy makers and voters appear to retain a keen appetite for punishment" (195).
6. Elizabeth Hinton, *From the War on Poverty to the War on Crime: The Making of Mass Incarceration in America* (Cambridge, Mass.: Harvard University Press, 2016).
7. Compare Western, *Punishment and Inequality in America*, and Michelle Alexander, *The New Jim Crow: Mass Incarceration in the Age of Colorblindness* (New York: New Press, 2010).
8. Western, *Punishment and Inequality in America*, 24–25. "Women Behind Bars" (editorial), *New York Times* (November 30, 2015), A22.
9. Sarah Wynn, "Mean Women and Misplaced Priorities: Incarcerated Women in Oklahoma," *Wisconsin Journal of Law, Gender & Society* 27 (2012): 290; Marne L. Lenox, "Neutralizing the Gendered Collateral Consequences of the War on Drugs," *New York University Law Review* 86 (2011): 77.
10. Francis Bacon outlined the inevitable connection of anger to the other emotions of contempt, dismissal, and condemnations. See Bacon, "No. 56. Of Judicature" and "No. 57. Of Anger," in *Essays or Counsels, Civil and Moral* (1625) in *Francis Bacon: The Major Works, Including "New Atlantis" and the Essays*, ed. Brian Vickers (New York: Oxford University Press, 2002), 446–450.
11. Richard Lazarus, "Hope: An Emotion and a Vital Coping Resource Against Despair," *Social Research* 66 (Summer 1999): 653, 674–675.
12. William E. Connolly, "The Desire to Punish," in *The Ethos of Pluralization* (Minneapolis: University of Minnesota Press, 1995), 41–74, esp. 41, 47, 49, 74.
13. See Harold J. Rothwax, *Guilty: The Collapse of Criminal Justice* (New York: Random House, 1996). Rothwax, who served for more than twenty-five years on the

New York State Supreme Court, admits that he punished more willingly and heavily over time until the defense bar came to call him the "Prince of Darkness," a title he came to welcome.

14. Elaine Scarry, "Speech Acts in Criminal Cases," in *Law's Stories: Narrative and Rhetoric in the Law,* ed. Peter Brooks and Paul Gewirtz (New Haven: Yale University Press, 1996), 166.
15. Brown v. Plata, 563 U.S. 493 (2011), at 563.
16. Jean Casella and James Ridgeway, "How Many Prisoners Are in Solitary Confinement in the United States?" *Solitary Watch* (February 1, 2012), http://solitarywatch.com/2012/02/01/how-many-prisoners-are-in-solitary-confinement-in-the-united-states/.
17. Jeremy Bentham, *The Rationale of Punishment* (1830), ed. James T. McHugh (Amherst, N.Y.: Prometheus Books, 2009), 128–129. Solitary confinement, writes Bentham, "if greatly prolonged, it would scarcely fail of producing madness, despair, or more commonly a stupid apathy." See, as well, *Solitary Confinement: Common Misconceptions and Emerging Safe Alternatives* (New York: Vera Institute of Justice, May 2015), 5–6, www.vera.org/publications/solitary-confinement-common-misconceptions-and-emerging-safe-alternatives. Anthony Kennedy, concurring opinion, Davis v. Ayala 576 U.S. __ (2015) No. 13–1428 (June 18, 2015): being locked up alone brings prisoners "to the edge of madness, perhaps to madness itself."
18. Margo Schlanger and Amy Fettig, "Eight Principles for Reforming Solitary Confinement," *Prospect* 26 (Fall 2015): 34ff.
19. Keramet Reiter, *23/7: Pelican Bay Prison and the Rise of Long-Term Solitary Confinement* (New Haven: Yale University Press, 2016), 145.
20. Prison Letters, 2014–2017, in author's possession.
21. "Why Are Violent Crime Rates Falling?" (editorial), *Washington Post* (January 2, 2010), www.washingtonpost.com/wp-dyn/content/article/2010/01/01/AR2010010101829.htmloilen.
22. Furman v. Georgia, 408 U.S. 238 (1972). Subsequent references in text. See, as well, Gregg v. Georgia, 428 U.S. 153 (1976).
23. Payne v. Tennessee, 501 U.S. 808 (1991).
24. Michael J. Graetz and Linda Greenhouse, *The Burger Court and the Rise of the Judicial Right* (New York: Simon & Schuster, 2016), 38.
25. "America and Its Fellow Executioners" (editorial), *New York Times* (January 10, 2016), SR10.
26. For fewer executions but sustained confusion over the death penalty with the relevant statistics used here, see "The Death Penalty Endgame" (editorial), *New York Times* (January 17, 2016), SR10. For the most recent corroboration, see James Forman Jr., *Locking Up Our Own: Crime and Punishment in Black America* (New York: Farrar, Straus & Giroux, 2017).
27. Furman v. Georgia, 408 U.S. at 238, 240. Emphasis added.
28. On the open contention in the Supreme Court over punishment, see, in addition to the Georgia cases, Baze v. Rees, 953 U.S. 35 (2008), and Brown v. Plata, 563 U.S. 493 (2011), 131 S.Ct. 1910 (2011).

29. For Powell's recantation over the death penalty, see John C. Jeffries Jr., *Justice Lewis F. Powell, Jr.* (New York: Fordham University Press, 2001), 451. For Blackmun's more openly public one, see his dissent in Callins v. Collins, 510 U.S. 1141 (1994).
30. Furman served time in prison instead of being executed. He was released on parole in 1984 and was convicted again of burglary in 2004 and is now serving a twenty-year sentence.
31. Jackson v. Georgia and Brunch v. Texas, consolidated in the Supreme Court's decision under 408 U.S. 238 (1972).
32. 408 U.S. at 307–308, 310.
33. 408 U.S. at 308.
34. 408 U.S. at 345, 347, 351–352.
35. 408 U.S. at 453–455.
36. 408 U.S. at 455.
37. 408 U.S. at 455–456. Emphasis added.
38. Jason Horowitz, "Cruz at Supreme Court: On Murders, He Wrote," *New York Times* (January 21, 2016), A16.
39. 408 U.S. at 467, 470, more generally 465–470.
40. 408 U.S. at 258, 269.
41. 408 U.S. at 25; Brennan quotes from Trop v. Dulles, 356 U.S. 86 (1958) at 103.
42. 408 U.S. at 269.
43. 408 U.S. at 286, 306.
44. *The Beautiful Prison,* ed. Austin Sarat, special issue of *Studies in Law, Politics, and Society* 64 (2014): 16.
45. Aristotle, *The Politics,* ed. Steven Everson (Cambridge: Cambridge University Press, 1988), 174 (7.1332a–10).

Chapter 10. The Architectonics of Reform

1. George Bernard Shaw, *The Crime of Imprisonment* (1946; repr. New York: Citadel Press, 1961), 26.
2. The Federal Bureau of Investigation's official "Anti-Piracy Warning," which appears on the screen before the beginning of every movie viewed on a DVD, reads as follows: "The unauthorized reproduction or distribution of a copyrighted work is illegal. Criminal copyright infringement, including infringement without monetary gain, is investigated by the FBI and is punishable by up to five years in federal prison and a fine of $250,000."
3. Brett Dignam, based on experience in prison work, writes, "confinement in American prisons has also become increasingly punitive." Dignam, "Learning to Counter Mass Incarceration," *Connecticut Law Review* 48 (May 2016), at 1220.
4. See "Shouldn't Criminal Defense Lawyers Prepare Clients for Prison?" *Sentencing Law and Policy* (December 30, 2015), http://sentencing.typepad.com/sentencing_law_and_policy/2015/12/shouldnt-criminal-defense-lawyers-prepare-clients-for-prison.html. A lawyer sentenced to prison for mail fraud says "during the

entire time I was incarcerated, I do not recall hearing of a single instance, my case included, where the defense lawyer provided any meaningful prison preparation or counseling for his or her client as part of the representation." He adds, "any defense attorney who offers clients the strategies they need to manage through confinement and emerge successfully would add substantial value to the legal representation provided."

5. See Steven Everson, introduction to *Aristotle: The Politics* (Cambridge: Cambridge University Press, 1988), xxii–xiv.
6. *Oxford English Dictionary*, s.v. "prison."
7. Epictetus, *Discourses: Books I and II*, ed. P. E. Matheson (Mineola, N.Y.: Dover, 2004), xx, 10n. The *Discourses* date from the second half of the first century CE.
8. On the primacy of dialogue in furthering truth, see Jürgen Habermas and Joseph Ratzinger, *The Dialectics of Secularization: On Reason and Religion*, trans. Brian McNeil (San Francisco: Ignatius, 2005).
9. Quote from a mother to her son in prison, in John J. Lennon, "Let Prisoners Take College Courses," *New York Times* (April 4, 2015), www.nytimes.com/2015/04/05/opinion/sunday/put-schools-back-in-prison.html.
10. Jones v. North Carolina Prisoners' Union, 433 U.S. 119 (1977) at 119–121, 125.
11. 433 U.S. at 125.
12. 433 U.S. at 125–126.
13. 433 U.S. at 132. Emphasis added to show just how little prison authorities must demonstrate for mere opinion to prevail.
14. 433 U.S. at 132, 127. Emphasis added.
15. 433 U.S. at 137.
16. 433. U.S. at 139, 147.
17. Sir William Blackstone's four volumes of *Commentaries* are organized around the public/private distinction of rights and wrongs, on which depends "civil liberty" or "the power of doing whatever the law permits." See Blackstone, *Commentaries on the Laws of England: A Facsimile of the First Edition of 1765–1769* (Chicago: University of Chicago Press, 1979), 1:6, 118.
18. Jones v. North Carolina Prisoners' Union, 433 U.S. at 134.
19. 433 U.S. at 136.
20. Keramet Reiter, *23/7: Pelican Bay Prison and the Rise of Long-Term Solitary Confinement* (New Haven: Yale University Press, 2016), 194–205.
21. Victoria Law, "California Prison Hunger Strike Ends After 60 Days," *Truthout* (September 6, 2013), www.truth-out.org/news/item/18649/-california-hunger-strike-ends-after-60-days.
22. Jones v. North Carolina Prisoners' Union, 433 U.S. at 123.
23. 433 U.S. at 123, 129.
24. Michael S. Gazzanica: "Imagination," in *Human: The Science Behind What Makes Us Unique* (New York: HarperCollins, 2008), 387.
25. Roy A. Sorensen, *Thought Experiments* (New York: Oxford University Press, 1992), 3, 36, 205.

26. "Connecticut's Second-Chance Society" (editorial), *New York Times* (January 4, 2016), A18.
27. Jesse McKinley and James C. McKinley Jr, "Cuomo Plans College Courses for Prisoners," *New York Times* (January 11, 2016), A20.
28. See "U.S. Department of Education Launches Second Chance Pell Pilot Program for Incarcerated Individuals" (U.S. Department of Education, July 31, 2015), www.ed.gov/news/press-releases/us-department-education-launches-second-chance-pell-pilot-program-incarcerated-individuals.
29. Baze v. Rees, 553 U.S. 35 (2008).
30. Travis Dusenbury, "My Life in the Supermax," *Marshall Project* (January 8, 2016), www.themarshallproject.org/2016/01/08/my-life-in-the-supermax.
31. Thomas Nagel, *Mortal Questions* (Cambridge: Cambridge University Press, 1979), p. 126.
32. Joseph Roth, "Hotel Kapriva," *The Hotel Years,* trans. Michael Hofmann (New York: New Directions, 2015), 77. Roth writes of the rise of fascism between the world wars.
33. Prison Letters, 2014–2017.
34. "A New York Prison-Yard Search and 10 Cases of Frostbite," *Marshall Project* (August 23, 2015), at www.themarshallproject.org/2015/08/23/a-new-york-prison-yard-search-and-10-cases-of-frostbite.
35. Martin Buber, *I and Thou,* 2nd ed., trans. Ronald Gregor Smith (New York: Charles Scribner's Sons, 1958), 11, 63; Martin Buber, "II: Person To Person," *To Hallow This Life: An Anthology,* ed., Jacob Trapp (New York: Harper & Brothers, 1958), 15, 19, 22. I am also indebted to Jürgen Habermas, "Martin Buber—A Philosophy of Dialogue in Its Historical Context," in *The Lure of Technology,* trans. Ciaran Cronin (Malden, Mass.: Polity, 2015), 123–136, esp. 125–126, 135. See also Buber, "Autobiographical Fragments" and "Replies to My Critics," in *The Philosophy of Martin Buber,* ed. Paul Arthur Schilpp and Maurice Friedman (London: Cambridge University Press, 1967), 26, 35–36, 705–712.
36. Marianne Constable, "Speech as Dialogue: 'You' and 'I,'" *Our Word Is Our Bond: How Legal Speech Acts* (Stanford: Stanford University Press, 2014), 91–98.
37. Paul Mendes-Flohr, "Introduction: Dialogue as a Trans-Disciplinary Concept," in *Dialogue as a Trans-Disciplinary Concept: Martin Buber's Philosophy of Dialogue and Its Contemporary Reception,* ed. Mendes-Flohr (Berlin: De Gruyter, 2015), 3.
38. Marshall B. Rosenberg, *Nonviolent Communication: A Language of Life,* 3rd ed. (Encinitas, Calif.: PuddleDancer, 2015), 6, 28, 164–165.
39. David Bohm, *On Dialogue,* ed. Lee Nichol (London: Routledge, 1996), 2, 6.
40. Chris Innes, *Healing Corrections: The Future of Imprisonment* (Boston: Northeastern University Press, 2015), 159, 137; David Bohm, Donald Factor, and Peter Garrett, "Dialogue: A Proposal" (1991), 3, www.david-bohm.net/dialogue/dialogue_proposal.html.
41. Chris Innes, *Healing Corrections: The Future of Imprisonment* (Boston: Northeastern University Press, 2015), 137–138, 163.
42. Innes, *Healing Corrections,* 135–136. The expert quoted is Peter Garrett, a long-time prison analyst and group therapist in a penal context.

43. Innes, *Healing Corrections*, 178–179.
44. Pierre Bourdieu, *In Other Words: Essays Toward a Reflexive Sociology*, trans. Matthew Adamson (Stanford: Stanford University Press, 1990), 137–138.
45. André Comte-Sponville, *A Small Treatise on the Great Virtues*, trans. Catherine Temerson (New York: Henry Holt, 2001), 7–14. The treatise first appeared in French in 1996.
46. Proverbs 15:1 (KJV).
47. Ken Belson, "No Foul Mouths on This Field: Football with a New Age Twist," *New York Times* (September 6, 2015), A1.
48. Rosenberg, *Nonviolent Communication*, 94, 17, 144.
49. Prison Letters, 2014–2017, in author's possession.
50. Lionel Trilling, *Sincerity and Authenticity* (Cambridge, Mass.: Harvard University Press, 1971), 2, 11.
51. Experience in the Devens Federal Correctional Facility in Ayer, Massachusetts. See Anita Raghavan, "Rajat Gupta to Finish Insider Trading Sentence at His Home," *New York Times* (January 21, 2016), B3.
52. A number of disputes in prison begin over prison mattresses. Prison Letters, 2014–2017. More formal prison narratives refer to the problem frequently.
53. I take these terms from Dr. Richard H. Fulmer, a practicing psychoanalyst in New York City.
54. An "aversive stimulus is an unpleasant event that is intended to decrease the probability of a behavior when it is presented as a consequence (i.e. punishment)." "Aversive Stimulus," *Encyclopedia of Child Behavior and Development*, ed. Sam Goldstein and Jack A. Naglieri (New York: Springer, 2011), http://link.springer.com/referenceworkentry/10.1007%2F978-0-387-79061-9_265.
55. Immanuel Kant, *Grounding for the Metaphysics of Morals* (1785), in *Ethical Philosophy: The Complete Texts of "Grounding for the Metaphysics of Morals" and "Metaphysical Principles of Virtue,"* trans. James Ellington (Indianapolis: Hackett, 1983), 11–12; Kant, *The Metaphysical Principles of Virtue*, trans. James Ellington (New York: Bobbs-Merrill, 1964), 122, 113 (second part of the Elements of Ethics, § 35, § 25).
56. Immanuel Kant, *Groundwork of the Metaphysics of Morals*, trans. H. J. Paton (New York: Harper Torchbooks, 1964), 61–62.
57. Drew Leder and the Jessup Correctional Institution Scholars, "The Enlightened Prison," in *The Beautiful Prison*, ed. Sarat, 19–22.
58. Steven Pinker, *The Stuff of Thought: Language as a Window into Human Nature* (New York: Penguin, 2008), 428.
59. Thomas Nagel, *Equality and Partiality* (New York: Oxford University Press, 1991), 84.
60. "Righting a Grave Injustice in Louisiana" (editorial), *New York Times* (January 29, 2016), A28.
61. Stefan R. Underhill, "Did the Man I Sentenced to 18 Years Deserve It?" *New York Times* (January 24, 2016), SR4.
62. Erwin James, "Bastoy: The Norwegian Prison That Works," *Guardian* (September 4, 2013), 1–6, www.theguardian.com/society/2013/sep/04/bastoy-norwe. For the

quotations in the paragraph on prisons in Denmark, Norway, Sweden, and Finland, see Doran Larson, "Why Scandinavian Prisons Are Superior," *Atlantic* (September 24, 2013), 1–10 at 2, www.theatlantic.com/international/archive/2013/09/why-scandinavian-prisons-are-superior/279949/.

63. Pinker, *Stuff of Thought*, 439.
64. Attempts by the Correction Officers' Benevolent Association in New York to shield officers accused of brutal conduct from public scrutiny by New York City's Office of Administrative Trials and Hearings give a recent example of entrenched interests blocking reform and siding instead with continued corruption. Jim Dwyer, "A Move to End Transparency for New York's Jails," *New York Times* (January 29, 2016), A23.
65. I use New York state here as a typical example of how correction officer unions control investigations. See "How to Get Brutal Guards Out of the Jails" (editorial), *New York Times* (May 2, 2016), A20.
66. Michael Schwirtz, "Guard Accused of Using Radio to Beat Inmate," *New York Times* (April 6, 2016), A22. Emphasis added.
67. For examples of union obfuscation in New York and the failure of the state legislature to do anything about the problem, see Michael Winerip, Michael Schwirtz, and Tom Robbins, "New York State Taking on Union of Prison Guards," *New York Times* (April 12, 2016), A1.
68. Tom Robbins, "Abused Inmates, Strong Unions and Hard-to-Fire Prison Guards," *New York Times* (September 28, 2015), A1.
69. Joshua Page, *The Toughest Beat: Politics, Punishment, and the Prison Officers Union in California* (New York: Oxford University Press, 2011).
70. Michael Winerip, "Rikers Officer Accused of Sex with Inmate," *New York Times* (February 8, 2016), A22.
71. Winnie Hu and Kate Pastor, "Rikers Cook and Guards Took Bribes, Officials Looking into Smuggling Say," *New York Times* (May 20, 2016), A20.
72. Winnie Hu and Kate Pastor, "5 Rikers Officers Convicted in Beating of Inmate," *New York Times* (June 8, 2016), A16; William K. Rashbaum, Michael Winerip, and Michael Schwirtz, "Fraud Charges Against Jail Officers' Union Chief with a Taste for Luxury," *New York Times* (June 9, 2016), A1.
73. Winerip, "Rikers Officer Accused," A22.
74. Michael Winerip and Michael Schwirtz, "Few Penalties for Workers in Escape of 2 from Prison," *New York Times* (June 24, 2016), A20.
75. Brittany Glidden and Laura Rovner, "Requiring the State to Justify Confinement for Mentally Ill Prisoners: A Disability Discrimination Approach," *Denver Law Review* 90 (2013): 55–75.
76. Jason Furman and Douglas Holtz-Eakin, "Why Mass Incarceration Doesn't Pay," *New York Times* (April 21, 2016), A29.
77. See Richard Pérez-Peña, "Rampaging Inmates Kill 2 at a Nebraska Prison Described as Understaffed," *New York Times* (May 12, 2015), A13; Richard Pérez-Peña, "Prison Riot Yields Few Answers," *New York Times* (May 13, 2015), A12; Jon Hurdle and Richard Pérez-Peña, "Delaware Prison Standoff Ends with Correction Officer Dead," *New York Times* (February 3, 2017), A9.

78. John W. Kingdon, "Problems," in *Agendas, Alternatives, and Public Policies,* 2nd ed. (New York: Longman, 2011), 90–115.
79. "Labels Like 'Felon' Are an Unfair Life Sentence" (editorial), *New York Times* (May 8, 2016), 10SR.
80. Alice Goffman, *On the Run: Fugitive Life in an American City* (New York: Farrar, Straus and Giroux, 2014), xiii, 109, 122–126, and more generally 109–141.
81. I paraphrase from Clayton M. Christensen, *The Innovator's Dilemma: The Revolutionary Book That Will Change the Way You Do Business* (New York: HarperCollins, 2011), 34, 40.
82. Doran Larson, ed., *Fourth City: Essays from the Prisons in America* (East Lansing: Michigan State University Press, 2013), 102.
83. Archibald MacLeish, "Apologia," *Harvard Law Review* 85 (June 1972): 1505–1511, at 1508, repr. as "Art and Law," in *Riders on the Earth: Essays and Recollections* (Boston: Houghton Mifflin, 1978).

INDEX